WATERMILLS

WATERMILLS

Peter Wenham

ROBERT HALE · LONDON

First published in Great Britain 1989

Robert Hale Limited
Clerkenwell House
Clerkenwell Green
London EC1R 0HT

British Library Cataloguing in Publication Data

Wenham, P. (Peter), *1936–*
Watermills.
1. Great Britain. Watermills
I. Title
621.2′1

ISBN 0-7090-3526-8

Photoset in Sabon by
Derek Doyle & Associates, Mold, Clwyd.
Printed and bound in Great Britain by
Butler and Tanner Limited,
Frome, Somerset.

Contents

Illustrations

Between pages 64 and 65

England

All photographs by the author

Dedication

To the memory of my father, rarest of men,
who made no enemies – only friends

Introduction

This is a book about mills which employ water, through the medium of a wheel, to provide power for whatever function the mill was constructed to perform. A few of my choices for inclusion may seem to be borderline, but they invariably possess something of relevance to the historical process of the use and development of watermills. And here I have to make plain that my main approach to the subject in this book is historical. When and where did mills develop, what effect did they have on the landscape, why did millers have, for so long, a questionable reputation? Just how much influence did the water-powered mill have on the industrial development of Britain, and what happened to cause its decline? Finally, since history is a continuous process, what is the present standing of the mill and what is its future 'history' likely to be?

The book consists of three main sections. One contains a short series of chapters tracing the history of the watermill, its effect on Britain's industry, how the mill works etc. The central section deals, county by county, with a number of mills in detail, with additional lists of shorter references. The last section contains a comprehensive glossary describing a wide range of terms.

How this works in practice can best be described by an example. The dramatic decline of the traditional mill in the late nineteenth century, following the arrival of roller-mills, is a frequent theme. Roller-mills are discussed in the detailed entry on Caudwell's Mill (p.82), where they were successfully employed, and they are considered in their historical context in the chapter on the history of milling. Finally, there is a glossary entry where the subject is briefly summarized. This apparent repetition is intended to serve three purposes. For the 'dipper' it provides necessary background knowledge when reading about or, better still, visiting a specific mill; the short introductory chapters are intended for those who wish to have a fuller 'over-view' of the subject, and the glossary supplies essential detail in an abbreviated 'dictionary' format.

A recurring problem in books written for the lay reader is the amount of technical detail to be included in the main text. Here one can only rely on personal taste – I do not enjoy being 'blinded by science'. Further, repetition of descriptions of machinery would soon induce boredom – and add considerably to the length of the book! The glossary therefore assumes more than usual importance, for it contains almost every technical word or term the reader is likely to encounter in this or other books and leaflets on the subject of mills and milling. Most entries are brief; many are linked to other, related terms; a few are extended; all are intended to expand on the inevitable use of 'shorthand' words employed in any broad treatment of a subject. Historically there is much variation in the spelling, by mill-owners, of the titles of their mills, we have chosen a uniform method of spelling.

I can confirm the experience of all those who have written previously on this subject; mill-owners, millers and the staff looking after the mills *are* unfailingly helpful, courteous and, most important, immensely enthusiastic about their subject. I only hope that my enjoyment of their mills is apparent in the book, but I must stress that the views and opinions expressed about mills in this book are entirely mine and are based upon my own experiences. Like the authors of some food guides, I rarely announced my visits in advance (South and West Wales were exceptions), but such is the enthusiasm of owners and staff that I was invariably 'rumbled' once I started making notes or even interested mutterings!

Inevitably in a book like this a great deal of reliance has to be placed on the available publications, and I acknowledge the immense debt I owe to the leaflets, booklets and, in some cases, treatises I have studied. Again, the conclusions drawn, and even some variations in always contentious 'facts' like dates, are my responsibility.

Certain people and staffs of organizations gave particular help and encouragement. Gerallt Davies of the Welsh Folk Museum gave the project a flying start in the chill days of February 1987. The long-suffering staff of Merton Public Library spent hours obtaining books and then more hours totting up the fines I so regularly incurred. The staffs of the Regional Tourist Boards are an unfailing source of assistance to anyone writing about Britain. Many of the staff of the National Trust (on this occasion, particularly Giles Clotworthy of the Cornish region, who drew my attention to at least two gems) are both helpful and valued friends. Without the calm assistance of Peter Shrubb and my cousin, Graham Wenham, the section on Scotland would have been less complete. Mike King of Millwrights International Ltd performed the vital task of checking the technical contents.

Several of my other friends responded, as they have over the years, to 'requests' for accommodation – the Austins, the Laceys, the

Parratts and the Parsonages among them. A great part of this book was written in the lovely River Wye home of darling Roxy – whose hospitality we so often abuse, whether writing or relaxing! I have left until last that member of the staff of the National Trust who is both friend and infinitely more. My debt to her is all-embracing.

London and Ross on Wye
August, 1988

I

The Development of the Watermill

CHAPTER ONE

History

The practice of producing flour from corn has probably taken place from the moment man first began to grow cereal crops. The earliest methods of grinding corn involved pounding, using a mortar and pestle, and they were followed by the backward-and-forward motion of the saddle stone or quern. These first querns appear to date from the neolithic period and were followed by rotary querns, in which the upper stone revolved around the surface of the lower. Querns were hand-operated – invariably by women or slaves; the harnessing of animal-power came much later.

The first reference to an ass driving a mill occurs in Cato (232-147 BC) but water-power seems to have been introduced some time later. Both the Greek chronicler Strabo and Antipater of Thessalonica, writing at around the time of Christ's birth, have been credited with the first reference to a watermill. The type of mill mentioned, it is universally agreed, was the 'Greek' or 'Norse' mill. This was a small mill with a horizontal wheel and vertical shaft still found in eastern countries and more remote parts of Europe; in Britain it was in use in the Hebrides and Shetland as recently as this century. In the isolated (often mountainous) areas where it survived, the Greek mill was often a true community mill, its doors open to all, asking no toll, exercising no soke rights (see below).

The major development towards water-powered milling, as we know it, came with the invention of the horizontal-shaft 'Vitruvian' or 'Roman' mill. It was described by the engineer Vitruvius in his *De Architectura* written a few years before the birth of Christ and only a little later than Strabo and Antipater. Suggestions have been made that this indicates an upsurge of interest in the engineering possibilities of the watermill. I think it more likely that Vitruvius was demonstrating a 'pure' interest in a solution to a problem. Certainly the Romans showed little interest in the potential of the vertical mill, and it is possible to identify three reasons for this – aesthetic, religious and practical. The Romans had an ambivalent attitude towards engineering and, in particular, mechanical sciences – they were never quite accepted as 'serious' subjects. Their early belief in gods of the elements may have conflicted with their appreciation of such a mechanism, although an increasingly cynical view replaced this belief over the centuries. But the most important factor was that they simply had no requirement to employ labour-saving devices – indeed, they positively encouraged the use of physically hard but menial tasks to keep their large 'slave pool' occupied. It was only towards the end of the Roman Empire that undershot (and, occasionally, overshot) water-wheels were widely adopted for corn-grinding.

With the fading-away of the Roman Empire, the use of slave labour in Europe began to disappear. By the end of the Dark Ages (AD 800) society was being organized in a very different manner and, although many men remained far from 'free', never again would the work-force be of sufficient size to permit such wasteful employment (colonial slavery is a separate issue). Of more immediate relevance was the growth of the Christian ethic. Men accepted, even embraced, the menial tasks they were expected to perform as a way of honouring Christ, but they did not consider themselves restricted in employing outside assistance. As a result, there was a growth of interest in mechanical devices, and many new ideas were introduced, often involving the use of animal-, wind- and water-power. Although the later 'Renaissance Man' affected to dislike the early Middle Ages, his roots, certainly in the sciences, can be traced to this period.

In Britain, the first documented reference to a watermill is in a charter of AD 762 which mentions a mill at Cert, east of Dover. The Saxons worked with both horizontal and vertical water-wheels – there are references to mills at Winchester in AD 983, during the reign of Ethelred II.

By the time of the Domesday survey, commissioned by King William at Christmas 1085 and completed, remarkably, within a year, watermills were already of great importance in parts of England, and over 5,000 were recorded. It is clear that most of the mills mentioned in Domesday must have originated in the Saxon period – they did not suddenly spring up when the Normans took possession of the land. The majority were almost certainly employing undershot wheels but it is likely that a percentage were Norse mills.

There was a widespread tendency at the time of the survey, and, indeed, much later, to refer to individual pairs of millstones as 'mills'. This applied equally to Wales, where the habit persisted for centuries – for example, at Melin Bompren (see p.203), which remained open until the 1950s, the last miller still called his stones 'mills'. Many of the records of 'mills' in Domesday probably relate to the pairs of millstones housed within the mill building.

To add to the confusion, there is little doubt that some mills, serving more than one settlement, were doubly listed. Inevitably there would have been a few errors; even some later references in sales and leases have led to the erroneous impression that an area or village possessed several mills when it simply had more than one pair of working stones under the one roof. Then, as now, these millstones were probably employed on different tasks. The effect of all this has been to make accurate assessment of the true number of mills – in the sense of mill buildings – very difficult, and I think the often-quoted figure of 5,624 mills at Domesday must be treated as an educated guess and no more.

It will be noticed that once or twice I have given a figure for the annual rental value placed on an individual mill. This could be based on a monetary valuation or it could be in kind – sometimes both. A common alternative was for the mill to supply eels in lieu of rent (see Bromham Mill p.58), and eel-traps are clearly illustrated beside an example of the increasingly popular overshot wheel in the fourteenth-century Luttrell Psalter.

One conclusion may be drawn from the briefest study of Domesday: the considerable number of settlements (parishes) listed which have retained evidence, if not of a mill, at least of a mill site, for nearly 1,000 years. Evidence as to the precise location of Domesday mills is rarely available but, with that proviso, it seems likely that a good site, once established, would be abandoned only with great reluctance. Compulsion in the form of eviction by landlord or military, the loss of a site due to natural causes, such as the diverting of the course of a river, economic pressure brought about by changing agricultural practice in an area – these were possible factors which might bring change. Even in these circumstances, it was likely that subsequent generations of millers would rebuild on the same or a nearby site. The possession of soke rights (see below) and the associated rights of freedom from tithes was another strong reason for retaining a mill on an old site – once the creation of manors died out in the reign of Edward I, the safest way of continuing to claim the rights was by rebuilding on old, recognized sites. Of course, wear and tear will have destroyed the original mill centuries ago, but there is a pleasing thread – almost a rope! – of continuity in the history of many a parish mill.

In the centuries following the arrival of the Normans, the majority of mills were manorial or monastic, contributing useful income to the estates to which they belonged. Inevitably there were disputes – for example, the villagers of Houghton had more than one argument with the abbots of Ramsey Abbey (see p.63). Their problems often arose from disputes involving the rights to water, who controlled it and who should pay for it. If you believe, as I do, in '*plus ça change* ...', it is worth comparing these common concerns with those currently being expressed by millers. They are raising similar queries over the possibility of the privatization of Water Authorities – who will 'own' the water, who will allocate its use and who will determine what sort of charges (if any) will be levied for water flowing past a water-wheel?

However, no matter caused more lasting dissension than 'soke rights'. Whoever owned a manorial mill in the Middle Ages had, and invariably enforced, these 'rights', which came to be bitterly resented by tenants. Soke rights were, in effect, a restrictive covenant giving the landowner the right to insist that all corn grown on his land be milled at the manorial mill. The origin of soke rights is shrouded in mystery and, if the rights existed at all in Saxon times – the evidence is uncertain – they could not have been widespread. More significantly, there is no mention of soke in Domesday, and William's commissioners would hardly have overlooked this obvious way of supplementing estate incomes.

Although soke rights never formed part of Statute Law, they survived for centuries, dying out only just over a hundred years ago. Cases – and there were thousands – were invariably resolved in favour of the landowner, to the fury of tenants, some of whom resorted to the most ingenious attempts to avoid conforming to the requirement. A not unusual ploy was for a group of tenants to build a new mill above the manorial mill, depriving it of water. The unsophisticated simply took their corn elsewhere and, when challenged, expressed surprise, ignorance or 'righteous' anger. And, if the manorial mill-owner's agents could be avoided, taking corn to another mill might be advantageous, for competition was fierce and 'special offers' of reduced tariffs were commonplace.

Reference to soke rights was invariably incorporated into leases, and the latest example affecting a mill mentioned in this book concerns Otterton Mill (see p.86) and occurs in a lease of 1814. There were later examples: Bradford was forced to buy a share in one of the town mills in order to obtain its release from soke as late as 1871, and Syson refers to Bedfordshire villagers who were still having corn milled by the mills of the abbey of St Albans at the end of the century, although this may have been custom and not in the terms of the lease, as it was at Otterton.

At first glance, the system of soke rights would appear to contain certain benefits for all. It was to the advantage of smallish communities to be self-sufficient, and poor transport limited opportunities to seek out alternatives, although the tenant did have the right to take his grain elsewhere if it was not ground within a certain period of being presented at the mill. 'Modern' mills were more efficient and labour-saving than the old hand-quern, producing better-quality flour with less waste.

There were, however, two major disadvantages. Because they were seen to be a valuable asset, mills were increasingly built to last, and that made them expensive. Their upkeep added to costs, and these were, inevitably, passed on. It is part of folklore around the world that farmers do not enjoy paying out more than they need to, and this is no twentieth-century phenomenon. So they resisted the charges by continuing to use hand-querns until forced to give them up by law; even then many were buried to avoid being confiscated, and they are still occasionally turned up by the plough.

In some respects the second disadvantage was more important than the first. I suspect that, granted good relations between the tenant farmer and the miller, the application of soke rights might have worked with a token degree of grumbling. The flaw in this argument is that relations were consistently far from cordial – in fact, downright hostile. There is no doubt that Geoffrey Chaucer was reflecting a common view of millers when, in both the Miller's and the Reeve's Tales of the fourteenth-century *Canterbury Tales*, he invests millers with a series of thoroughly unpleasant traits, including dishonesty.

The charge of dishonesty was levelled against millers for centuries – it certainly didn't begin or end with Chaucer. The miller was allowed to take a toll, usually a sixteenth, of all the flour he produced. The question was, when is a sixteenth not a sixteenth? The problem stemmed from what Chaucer termed the miller's 'thumb of gold'. Many things affect the density and content of corn, and no one possessed the necessary experience to judge how much flour the miller should take for his own 'ark' (bin). With experience, a miller could gauge the quality and condition of grain by testing it between thumb and forefinger. From this he judged how much flour could be produced. The complaint was that he regularly falsified the figure, allowing him, if Chaucer is to be believed, to take three times his due. As a precaution, housewives were warned to 'measure before and after' sending their corn to be ground, but this advice had little practical value.

Nonetheless, millers were always being charged with dishonesty, suggesting either that prejudice was affecting judgement or that some were not only dishonest but stupid. In an attempt to ease the problem, the right to make financial payment in lieu of tolls began to be accepted as early as the thirteenth century, although it was not placed on the Statute Book until 1796. The only effect was to lead to prosecutions relating to over-charging in monetary terms!

All in all, a classic situation where bad laws lead to dissatisfaction.

The majority of millers were probably no more dishonest than most men of the age, but they were the focal point of what was seen as an unfair system; even in our more sophisticated times, we tend to blame the Collector of Taxes more than the Chancellor who imposes them.

The miller must have been keenly aware of his position. A good miller was an important asset to an estate, for, in addition to his other skills, he could provide useful information on the farming abilities of tenants. As a result he had the ear of the landowner, and that increased the suspicions of the farmers. Yet he was still a tenant and ultimately as much a potential victim of the feudal system as other tenants. After all, in times of plague or famine, his income suffered as much as anyone's.

I doubt that any society is more ambivalent in its attitudes towards the 'man in the middle' than ours, for we have never decided how to regard foremen, NCOs, supervisors – some would say, even the middle class – for they belong neither with 'them' nor with 'us'. Perhaps, feeling his isolation, the miller was tempted occasionally to use his skills to take a small revenge on both sides.

The very clear division of society which existed in the centuries following the arrival of the Normans had already begun to break down by the time Chaucer was writing, and the peasant farmer was increasingly his own man. The plague of 1348-9 reduced the population by between thirty-three and fifty per cent, and the result was an increase in the amount of land available, leading to a growth in the size of smallholdings. Only the relationship between the newly independent peasant farmers and the miller was not changed – mutual suspicion continued to dog their dealings.

The function of the mill began to undergo a change as early as the thirteenth century. Wool was very much the staple industry of Britain but the cloth trade was also developing. The first record of a mill being used for fulling (a vital process in cloth manufacture) occurs in about 1168, and within fifty years the tilt-hammers used in that process were being adapted to tanning. A century later several paint-mills were established, but it was the development of the metal industries which triggered the next major role for water-power. The ironmasters of the Weald of Kent and Sussex used large quantities of water to power their furnaces and, by building hammer-ponds, many of which still survive, they irrevocably changed the face of the Weald. These and other uses for the 'mill' will be looked at later (see p.39 on).

In the meantime, the miller was establishing himself (and, not infrequently, herself) as an increasingly prosperous member of the community. In Tudor and Stuart times millers began to move out of the mill they invariably now owned and into the newly built adjoining millhouse – a building of greater quality, with pretensions to architectural merit, befitting its owner's position. A pattern was being established, one which would lead ultimately to the many, often remarkably fine Georgian mills which now survive, usually as country residences for families with neither country nor milling connections.

How was this change in status effected? Agriculture continued to dominate the economy during the late fifteenth century, although tenants gained little, but the population was once again rising, and land, much of it lying fallow or having been uneconomically husbanded, was again in demand, albeit at high prices. There were still profits to be made in the wool trade, which led to problems with enclosure and in some respects at least held back development, but the increased demand for food caused by the higher population produced two major effects.

First, the introduction of a whole range of new farming techniques led to increased productivity – by the early years of the eighteenth century Britain was capable of feeding its own greatly increased population and still had a grain surplus producing a profitable export trade. Second, for those who had land, either owned or, as in the case of the miller, more probably leased, it was a time of almost unrivalled opportunity. Anyone controlling land was able to switch from wool to arable production, and some, admittedly usually the larger landowner, profited from purchasing land at the time of the Dissolution of the Monasteries (the 1530s). Even for the smaller land-holder, subject only to the vagaries of the harvest, there was at the very least a comfortable living to be made.

And so millers had two opportunities to increase their wealth and their standing in the community. If they continued to work for a large estate, they were involved in its growth and prosperity, and if they were fortunate enough to lease their mill and, perhaps, some land, their future was equally assured. For this reason, the rise of the miller, as a person of influence in society, continued between the seventeenth and nineteenth centuries. There were exceptions, notably in the north of England and Wales, but by and large the corn-miller, whether in a rural community or close to a developing urban area, continued to prosper until almost the end of the nineteenth century.

Throughout this book there are examples of mills being enlarged in the middle part of the last century, only to run into trouble in its latter years. This was not due to a decline in the demand for flour; rather, the reverse was true. The population might be expanding, demand increasing, but the simultaneous introduction of the new roller-mills would come close to destroying the small corn-mill.

'Mixed' mills first appeared in Britain in the 1860s, and a 'stoneless' mill was operating successfully by 1878, but it was only following a major exhibition in London in 1881 that the value of the system was widely recognized. Influenced by a number of new or previously unconsidered factors, roller-milling had almost replaced traditional milling by the end of the century. A major factor was that hard winter wheats, developed in the United States, proved difficult to grind using millstones. This cheap grain, introduced to Britain in the 1870s, was ground immediately on arrival at large commercial roller-mills centred in the docks. The result was a uniform, fine white flour lacking nutritional value, character and flavour – but it gained immediate popular acceptance, and whole-grain bread would not regain favour for almost a hundred years. At the same time, the growth of an efficient transport system permitted rapid distribution to an increasingly urbanized population.

There were two choices open to mill-owners at the turn of the century. Either they adapted to the new roller-milling methods or they could attempt to carry on milling in the traditional manner. Rarely, very rarely, they made the choice to adapt; one of the pioneers of adaptation was Caudwell's Mill (p.82). The more usual reaction was to struggle on, combining flour- and grist-milling in an attempt to remain in profit. In practice this invariably led to mills becoming grist-mills – that is to say, manufacturers of animal feed – at some time during the early years of the twentieth century. Those that survived until the start of the Second World War were invariably put back to work briefly as corn-mills – Orchard Mill (p.142) is a case in point.

But the days of the small rural corn-mill appeared to be drawing to an end, and in the 1950s many limped to a close and were soon deserted and disintegrating. At the important new museums of rural life at St Fagans, York, Stowmarket and Singleton, mills were saved and re-erected as examples of what was then considered to be a fast-disappearing type of vernacular building.

However, almost at the time the Weald and Downland Open Air Museum at Singleton was being established in the late 1960s, the situation began to undergo a dramatic change. A series of books extolling the virtues of vernacular buildings, including mills, began to appear. Industrial archaeology took its place as an established discipline, and such experts as the late Alec Clifton-Taylor brought the broader subject of architecture to the television screen. Nonetheless, as late as 1970, John Reynolds in his fine introduction to the subject *Windmills and Watermills* was drawn to a pessimistic conclusion regarding the future of the mill.

What Mr Reynolds could not have foreseen was that two new factors would change the situation radically from the mid 1970s onwards. The first of these was an enormous growth in interest in conservation in the broadest sense. Membership of the country's premier conservation organization, the National Trust, some 300,000 at the beginning of the 1970s, passed the 1½ million mark in 1987. Other conservation bodies were created and flourished, as did many new and established magazines and publications devoted to countryside topics. Newspapers appointed writers on conservation, and the whole subject received 'official' approval when the major political parties expressed their commitment to 'green' subjects in the general election of 1987.

Helpful as all this was to the cause of preserving mills and mill buildings, it was necessary for there to be a practical input. Initially, that input came with a movement 'back to the land' by people who had become disillusioned with an increasingly commercial world. Their prime interest lay in using the framework of disused mill buildings to house a variety of craft and other workshops, sometimes organized as co-operatives (see Otterton, p.86). A few pioneers began the task of restoring mills to their former function, often working unaided and with little financial support. If they were lucky, local craftsmen would give them assistance, and occasionally a retired miller could be called upon for invaluable advice (see, for example, Dunster Mill, p.140). Grants were obtained from enlightened local authorities and other public bodies, while one or two successes in gaining conservation awards brought welcome publicity.

The most recent tendency has been for those who have been made redundant or have taken early retirement to explore the possibilities of a new life-style. They have been aided by the earlier pioneers giving generously of their time and hard-won knowledge. It may be that some of the newcomers will engender, of necessity, a harder, more commercial view of milling in future than did the gifted amateurs – in the best sense – who began the process of rediscovery. Whatever the future, I find it exciting that scattered throughout this book are examples of watermills which have been restored and re-opened in the last two to three years – indeed, in a few instances restoration work has yet to be completed.

Problems remain: there are areas of England and Scotland – not so much Wales – which, as can be seen by glancing through the county introductions (where I make some harsh comments), have very little of interest to the molinologist (mill buff). In many instances, particularly those areas where the mills were small and remote, they have simply fallen into disrepair; Leicestershire is a sad case in point. By contrast, where the mills are large and of architectural value, they have increasingly been taken over as private houses, and their new owners invariably allow no access to the public; many East Anglian mills have been effectively lost in this manner.

I believe, however, that there is cause for cautious optimism. The numbers of enthusiasts appear to be growing, and if only one or two are able to translate their enthusiasm into practical terms – well, there are mills throughout Britain which have not deteriorated beyond repair. But, even if we are unable to add many 'new' names to the list of surviving watermills in the next few years, a seemingly irredeemable decline has already been halted and a new chapter opened in the thousand-year history of the watermill in Britain.

CHAPTER TWO

The Mill in Architecture and Landscape

Contrary to the fashionable, but misguided, view among the more romantic recent converts to 'conservation', much of the landscape of Britain is man-made. In some instances, such as the currently sensitive issue of the loss of 'our' hedgerows, not only were they man-made but in most cases they are a relatively recent imposition, dating only from late-Hanoverian times.

What one might term the broad brushstrokes, on which the picture of much of the countryside is based, were laid down during the early Middle Ages, when such structures as castles, churches and large manor-houses created oases of order in a previously primitive landscape. Around these centres, new or enlarged village communities developed and with them the monastic or manorial mill. Many mills were, of course, already in existence by the time of the Domesday survey, and it is likely that the majority of remaining sites have existed at least since the fourteenth century.

The effect of the mill on the landscape has varied enormously. In the case of a corn-mill forming part of a small group of buildings in a sheltered valley, it will contribute only to the overall effect. By contrast, a mill in an open landscape away from a village will influence the landscape far more, drawing and focusing the eye. In some areas where large industrial water-powered mills have been built, the effect will be quite dramatic, and very visible. And it is not just the mills which can alter a landscape. The various channels into which the Itchen was diverted to provide power for a number of mills greatly influenced the countryside surrounding Winchester – an influence which can still be glimpsed amidst the chaos of motorway development.

Because no medieval examples survive other than in much altered forms, it is impossible to do more than guess at the size of early watermills. The few illustrations that are available hint at relatively small buildings attached to large under- or overshot wheels (the Luttrell Psalter has an illustration of the latter), and there is no reason to suppose this was not so. A factor to be borne in mind in this connection is that millers did not become responsible for the storage of grain until the end of the sixteenth century. As a result, and with the expansion of trade in the eighteenth century, mills needed more space. The upper, granary floor with its large storage provision and hoist was a product of this expansion.

Mills are true vernacular buildings in that, almost from the start, they were built in the local style and of materials easily available in the locality. Originally, the mills would have been constructed of wattle and daub with a thatched roof but, as their value grew and was recognized, later examples were built in stone, brick or half-timber, depending on the local tradition. This tradition continued, with very few exceptions, until the eighteenth century.

By and large the earlier mills which have survived are not outstanding buildings, although there are one or two exceptions – West Harnham (p.174) at Salisbury is one, while Bourne Mill, near Colchester, is a quite remarkable conceit (p.95). Suggestions have been made that both may have been built with other purposes in mind.

It was not until the eighteenth and nineteenth centuries that the rather grand white-painted and weather-boarded mill, which many would consider the 'traditional' mill, made its appearance in the south-east and East Anglia. The handsome stone or brick-built millhouses, now so much in demand for conversion to private homes or restaurants, start to appear at the same time – many are, of course, 'Georgian' in style if not period.

The placing of mills along rivers and streams clearly affected the landscape – in some areas they were the first buildings to be built in isolation from the village they served. This certainly happened in the Weald of Kent and Sussex, where a small community often followed the establishment of a forge. A good example is Burton (p.163), a Sussex hamlet where the present buildings are the successors to those which had occupied the site from its beginnings as an iron forge in the early years of the seventeenth century, through its subsequent development as an estate mill. Burton is still unexpectedly remote, considering its proximity to major roads leading to Chichester and the coast, and it is clear that no hamlet would have existed there if the first forge had not been built.

The effect of its many, now vanished, mills on the valley of the Wandle in south-west London can only be guessed at, but if the claimed figure of thirty-eight is accurate, this must go a long way to justify the assertion that it was 'the hardest worked river of its size in the realm'.

It is still possible, by the exercise of a little imagination, to gain an insight into the influence of the thirteen or so watermills which, until recently, adorned the valley of the River Loose, near Maidstone (p.116). A few of these mills have now gone but the majority, of different periods and purpose, remain in a valley that has only in the last twenty years succumbed to the inroads of urbanization. Most, on early sites, spawned little clusters of associated buildings, many of which, though converted, are still recognizable. The physical differences between the Loose and the Wandle are very considerable – the Loose runs down through a steep, claustrophobic valley, far from typical of the south-east – but the activity along them must have been equally fascinating to observe.

Similar situations in the north are often even less clearly defined because of the much greater expansion of the towns. Abbeydale (p.181), now part of Sheffield, was once one of several industrial hamlets in the area. By contrast, Shepherd Wheel (p.182) lies deep in a narrow, heavily wooded valley, just three miles from the centre of the city, yet often ignored by passers-by. It is possible that there was a mill on this site in the late 1500s – if so, it could hardly have been more self-effacing than the present building. Shepherd Wheel is a very rare example of a commercial mill (other than gunpowder mills) not attracting other buildings or having more than a limited influence on its locality. Certainly, it is not representative of Lancashire and Yorkshire during the last two centuries, when the cotton and woollen industries reached a peak of concentrated activity. Any observer of the great factory mills – at least up to the 1950s – must have felt that the landscape had been irrevocably changed.

It is a nice debating-point as to whether the silk-throwing mill built for the Lombes at Derby or Boulton's Soho Manufactory in Birmingham was the first true 'factory', but the influence of the new mills cannot be disputed. Their sheer size made them highly visible, and their siting, often in remote and lovely settings, made it impossible for them to be ignored. A series of romantic writers were quick to voice their horror of the violation of the 'soft, romantic, consecrated scenes' ('Coalbrook Dale' by Anna Seward). But for each Seward or, indeed, Wordsworth there were those who recognized the grandeur of the new structures. Joseph Wright of Derby painted Cromford and other mills and foundries in a romantic, almost Claudean, style. A visitor to Cromford Mill (p.81), ablaze with light at night (as Wright had painted it), could refer to its looking 'luminously beautiful'.

It is worth noting here that, granted its basically simple design, the mill has rarely proved to be an architectural disaster. It is possible that proximity to water has produced a softening effect on the architecture – or on our critical faculties. Nor can it be denied that some buildings have genuine architectural merit. Ruskin may have raged at the building of the viaduct in Monsal Dale but he made no criticism of the fine Georgian Cressbrook Mill (p.79) of 1814-15 (what he might write of the mill in its present state is a different story).

Not only could mills be attractive, but over the centuries many fine buildings were put up by men whose wealth came from the workings of mills in all their manifestations. Good examples of this 'spin-off' can be seen in both Bradfords. If the fine houses of Bradford-on-Avon are the enduring symbols of the success of early clothiers, the remarkably confident public buildings of West Yorkshire's Bradford are reminders of enterprising Victorian industrialists.

Just three miles north of Yorkshire's Bradford is one of the most significant examples of the effect milling has had on the landscape – the community of Saltaire. Saltaire was not only a model of its type; it was, in a sense, the ultimate expression of the importance the mill had assumed in the lives of men. The great textile-mill, six storeys high and 546 feet long, stands beside the River Aire, a shrine round which the homes of those who worked in it are grouped, reverentially.

But at Saltaire we have moved far from the small estate corn-mills with which the history of milling began. Inevitably there are very few 'traditional' mills still operating, and their discovery is a source of great pleasure.

Because each of us has our own, unique picture of 'the mill', I will do no more than suggest that such mills as Howell Mill on Anglesey, Priston Mill near Bath, Lode Mill in Cambridgeshire and Montgarrie Mills in Grampian come close to fitting my own picture – and stress that there are others to be discovered in the Gazetteer section of this book. These mills are all vernacular buildings in unspoilt country: ducks or other waterfowl float on most of their millponds or streams; all grind corn or oats and are satisfyingly dusty – is this not the fundamental impression most of us retain of the watermill in the landscape?

CHAPTER THREE

Art and Literature

In the visual arts, the earliest, if indirect, references to mills come in the form of the saddle querns depicted in Egyptian paintings. Several examples survive of statuettes showing women servants or slaves grinding meal, possibly as an accompaniment for the dead on their journey towards the afterlife.

The earliest known illustration of a watermill can be found on a mosaic in the ruins of the Great Palace of Byzantium (Istanbul). A large undershot wheel leans against a tall building – though the work dates from the fifth century, the effect is remarkably modern. In England, one of the first depictions of a mill occurs in the fourteenth-century Luttrell Psalter, showing a timber-framed wattle-and-daub building under a thatch roof. Beside the mill is an overshot water-wheel, and in the millrace are two eel-traps.

In the Middle Ages a representation of the mill-rynd, known, in heraldic terms, as the *fer-de-moline*, was commonly employed, most significantly on the arms of the Court of Lincoln's Inn in London.

Joseph Wright of Derby saw a fresh and dramatic beauty in the new mills as early as 1789, when he painted his friend Arkwright's large mill at Cromford by night and ablaze with lights. There is, as Professor Hoskins has pointed out, a little mystery about this work, for Murdoch did not demonstrate the potential in the use of coal gas for lighting until 1792, and the idea was not commonly adopted until the early 1800s. Like most of the romantics, Wright had a ruling interest in light and, although he completed several industrial paintings, they seem to owe more to the effects created by, for example, furnace fires against the sky, than to a deep desire to portray the buildings! This was not uncommon and, to demonstrate my meaning, there is a much reproduced painting in the Ironbridge Museum by de Loutherbourg where a very romantic Coalbrookdale is depicted bathed in a fiery orange light.

Turner painted Marford Mill in 1795, but the paintings we most commonly associate with mills are undoubtedly those of John Constable. His famous series set in and around the Dedham Vale area effectively begin with *The Mill Stream* of 1814. In a sense this is a prophetic title, for it has to be said that few of Constable's paintings actually show a mill! For example, *The Mill Stream* shows Willy Lott's cottage but not Constable's father's mill at Flatford, and the year-later *Boat-building near Flatford Mill* depicts some of Golding Constable's men building a barge but again does not include the mill. *Flatford Mill*, painted in 1817, shows the mill in the background and hardly the focus of the painting. Only in *Dedham Lock and Mill* (1820) does Constable highlight a mill and its buildings. With *The Haywain* we return to Willy Lott's cottage, yet no less an expert than Gombrich is drawn into referring to 'lingering by the mill' when analysing the picture. It can, I think, be explained by the application of that much-abused word 'perception' – our minds perceive a mill, *ergo* there is a mill.

In the latter half of this century mills have appeared, with some regularity, on up-market Christmas and birthday cards – often featuring the work of some hitherto unknown Victorian artist. A popular modern artist who has featured mills in his work is Rowland Hilder, a painter with an unfailing eye for the artistic possibilities to be found in attractive groupings of buildings.

The earliest published references to the mill occur in the writings of the Greek geographer Strabo and in the work of Antipater of Thessalonica. Vitruvius gives the first 'scientific' description of a water-wheel in *De Architectura* written some fifteen to twenty years BC. It must be said that only Antipater's epigrams may truly be termed 'literature'. The first reference to the Bible is in the Book of Exodus, while St Matthew refers to 'grinding at the mill'. Both he and St Luke say of anyone harming a child who believed in Christ that, '... it were better for him that a millstone were hanged about his neck, and that he were drowned in the depths of the sea'.

One of the first works of English literature, *The Canterbury Tales*, written in the fourteenth century, has extensive and unflattering references to the miller. Geoffrey Chaucer, it appears, was reflecting a widely held view of the miller when he presented him as a foul-mouthed, drunken churl during the telling of his own tale, and followed this by making the crooked miller of Trumpington, Simpkin the Swagger, the cuckolded butt of the Reeve's Tale. For fourteenth-century listeners this (and the parallel seduction of his daughter) would have provided a certain piquancy to the tale, for there was a widespread belief that, in addition to being thieves, millers themselves had a 'facility' with women.

In *Titus Andronicus* Shakespeare takes one of his occasional sideswipes at women, drawing an allegorical reference to the mill when saying of Lavinia:

> She is a woman, therefore may be won;
> She is Lavinia, therefore may be lov'd.
> What, man! more water glideth by the mill
> Than wots the miller of; and easy it is
> Of a cut loaf to steal a shive, we know.

Ill-feeling towards millers persisted for many years. The famous Essex epitaph to miller Strange is eighteenth-century and says it all:

> Here lies an honest miller
> And that is Strange

Elsewhere in this book I have referred to the miller's sense of isolation, and it is nowhere better portrayed than in the old song of the miller of Dee, written by Isaac Bickerstaffe in 1762. However, despite the sentiments below, the miller of Dee still remained both jolly and blithe:

> I care for nobody, no not I
> And nobody cares for me.

In *Gulliver's Travels*, written in 1726, Jonathan Swift makes the little Lilliputians know about watermills, if not clockwork: 'He put this engine [a watch] to our ears, which made an incessant noise like that of a water-mill; and we conjecture it is either some unknown animal, or the god that he worships, but we are more inclined to the latter opinion.'

References to mills by both poets and novelists have increased in the last two centuries. Shelley, in 'Charles the First', refers to 'little motion in the air except the mill-wheel's sound.' Tennyson, who grew up at Somersby in Lincolnshire, near Stockworth Mill, is presumed to have had the mill, and specifically the mill-stream, in mind when he wrote in 'The Miller's Daughter':

> For men may come, and men may go,
> But I go on for ever.

Perhaps it was the stirrings of a romantic nostalgia in the hearts of people confined increasingly to towns which led to the popularity of 'Nellie Dean'. In this perennial music-hall favourite the imagery is of a quiet place 'where I used to sit and dream'.

Novelists of the nineteenth century were very fond of mill locations. *The Mill on the Floss*, by George Eliot, is set on a tributary of the Trent and has obvious connections with Gainsborough, Lincolnshire. However, Mary Ann Evans ('Eliot') grew up near Nuneaton, and 'St Oggs' in the book is probably based on the now-vanished Arbury Mill in that area. *John Halifax, Gentleman*, by Mrs Craik, has references to the mills in the Nailsworth area of Gloucestershire, and the Abbey Mill in Tewkesbury is the site for Abel Fletcher's mill. Wool, in Dorset, is 'Wellbridge' in Thomas Hardy's *Tess of the d'Urbervilles*, where Tess spends her wedding night at the manor-house, and it is to Bindon Abbey, with its adjacent mill on the River Frome, that Angel Clare carries her, in his sleep, placing her in an empty stone coffin.

The less romantic implications of the various industries involved in milling in the eighteenth and nineteenth centuries did not go unremarked. Blake's 'dark Satanic mills' is, perhaps, the briefest, yet most quoted and scathing reference to the bleaker side of milling at that time. But it does not stand alone. Anna Seward, in 'Coalbrook Dale', attacked what she saw as the violation of that valley. That most exquisitely middle-class poet, Wordsworth, described one of the undoubted problems of the new industrial processes – the exploitation of workers – in abstract 'middle-class' terms, preferring to sneer, in 'The Excursion', at the idol of the new capitalists, while offering no alternative whereby the masses might obtain betterment:

> ... where the rumbling stream,
> That turns the multitude of dizzy wheels
> Glares, like a troubled spirit, in its bed,
> Among the rock below. Men, maidens, youths
> Mother and little children, boys and girls,
> Enter, and each the wonted task resumes
> Within his temple, where is offered up
> To Gain, the master idol of the realm,
> Perpetual sacrifice.

Not all of us are fortunate enough to be born to dwell, with Lucy, 'among the untrodden ways'.

In more general terms, the agricultural and topographical writers who proliferated between the sixteenth and eighteenth centuries have left a series of interesting pictures of the patterns of agriculture, including the distribution of cereal crops and their harvesting and disposal. Defoe refers to the industrial processes in a note on Sheffield and to problems with gunpowder works in Faversham, while Celia Fiennes makes several references to industries dependent on water-power in her late seventeenth-century travel writings. Both these most reliable of sources for modern writers on Britain are quoted in the main part of this book.

CHAPTER FOUR

Mill Mechanics

Certain terms recur throughout this book, not least references to the types of water-wheel which produce the power to turn the mill machinery. I have included brief technical descriptions of the various types of wheel in the Glossary but include a summary in this chapter which also includes a section on how grain makes its way through the mill as it is processed. Many additional terms found in this and other books and leaflets on milling are, for convenience, included in the Glossary, which is intended to be the prime technical section of the book.

Types of Water-Wheel

The earliest and simplest is the *undershot wheel* – still very common. It is, like all the 'modern' wheels referred to throughout the book, a vertical wheel. An earlier form of wheel, the Greek or Norse wheel, is described in the Glossary. Overshot wheels have blades or paddles around their circumference and stand in moving water. The effect of water striking the blades is to turn the wheel in the same direction to the flow of the water.

The result of this action is to produce power which is used to operate the mill. The method of transferring power is invariably the same, regardless of the type of wheel involved. The wheel is mounted on a horizontal axis, often called an *axle tree*. Also on this shaft is the *pit-wheel*, the teeth or cogs meshing with those of the horizontal *wallower*. The wallower is fixed to, and turns, the upright *main shaft*. Immediately above the wallower and also fixed to the main shaft is the great *spur-wheel*. Beside the spur-wheel is a much smaller gear-wheel (or several, depending on the number of pairs of stones operated by the mill) called the *stone nut*, which, when meshed with the spur-wheel, turns the runner stone. Set higher up the main shaft is the *crown-wheel*, used to drive ancillary equipment, such as the sack-hoist, through a straightforward belt-drive system.

Any stream or river with a consistent, strong flow is suitable for the undershot wheel, as is the leat, an artificial water-course. Leats are used in many instances for convenience. The mill can be built away from the river and a channel cut from a point above the building to pass under the wheel, returning to the river through a continuation of the channel, now called the tailrace. Water-flow can be controlled by sluices at the beginning of the channel, and, by narrowing the channel and increasing the velocity of the water a greater force can be concentrated onto the blades. Where the natural water-flow is sluggish, a long leat is used to build up the water-speed. The undershot wheel is not very efficient: John Smeaton, who carried out controlled experiments on model wheels in the eighteenth century, calculated its efficiency at no more than twenty-two per cent.

The *Poncelet wheel* is a nineteenth-century development, by the brilliant French engineer General J.V. Poncelet, of the undershot wheel. Essentially, Poncelet's improvements were intended to produce greater control of the water-flow, 'squeezing' the water and guiding it more effectively onto improved paddles. For this, relatively simple adjustments were made to the shape of the paddles and, by angling the control gate or hatch, which he made adjustable, Poncelet increased the efficiency of the undershot wheel to a claimed sixty-five per cent. The idea was first introduced to England in the 1820s, and the well-known Dorset company of Maggs & Hindley had considerable success with their installations of the Poncelet wheel.

Undershot wheels are turned by kinetic energy, while the *overshot wheel*, which was introduced during the early Middle Ages, requires potential energy which arrives on the wheel in the form of falling water. All the remaining types of water-wheel consist essentially of buckets into which the water falls from various positions and heights, which determines the name by which the wheel is described. In the basic overshot wheel the water is fed onto the top of the wheel and is collected into buckets; the weight of water in the buckets carries the wheel down, the water spilling out into the tailrace as the wheel reaches the bottom of its circle. A simple but effective method, requiring a small but reliable supply of water. This is invariably achieved by creating a dam and collecting water from one or more small streams into a millpond.

A *pitch-back wheel* is essentially an overshot wheel but the water is now supplied to the buckets at the back, i.e. the upstream side. The effect is to turn the wheel in the opposite direction to an overshot wheel, and the discharged water is therefore flowing with the water of the tailrace. This method works particularly well using small buckets on a large wheel – an obvious example is the Lady Isabella Wheel at Laxey, Isle of Man (p.111).

The latest and, with the Poncelet, most efficient types of wheel, developed in the eighteenth and nineteenth centuries, were the two types of *breastshot wheel*. Again water falls into buckets, but now the entry is either just above the axle at the back of the wheel, when it is known as a *high-breast wheel*, or below the axle – *low breast*. The wheel turns in the same direction as the pitch-back. Breastshot wheels are, in general, associated with a fairly lengthy leat and a good, well-controlled supply of water.

Occasionally wheels were operated in pairs. Good examples can be seen at Cheddleton Mill (p.145) and Felin Geri (p.191), where the wheels operate side by side and at Oldmills, Elgin (p.211), where they are on opposite sides of the building. The alternative is to have the wheels in series, and there are several examples in this book, including Little Salkeld Mill (p.77).

Mill Machinery

The working of a water-powered corn-mill is delightfully simple and, in its essentials, varies very little. I shall promptly appear to contradict that comment by adding that it must be emphasized, as I frequently do in the course of the book, that no two mills are alike. They vary because sites vary; materials vary; the purpose of the mill varies and – most important – millers vary! Each man had his own ideas, foibles, even different physical characteristics which affected the layout of 'his' mill. Historically and in fiction, millers have invariably been represented as individuals – certainly many chose to express their individualism in little refinements to an age-old practice.

Because this is not a technical book, I have chosen not to dwell on involved methods of gearing or unusual machinery, although some mention of variations is made in individual entries, and millers will always be prepared to explain these variations to those who are interested.

Let me repeat that the Glossary (pp.223-36) contains many descriptions and definitions used in milling practice. In the entries I frequently refer to conventional gearing or machinery. This is intended as a 'shorthand' way of suggesting that the specific example does not depart in too startling a fashion from the basic methods employed for centuries. To explain the broad principles, I give below a description of what happens to grain from the moment it enters the mill.

A 'typical' mill will have three floors, with possibly a *lucam* projecting from its upper floor and containing hoisting-gear. A *sack-hoist* lifts sacks of grain from carts driven under the lucam. The grain is stored in bins on the top floor – the *bin* or *granary floor*. When required for grinding, the grain is released from the bin and flows down *chutes* by gravity to the first floor; the whole 'journey' to the ground floor is, in fact, by gravity.

On the first floor, commonly called the *stone floor*, the grain enters the *hopper* and is fed into the centre or eye of the top stone of the two which comprise the grinding-tool. This top stone is called the *runner stone*, and it is turned by power supplied through wheels and gears from the main water-wheel. The bottom or *bed stone* is fixed, and the grain is nipped in the gaps between the stones, is broken down into flour and works its way to the edge. The height of the runner stone above the bed stone is controlled by the miller, and it governs the degree of fineness in the flour produced. The process is assisted by the pattern – hardly changed since it was developed by the Romans – etched into the surface of the stones. The grain is effectively cut in a scissor-like motion as the runner stone revolves with the flour working its way by centrifugal force along channels in the surface of the bed stone. The stones and flour are enclosed in a wooden box called a *tun*. From the tun the flour falls to the ground floor, where it is bagged up for transporting away from the mill or taken back to the third floor for further processing.

CHAPTER FIVE

The Watermill and Water-Wheel in Use

It is always difficult to study any industry in isolation – never more so than when attempting to divorce a study of the history of the water-wheel and water-power from the continuing industrial revolutution which has been a feature of Britain's history for longer than any other nation. Not only did water-power play a significant, often similar, role in all the industries to be discussed but it is interwoven with the overall pattern of industrial development.

My intention in this chapter is to look briefly at a number of the industries which operated in mills and relied on water for power, studying how they progressed in an historical context. Inevitably the study is related to the chapter on the mill in history and to individual entries in the main body of the book dealing with mills of significance in the development of specific industries.

Historically, the growing of corn and the trade in wool were the most significant of the nation's early industries, and both were vitally dependent upon water-power. Then, as successive major industries, such as iron and textiles, were developed, each passed through a phase when water-power was of paramount importance to its success. Even silk- and needle-making, smaller, specialist industries, reflect this dependence.

Only as new forms of energy – steam and electricity – were developed did the hitherto indispensable role of water-power begin to fade. To an increasing degree, its limited survival in the twentieth century depended, like that of the watermill, on a reluctance to consign it to history and not on strict commercial values.

Corn-milling

The first purpose to which the mill was put was the grinding of cereals. While other cereals played an important part in the diet of early man, the most valuable has almost always been corn. The original mill was the hand-quern, while the water-wheel was used for irrigation. Once the two were combined, the pattern of growth of the watermill closely followed historical trends in agriculture.

In Britain – indeed throughout Europe – the rapid expansion of population between the eleventh and thirteenth centuries placed enormous pressures on both the available land and current farming practice. Draining the wetlands and clearing forests and wastelands took on considerable significance at this time. Monastic settlements often led the way in clearing and reclaiming land and in investigating new ways of farming. Many schemes involved creating small hamlets in hitherto unproductive areas, but when, as a result of declining climate, poor harvests and the plagues which afflicted both animals and humans, the population decreased in the fourteenth century, many hamlets were abandoned. Nonetheless, the basis for improved levels of cultivation had been laid.

It is uncertain when such ideas as the use of fields for alternate grazing and tillage were introduced. New crops, larger, more productive farm units – each played a part in the so-called agrarian revolution which was to lead, by the end of the Stuart period, to an established industry capable of supplying a much-expanded home demand and a burgeoning export trade. The process continued long into the nineteenth century, when Britain – with a greatly increased population – was still largely self-sufficient in grain. In recent years there has been a tendency to minimize the 'revolutionary' aspects of the early history of agriculture (concentrating them into the developments of the last century) and to lay greater emphasis on overall achievements: an 'agrarian evolution'. Farm and estate records have proved to be valuable sources of data, and surviving mill records could surely supply equally useful information.

The miller profited during the gradual development of agriculture and of society. After the bad years of the Middle Ages his standing slowly increased until he often reached a status reflected in his fine millhouse. In this he was assisted by several factors. He – and, not infrequently, she – was in a position to study the workings of the efficient tenant farmer and, when he became a working tenant or landowner himself, to employ good farming practice based on observation of the successes and failures of others. Corn-milling was a lucrative business, supplying a steadily expanding population with a staple part of their diet. On balance, those millers who failed in later centuries did so because they had overstretched themselves with loans for new premises.

That at least was the situation until the late nineteenth century, when a rapid expansion of population led to a demand for more flour. It was provided by a combination of relatively new ideas. Roller-mills had been tested in the late eighteenth century but the first all-roller mill was not opened until 1870, and roller-mills did not begin their remarkable 'rise to power' until they were demonstrated in London in 1881.

The introduction of steam-engines (first used commercially at the Albion Mills in London towards the end of the eighteenth century but not widely adopted until the latter half of the nineteenth century) removed the need to site a mill by a convenient water-source and allowed large new mills to be built at ports. Here they could take advantage of increasing imports of grain arising from the repealing of the Corn Laws in 1846.

The importing of hard winter wheats from North America forced a major re-appraisal of milling methods. As discussed elsewhere (p.24), traditional mills did not cope well with these new wheats and, once forced to give way to roller-mills, the corn-mills passed, in a remarkably short time, from playing a central part in many local economies to being an archaic reminder of a lost world. Only in the latter half of the twentieth century did 'real' bread stage a recovery and a trickle of mills return to production on a quasi-commercial basis.

Woollen Industry

From the twelfth to the end of the eighteenth century, wool was the staple industry of England, affecting the nation's fortunes, inextricably bound up with the very fabric of society. At first wealth was created through the export of wool, often by the monastic foundations which maintained large flocks of sheep on their vast estates and which possessed Continental connections to whom they could sell the fleeces they produced. Great Cistercian abbeys like Fountains were almost literally built on the backs of the flocks which roamed the Yorkshire Dales.

Interest in overseas trade declined as the production of good-quality woollen cloth for the home market began to expand in the fourteenth century. Soon the export of wool was actively discouraged, and by Tudor times it had disappeared. Edward III introduced new skills when he encouraged Flemish workers to settle in England in the 1330s, and other factors led to expansion of the industry in many parts of the country.

This development was made possible, at least in part, by the introduction of water-powered fulling-stocks. Fulling was a vital process in the production of broadcloth, converting a relatively loosely woven fabric into a close-knit one, by soaking it in water and fuller's earth and then pounding it by foot. Fulling-stocks, heavy wooden hammers, achieved the same result with less labour and greater efficiency and were constrained only by a lack of water.

Weaver's guilds had been established in towns as early as the twelfth century, but the restrictive practices and attitudes the guilds introduced hampered progress, a problem repeated in the seventeenth century when the needle-making industry suffered in a similar fashion (p.44). Although the migration of the woollen industry away from the guild-dominated towns was to take some centuries to complete, it really began with the appearance of water-powered fulling-stocks. Once the power of the guilds was broken, the manufacture of woollen cloth became very much a cottage industry, remarkably well organized if often poorly paid, until the eighteenth century.

Apart from the prosperity it eventually brought both regionally and nationally ('the richest and most valuable manufacture in the world', said Defoe of woollen goods), the success of the woollen industry had a lasting effect upon the townscape, with the building of fine, large town houses, still a major feature of many towns, particularly in the West of England. Many of these houses were built by the clothiers who had replaced the guilds in organizing the industry.

The eighteenth and nineteenth centuries continued to be periods of great prosperity for much of the industry, but it had entered a period of rationalization which would lead to the rise of Yorkshire to a position of pre-eminence. A cloth-producing area from the fourteenth century, Yorkshire's movement towards dominating the woollen industry began early in the eighteenth century with the success of its cheap, narrow cloth. Although there was initial, and violent, resistance to the introduction of new machinery (already revolutionizing the cotton industry), Yorkshire workers ultimately responded better to the demands of mechanization than did those of East Anglia and the West Country. Five centuries earlier, these had been among the earliest areas to accept change, including the arrival of workers from the Continent – now their labour force resisted the new machines and lost ground they would never recover.

In the event, and because wool did not lend itself to mechanical handling in the way cotton did, machines took longer to penetrate the industry. By the time they had become established, steam had replaced water as the major source of power; indeed, many of the large new mills, although sited by rivers, never employed water-power. As in so many industries, the nineteenth century sounded the death-knell to the long connection between water-power and wool.

One of the most beautiful mill buildings anywhere in Britain is the fulling-mill at Alresford. It's now a private house and not open but can be enjoyed from a public footpath beside the lovely River Itchen (p.99). The Nailsworth area of Gloucestershire (p.97) still contains several, generally dilapidated examples of large mills built during the early nineteenth century. Newmill Woollen Mill in Elgin (p.210) was responsible for the introduction of several of the more exotic cloths introduced in the last century or so. Conversely, Newtown in Wales was a great centre for cheap cloth in the nineteenth century – and the site of the first mail-order factory – and Esgair Moel (p.202), now re-erected at St Fagans, is an important survival from an area once called 'the Leeds of Wales'. By contrast, Armley Mills in the real Leeds (p.184) was once the largest woollen-mill in the world.

Iron Industry

The iron industry in Britain has an immensely long history, stretching from the Iron Age to the present day. For the early part of its existence the industry relied on a low-temperature method which, after lengthy working, produced wrought-iron. The development of high-temperature methods – first employed at Buxted in Sussex in 1543 – transformed this ponderous process, introducing the possibilities of industrial expansion.

Essentially, the new process depended upon improved 'blast' furnaces operating at high temperatures achieved by the use of water-powered bellows. The temperatures were capable of melting the iron, enabling it to be cast in finished form, giving the industry an alternative to wrought-iron; equally significant for the future, the process allowed much larger quantities of iron to be produced than by the low-temperature method.

Until the early years of the eighteenth century, when Abraham Darby of Coalbrookdale showed how charcoal could be replaced with coke, the industry was limited to areas where there was a good supply of wood for charcoal and of water to power the bellows and tilt-hammers, a vital component of the iron-making process. The Weald of Kent and Sussex possessed both in good measure and also yielded generous supplies of iron ore. As a result of all this, the industry underwent a dramatic expansion in the Weald during the sixteenth and seventeenth centuries. The combination of wood, water and iron ore made the site on which Warnham Mill now stands (p.166) an archetypal Wealden furnace.

But the Weald had disadvantages for the long-term future of the industry. Many of the furnaces were in remote sites, far from potential markets, and were hampered by lack of an adequate transport system. More important, the great Wealden forests were virtually exhausted by the end of the seventeenth century (the dates of remaining sites demonstrate how the forests were denuded in an east-to-west direction), and the iron industry began its migration away from the south.

Not that Darby's discoveries had a dramatic effect. Indeed, the history of the iron industry in the eighteenth century is one of gradual development of new ideas. In the meantime, the Coalbrookdale Company was successful and, to ensure a regular supply of water whatever the conditions, it installed a Newcomen engine to pump water to its millpond. Once John Wilkinson had discovered how to produce accurately bored cylinders for the new steam-engines being developed by James Watt, steam began to replace the water-wheel in supplying a constant air blast to furnaces – the second Boulton & Watt steam-engine to be made was installed at Wilkinson's foundry.

Although large-scale production of steel did not begin until the Victorian period, there were developments affecting the smaller foundries, beginning with Benjamin Huntsman's process first demonstrated in 1742. Water-power would play no significant part in the large industrial plants but it could, and did, contribute a great deal to small hamlets like Abbeydale (p.181). Production of a range of scythes, knives and various agricultural edge-tools continued until 1933, employing water-wheels to supply power to the tilt-hammers, blowing-engine, grindstones and boring-machines. The situation was almost identical at the Finch Foundry (p.88) which survived until 1960.

Needle-making

In the early Middle Ages needle-making tended to be a sideline for village blacksmiths. But, although remaining very much a 'cottage' craft until the early years of the seventeenth century, it ceased to be restricted to country areas once needle-working machines were introduced. Needle-pointing, scouring (brought to England from Italy in the fourteenth century, and polishing were all processes where the presence of a good supply of water could be valuable in powering the new machines. As early as 1250 there are references to needle-makers at Wilton, near Salisbury, and other major centres included London and Chester. At both these sites, communities were set up close to the city bridges, and it has been suggested that they may have had access to working mills such as those under the arches of London Bridge.

The expansion of the industry in the seventeenth century led to the setting up of a guild, its charter granted by Cromwell in 1646. But, as happened with other guilds and associations (the wool trade is one example), problems quickly arose because of increasingly restrictive practices. Dissatisfaction among members led to the break-up of the guilds, with many needle-makers seeking new areas in which to operate.

The history of Redditch, where many settled, is closely interwoven with the history of the River Arrow and the Cistercian Bordesley Abbey built beside it in 1138. The abbey had extensive lands in the area, developing a large and thriving trade, particularly in wool. The monks used water-power for many of the more exacting of their tasks, and among the fascinating discoveries made on the site in recent years are the remains of an early post-Norman watermill.

A factor contributing to the rapid expansion of the needle-making industry in Redditch was the number of enterprising local families prepared to adapt to new developments. The first necessity was to change the function of some of the existing corn- and forge-mills along the Arrow and the Alne. Forge Mill (p.106) was one of the earliest mills to be adapted to the new, industrialized processes which were to make Redditch the world centre of the needle-making industry. With relatively little change, it operated until 1958, by which time it was the only surviving water-powered needle-mill in the world.

Forge Mill was reopened in 1983 as the National Needle Museum and presents, in its various exhibitions, a comprehensive history of this fascinating industry from 'cottage' to major exporter – and of the vital role of the water-wheel in that history.

Silk Industry

Silk-weaving did not develop in Britain until the late Middle Ages. To a degree its progress was governed by the religious persecution of the period, with Protestants and Huguenots arriving in England in great numbers after such incidents as the massacre of St Bartholomew's Day in 1572. The Edict of Nantes in 1685 produced a further 50,000 refugees, many of whom settled in and around Spitalfields, bringing much-needed expertise to a languishing industry.

Interestingly, water-power was not used until the silk trade had become well established. Then, in 1721, a five-storey throwing-mill was built in Derby for Thomas Lombe. 'Throwing' is a process in preparing silk threads for weaving, and Lombe, whose half-brother John had secretly studied the working of the machines in Italy, installed Piedmontese throwing-machines, powered by water from the River Derwent.

After the Lombes had lost their exclusive rights to the use of the machine, a number of water-powered throwing-mills were opened, almost all in the north-west, with a further centre at Paisley. The industry entered a period of change in the 1770s, and towns such as Macclesfield and Congleton, major centres of the silk industry, began to turn to broadloom weaving. There is a working silk mill, Paradise Mill, in Macclesfield, with machines and an exhibition.

As a result of the free-trade policies of the 1820s, there was an all too rapid expansion of the industry which led for a time to a decline. However, by the 1850s the industry was once again operating at peak output, but by this time steam had begun to replace water-power in many industrial processes, and silk-throwing was no exception. Yet the mill Thomas Lombe built, effectively the first true factory to be built in Britain, had a relevance beyond the silk industry, for it pointed the way to the rapid expansion of the cotton industry, which, for a long time, was to rely heavily on water-power. Today there is a mill on the site (but not the original) which houses the Derby Industrial Museum.

Cotton and Other Textiles

The cotton industry led the way in developing the power-driven machines which would irreversibly change the face of British industry. An industry which had functioned efficiently by employing home workers, it faced, in the early eighteenth century, a rapid increase in demand. It needed a new direction, and a series of inventions involving the use of powered machines provided the stimulus. Of these the one which concerns us, in our study of the influence of water-power on industry, is Richard Arkwright's spinning-frame, patented in 1769. With it Arkwright set up a mill in Nottingham.

These first machines were driven by horses, but in 1771 Arkwright built a second mill at Cromford powered by water. The mill prospered, as did the village which Arkwright developed for his workers, based on the success of Matthew Boulton's Soho Manufactory, an engineering works with its own cottages, opened in 1762. Both concepts owed something to the silk-throwing 'factory' built by the Lombe half-brothers at Derby in 1721 (p.45). Like the Lombes and Boulton, Arkwright relied heavily on water, yet, ironically, the water-supply at Cromford was a continuing source of concern (p.82).

There is a wider irony concerning the cotton industry for, having been the first to adopt the new techniques of the late eighteenth century, all it did for the next 150 years, until its abrupt decline, was to refine them – no major technical developments occurred in the industry. Later mills might be better sited, mainly in Lancashire to which the cotton industry steadily gravitated; they were certainly larger, providing whole towns with employment; but the machines had their genesis in the eighteenth century. Even though the larger mills turned increasingly to steam, it too had already begun to be employed by the end of the eighteenth century.

Whether this was a reflection of an innate conservatism – even complacency – re-asserting itself after the heady pioneering days of the early 1800s, when cotton overtook wool as the main source of Britain's export trade revenue, is beyond the scope of this book. And whether that conservatism was, at least partially, responsible for the sudden decline of the industry is something for historians to decide. All that can be said with certainty is that water-power played a key part in the dramatic rise of this remarkable industry and that, in a few mills, it continued to be the prime source of power until well into the twentieth century.

Any study of the cotton industry must take in Arkwright's Cromford Mill (p.81), where the expansion of the industry virtually began. Higher Mill at Helmshore (p.120) and the interesting Calder Vale site (p.119) supply valuable insights into the development of the industry. The Lewis Museum of Textile Machines in Blackburn includes examples of almost every type of machine from the classic period of the industry. In Scotland, the two major developments were New Lanark (p.219) and Stanley Mills (p.221) with both of which Arkwright was also associated.

II

The Watermills of England, Wales and Scotland

Introduction and Abbreviations

This, the main part of the book, contains details of a selection of watermills to be found in the counties of England and Wales and the regions of Scotland.

Each individual county or region has an entry with a brief introduction considering the current status of its mills. English references usually include mention of the state of the individual shire as it obtained at Domesday. The introduction is followed by a list of mills consisting of either abbreviated entries giving basic details, or page references relating to main entries.

The mills have been included for a variety of reasons: some are of historical importance; some represent a specific application of water power to an industry or process; many are aesthetically appealing (at least to their proud owners – and me!). Some of these mills still perform their original functions; many do not and the range of applications to which they are currently adapted almost beggars belief. There are craft shops and tea shops, folk museums, mills which have been removed from one site and re-erected on another as part of a museum of vernacular buildings. Some sell flour although they do not all grind their own; others produce and sell animal feed. At least two are part of activity holiday centres for children. Among those being used as stores, two house theatrical properties – by a remarkable chance, both are in Surrey! One mill is used as a theatre, others as restaurants, a few as pubs, one as a brewery and many have been lovingly restored as homes. One or two are included here because, unless action is taken soon, they will not exist to be included in any future book on mills.

Some counties of England and Wales are dealt with in considerably greater length than others – I refer to them in the text as 'core' counties. The obvious reason – that they possess more mills than others – is only part of the explanation. Those with limited time will be able to sample a range of mills in a relatively small area and obtain an indication of how much variety exists in a seemingly narrow subject. Most of the 'core' counties have good holiday facilities.

Scotland is described in slightly less detail; only Grampian qualifies as a 'core' area.

I have deliberately avoided a set format in the entries with the result that in some the concentration is on the history of the mill, in others, on the industrial process it embodies. Some of the small, lovingly-tended family mills, have, perhaps rightly, drawn a less critical reaction from me than might a professional museum. In the final analysis, what appears here are my impressions, my opinions. They may be wrong, they will certainly contain factual errors, but they are expressed honestly and, invariably, with a sense of excitement. If they encourage you to turn the page and discover another mill, another county, they will have achieved their purpose.

No opening arrangements have been given, for experience shows that these are liable to review at short notice, even in the case of mills which regularly open on a commercial basis. It is always advisable to check times and dates of opening before visiting. Many mills listed here do not open on a regular basis, but their owners are usually willing to show their mills to interested visitors who contact them in advance. Where mills are shown as NOT OPEN no attempt should be made to enter either grounds or buildings – most of which are private homes. Almost all can be viewed from public roads or paths.

Facilities for disabled visitors: inevitably these are limited as mills are not easily accessible even to the more able-bodied. I have indicated those mills where particular attempts have been made to ease access for disabled visitors.

Abbreviations

The following abbreviations have been used:

CADW: Welsh equivalent of EH & SDD.

EH: English Heritage, the popular name for the Historic Buildings & Monuments Commission. Details of opening arrangements are included in their literature.

NGS: on certain days of the year some garden owners open their gardens to the public under the National Gardens Scheme. The proceeds are used to benefit certain charities; open days are published in the NGS annual guide.

NT: National Trust. Details of opening arrangements for the mills listed here are included in their literature.

NTS: National Trust for Scotland. As for National Trust.

SDD: Scottish Development Department (Ancient Monuments). Roughly equivalent to EH in England.

TCG: The Traditional Cornmillers Guild. Set up in March, 1987 by a group of independent wind- and water-millers, all using natural power to produce unadulterated stoneground meals and flours. The sixteen mills currently comprising the Guild are located throughout England and Wales; all fourteen of the watermills are listed in this book. TCG has already published a recipe book by Desna Greenhow of Otterton Mill (p.86) and it is of interest both historically and as an indication of a welcome current trend in milling that four of these mills list women among their millers.

England

Avon

All four of the areas shown in this brief gazetteer of the relatively new administrative area of Avon did possess a mill in 1086, but the mill at Claverton would have been very different from the present pump-house.

The disappearance of many small mills which must have functioned here at one time can be traced to the growth of roller-milling in large dockyard areas, such as those at Avonmouth. Many of the mill buildings associated with industry which do remain in Avon have been converted to unattractive uses or allowed to become derelict in recent years. Conversions to private dwellings are relatively rare; both Stanton Drew and Wellow have examples but, unlike Algar's Mill at Iron Acton, they are not open to the public.

Bristol: Stratford Watermill, Blaise Castle House Museum, Henbury – In 1956 the mill was moved from West Harptree, where it had worked for approximately 250 years, up to 1952, when the Chew Valley reservoir was constructed; open only by appointment.

Claverton Pump-House and Water-Powered Beam-Pumps, near Bath – below.

Iron Acton, near Chipping Sodbury: Algars Mill – 300-400-year-old millhouse through which millrace runs; edge-runners by door; two-acre garden beside River Frome; occasionally open through NGS.

Priston Mill, near Bath – p.56.

Claverton Pump-House, near Bath

From the outside, Claverton may look relatively unimpressive, for it bears a superficial resemblance to an old-fashioned electricity sub-station, although with some touches of what might be termed restrained dignity – it has good round-headed windows. Inside, the beam-engine is a splendid example of its kind (see also Coultershaw, p.164); the Crofton beam-engine near Marlborough is similar, but steam-driven.

Built between 1810 and 1813 to pump water from the River Avon to the Kennet & Avon Canal, forty-eight feet above, the engine was designed by John Rennie. It stopped working in 1952 after an argument with a floating log but, having fallen into disrepair, the pump-house was restored and reopened in 1975 as a result of heroic efforts by members of the Kennet & Avon Canal Trust.

The enormous cast-iron breastshot wheel with its wooden floats is 17½ feet in diameter and twenty-four feet wide and is housed in a wooden shed set at right-angles to the engine-house. It drives a sixteen-foot-diameter pit-wheel, and a series of other wheels and shafts operate the cast-iron beams through connecting rods in each of the pump's two cylinders. Working at full power of sixteen strokes per minute, the two bucket-pumps could raise an estimated 70,000+ gallons of water per hour from the Avon to the canal.

Priston Mill, near Bath

Priston Mill was worth 7s. 6d. when Domesday was compiled, making it very much the poor relation of the Abbey Mill at Pulteney Weir, which was worth 20s. Both were owned by the Benedictine monks of Bath Abbey – or rather 'the Church of Bath', as it then was. Perhaps the most exciting aspect of Priston is the possibility that it is on an Anglo-Saxon site, which would place it firmly among the oldest sites still operating in Britain. Furthermore, it is still proving commercially viable after a thousand years of producing flour, although for a brief period in the eighteenth century it was a fulling-mill.

At first glance, the mill hardly seems to be in an ideal position, for it stands in a quite remarkably remote and untouched rural area away from the village of Priston, but, of course, it is this very degree of isolation from other mills which made Priston – and many others – so valuable to the scattered communities they served.

The air of detachment at Priston is compounded by the austerity of the mill building – an early eighteenth-century three-storey building of Bath stone, functional but not lacking in proportion. Approached along narrow lanes, it sits behind a small millpond, appearing, as do so many of its type, to be just two storeys high. From the large farmyard, the effect is totally different, for the mill appears to be of considerable size, an impression heightened because the wall at its east end is almost blank.

The supply of water to the pitch-back water-wheel is unusual – the wheel is set at an angle of 90 degrees to the water-flow, which passes through a grill in the wall of the mill onto an iron launder and then spills over into the wheel-buckets. The cast-iron wheel is twenty-two feet in diameter and was installed in the 1850s, along with much of the machinery. The Conygre Brook has never been an entirely reliable source of water during dry spells, and at one time a long leat was cut from another stream running through the village.

The gearing of the machinery for the transfer of power from the water-wheel to the stones is basically the same in the majority of mills, with subtle variations brought about due to the structure of the building, local custom and, frequently, the individuality of the miller. Here, the two iron stone nuts have loops built into them, and they and their spindles are lifted out of mesh by 'spearing' them on a 'fork', technically called a rigger.

Variations also arise in the terminology associated with mill machinery. At Priston the wooden vats or tuns which encase the millstones are called 'hurstles', one of many localized terms for them. There are two pairs of stones – one modern (1963) composition pair and an older pair of Derbyshire Peak stones. Outside the mill there is an interesting old stone of a type restricted to the south-west. Cut in one piece from quartz conglomerate, it provided a cheap substitute for Peak or French Burr stones. A possible source for this stone would be the Penallt area near Monmouth, where cut stones were rolled down the steep sides of the Wye Valley to await transport by boat.

A high proportion of the corn used at the mill is still bought locally, and the flour produced is on sale at the farm and craft shop. Whatever the cost, it is a small price to pay for a bag containing a thousand years of milling history!

Bedfordshire

Bedfordshire was, in the literal sense of that word, one of the most 'civilized' counties when Domesday was compiled. There were a great number of mills – Luton alone had six (some say seven) – but the modern county has remarkably few which may be viewed by the public. The problem was, as elsewhere, that the majority of small estate mills did not survive the upheaval in 'taste' brought about by the introduction of white bread of uniform quality. Largish establishments, such as Jordan's, were able to continue and remain successful by diversifying their range. Bromham Mill is a good, if rare, example of what sensible County Council authorities can achieve in the field of conservation.

Biggleswade: Jordan's Mill – Large, family-run mill, still producing a wide range of products.

Bromham Mill, near Bedford – p.58.

Bromham Mill, near Bedford

Though few, references to Bromham Mill occur with tantalizing regularity throughout the centuries, ensuring that we at least have some sort of picture of its history. It is obviously one of the pair of mills listed for Bromham in Domesday which together rendered 225 eels as part of their dues. Records show that as much as 1½ hundredweight of eels were taken in a single night in the eel-trap at Bromham (demolished as recently as 1961). As a point of interest, Domesday confirms that the majority of Bedfordshire mills rendering eels 900 years ago were situated along the Ouse – eels clearly don't learn much from history!

What we can learn is that both the mill and the manor of Bromham belonged to the Dyve family in 1565, passing in 1708 to the Trevor family, in whose hands it remained until the present century. The major tenants were the Biggs family, who were living in the mill in 1792 and remained in occupancy until 1905.

The construction of the older part of the mill straddling the mill-stream is interesting: red brick on stone with a small section of the upper part half-timbered in an almost decorative fashion. It is early eighteenth-century and was possibly extended by the Trevors in the years after they bought it. The smaller and newer section, containing the reception area and natural history display, is Victorian and built entirely of stone.

Inside the mill there is a range of machinery – more than could be driven by the one remaining wheel. A wheel at the eastern end collapsed in 1939 and was not replaced. The low-breast iron wheel (fourteen feet in diameter, seven feet wide) was installed in 1908 and repaired in 1980. The Derby Peak stones it drives have experienced every variety of power source during this century, water giving way to steam in the 1920s. A Petter oil-engine was employed in the 1930s and became almost the only source of power as the mill-stream silted up. The oil-engine gave way to electricity for a period in the 1940s, but milling was already proving uneconomic and was abandoned in 1943. The last tenants left the mill in 1970, and it was then occupied by squatters. Interestingly, they used Bromham for the production of pottery and leatherwork, foreshadowing the trend in the later 1970s to convert mills to craft centres. Near disaster struck the mill in 1974, when fire destroyed the roof and upper floor of the old part of the building.

Bromham Mill had already been bought by the County Council, who have now renovated it, incorporating material salvaged from the site. The renovation seems to have been aesthetically and historically successful; only the pantiled roof shown in old photographs has been replaced by slate. Inside the mill the machinery is in good condition, clean and well lit. I am not convinced that some of the ancillary displays are an asset to the mill – they include an art and craft gallery as well as the natural history section. By contrast, the descriptive panels outlining the history of this and other mills in Bedfordshire are models of what such things should be: concise yet informative, sensibly illustrated and well displayed.

Berkshire

The savage redistribution of Berkshire as a result of the Redcliffe-Maude recommendations has deprived the county of many of its best mills. At the time of Domesday it had large numbers of mills, particularly along the Thames and Kennet. As will be seen from the following gazetteer, very little is left to public view – even the National Gardens Scheme appears to have 'lost' two gardens on mill sites in the last couple of years. The Sheepbridge Mill site is included mainly for sentimental reasons (I passed it every day on my way to school for several years!).

Aldermaston: The Old Mill – good brick-built mill; NOT OPEN; River Kennet flows through garden; sluices and hatches; garden sometimes open under NGS.

Bagnor, near Newbury: Watermill Theatre – A very attractive village with immensely long history; on Domesday site, the long, low 1830s mill was converted to a theatre in 1967; twenty-foot cast-iron wheel but no other machinery; beautiful garden compensates; restaurant.

Sonning: The Mill – Sonning had three mills at Domesday; this mill provided flour for Cromwell's troops based at Reading during the Civil War; it continued to work until 1969, latterly providing flour for Huntley & Palmers; converted to a theatre in 1982; two wheels remain, the smaller a feature of the bar area, the larger, one of the most powerful on the Thames, no longer turns.

Swallowfield, near Reading: Sheepbridge Mill – Valued at only 50d. in Domesday; mentioned by Mary Russell Mitford in *Our Village*, the last mill on the site was destroyed by fire in 1961; the present house was built in 1967; next door is the mill house – much altered but still a fine example of well-to-do miller's home; long a restaurant; house NOT OPEN – restaurant only to patrons.

Buckinghamshire

Many of us complain about the 1973 local government reorganization of county boundaries, but when Domesday was compiled by eleventh-century Normans, Buckinghamshire, a Saxon creation, was only a century old and very possibly resented by 'locals'!

The distribution of settlements and of the 114 mills recorded in the county at the time of the Domesday Survey is very uneven, with a heavy bias to the north. To a degree this reflects the striking variety of terrain still obvious to anyone travelling from north to south of the county. But it also confirms that the farming communities of the north were more advanced than those on the hilly Chilterns or in the wet Thames basin.

Ironically, all but one of the mills included here are in the south of the county. However, Olney proves the point, for it has the longest recorded history. Hambleden is one of the most visited and photographed mills in the whole country, although not open to the public. The two mills at High Wycombe (which is worth exploring for other sites and mills) offer a great contrast in size and beauty but have individual attractions, while the Pitstone Local History Society are continuing with their efforts to repair Ford End, a mill of architectural interest.

Hambleden: Hambleden Mill – below.

High Wycombe: Bassetsbury Mill – beautiful late seventeenth-century red-brick building set in a delightful small garden; large wheel remains, visible through trees surrounding house; water still flows under building, once an inn, and now converted to flats; can be seen from drive leading to adjacent Community Centre. NOT OPEN.

High Wycombe: Pann Mill – Small building beside A40 on edge of public space known as the Rye; whitewashed brick mill sadly demolished in 1967 – undershot wheel remains as landscape feature; High Wycombe Society have reconstructed building and reassembled machinery; work in hand to supply water to wheel through leat; difficult parking.

Ivinghoe: Ford End Mill – Three storeys, although comparatively small building, with a distinctive mansard roof, uncommon in this area; small iron overshot wheel with internal machinery and two sets of stones; last worked early 1960s; slow progress being made in restoring mill.

Olney: The Mill – A four-storey mill on the Ouse, with lucam; probably on the site of the Domesday mill, valued then at the relatively high price of 40s. and 200 eels; there were two manorial watermills here in the fourteenth century. NOT OPEN.

Hambleden: Hambleden Mill

An exceptionally attractive, white weather-boarded mill in an area of great beauty where heavily wooded hills still sweep down to cradle the Thames. The only problem is the difficulty in parking nearby (impossible on the busy, narrow road from Henley to Marlow), and therefore a hazardous walk of some 400 yards must be taken from the signposted car-park on the minor road almost opposite the mill.

Hambleden Mill is approached along a public footpath which leads to the weir across the river. The sound of water pouring over the weir is always pleasing but there is a reminder of the inherent dangers of such places in the parish register for 1753, when a bargeman was 'kill'd by accident, shooting ye lock'. Although there are parking-spaces and other paths near the mill, all are private and rather aggressively signposted as such.

The mill stands at Mill End, a mile or so away from Hambleden village, and is one of the seventy-eight in the county recorded in Domesday. It was held by Queen Matilda and, like most of the Thames-side mills, 'Hambledene' paid its dues in eels – in this case a thousand of them. Rent was a not excessive £1 a year. Like many mills Hambleden spent some time in monastic hands – ownership of the mill passed to the abbot of Keynsham in about 1235. Records of the fourteenth century are taken by some to refer to a second mill, although no trace of it survives. Rather confusingly, the present mill is sometimes dated to the same period but seems to be largely sixteenth-century. Let us just say that milling has been carried out on the site for close on a thousand years. Corn-grinding continued until 1955, although the water-wheel was replaced by a water-turbine early in this century.

The mill has now been extensively renovated and converted into flats; not perhaps ideal from the point of view of the purist but retaining a beautiful structure in a recognizable and acceptable form. The well-maintained Mill House and Mill End Farm play their part in heightening the aesthetic appeal of an always popular grouping.

The first Universities' Boat Race was from Hambleden Lock to Henley Bridge – Oxford winning after a false start. Today the world-famous Regatta course starts at Temple Island, about half a mile from the weir at Hambleden. NOT OPEN.

Cambridgeshire

Cambridgeshire in the eleventh century was very much more of a wetland than it is today, possessing a high percentage of mills to settlements, the bulk of which were in the lower half of the county. In this century many of the surviving mills have disappeared or are privately owned and do not welcome visitors.

By contrast, the part of the county still thought of by most of us as Huntingdonshire had a much more even distribution of population, except in the north-east where it bordered Cambridgeshire. The majority of its settlements were dominated by abbeys, such as Ely and, in particular, Ramsey, which held lands in twenty-two settlements in addition to Houghton.

Of the mills included in this section, Duxford and Maxey both have literary connections, and Lode, Maxey and Sacrewell retain much of the 'feel' of small community mills. The history of Houghton Mill is remarkably well documented and the site dates back to Anglo-Saxon times.

Anglesey Abbey, Lode: Lode Mill (NT) – below.

Duxford Mill, Duxford – At Domesday there were four mills strung out along the River Cam at Duxford – this is almost certainly one of them; many historical connections – Cromwell stayed here during the Protectorate; Kingsley said to have written parts of *The Water Babies* here (I know of at least three other places where this claim is made!); regular openings of garden under NGS.

Houghton Mill (NT), near Huntingdon – p.63.

Maxey Mill (TCG), Maxey, near Market Deeping – The present handsome three-storey mill, dating from 1779, is the third mill on this site and the last to be working on the River Welland; produces pig food for own herd; two pairs of stones driven by clasped arm, breastshot wheel, 13½ feet in diameter; mentioned in Clare's 'The Fall of the Year' – he regularly brought corn here from home village of Helpston; mill works most afternoons but is part of working farm and visits MUST be arranged in advance; no charge, donations requested for MENCAP.

Thornhaugh: Sacrewell Watermill, near Peterborough – p.64.

Anglesey Abbey, Lode: Lode Mill (NT)

On the edge of the village, with open fields on one side, Lode looks as many small estate mills must have done at the end of the eighteenth and throughout much of the nineteenth century. Part of the Anglesey Abbey estate, Lode Mill is a tall, three-storeyed building, built in the eighteenth century. The illusion of height is furthered by the unusual application of vertical weatherboarding. Originally a corn-mill, it ceased producing flour in the early years of this century, turning to the unlikely but commercially viable grinding of materials used in cement manufacture, finally ceasing to work in 1934.

The machinery, including two pairs of millstones, remained intact and has been restored by the Cambridgeshire Wind & Watermill Society. It is powered by an iron breastshot wheel with conventional gearing, and now grinds flour for demonstration purposes on average once a month. In mid-1988 the National Trust launched an appeal to provide more mechanism for the almost empty second floor – and to enable the mill to produce *white* flour! Entrance to the mill is free to visitors to Anglesey Abbey.

Houghton Mill (NT), near Huntingdon

When Domesday was compiled, Huntingdonshire boasted twenty-three mills, all powered by the Great Ouse or its tributaries. Several survived into this century, including an unbelievably romantic mill in that loveliest of villages, Hemingford Grey. The area between Huntingdon and St Ives contains the best of the Ouse, soft, lush scenery of great charm where green meadows border the slow-moving river as it drifts through avenues of willow and past a series of villages with tempting names.

Most of the mills have disappeared but one of the most significant mills in England remains. The tall, five-storeyed brick-and-timber structure with tarred weather-boarding of Houghton Mill (locally pronounced 'Hoton') is a fine specimen – probably even more attractive when it was thatched. The present mill, on an island in a backwater of the river, was rebuilt in the seventeenth and eighteenth centuries.

The mill at Houghton was purchased by Aylwin in 974 as part of the endowment of the Benedictine Abbey of Ramsey which he had founded, with St Oswald, in 969. Domesday records the value of the mill at 20 shillings, but this had risen to 100 shillings by 1165. Relations between tenants and abbey were often strained, and not just because of the fines imposed on any tenant who failed to take his corn to the mill for grinding. In 1515 the villagers obtained a judgment restraining the abbot from obstructing the river with floodgates. These may have improved the flow of water past the mill but had a disastrous effect on the surrounding meadows. After the Dissolution, the land became Crown property, and it was sold by Charles I in 1625. In the next 300 years it had many tenants – perhaps the most successful was the Quaker and 'village philanthropist' Potto Brown. During his tenancy the annual rent reached £352.

The mill contained three water-wheels, one on the north side and two on the south. In the 1930s they were replaced by sluices which still produce a very satisfying swirl of water when required. Much of the internal machinery remains and has considerable historic significance. The drive to the millstones is remarkably complex, achieving a highly efficient end result – ten pairs of millstones driven by the three wheels. In effect, Houghton represents the best example of the application of nineteenth-century engineering skills to mill design. But others were already applying their skills to developing roller-milling, soon to change the future of corn-milling irrevocably.

The National Trust acquired Houghton in 1939 and leased it to the Youth Hostels Association. The mill returned to the control of the Trust in 1983, when restoration work was initiated. Nowadays the machinery is electrically powered to produce small quantities of flour during demonstrations. The nineteenth-century miller's house and some land on the north bank of the river have recently been added to the property. The land may look a little run down but it is of considerable ecological interest, as there is no record of its ever being developed – a sort of 'unimproved marshland'.

Thornhaugh: Sacrewell Watermill, near Peterborough

The present mid-eighteenth-century three- and four-storey, T-shaped Sacrewell Mill is part of a delightful group of buildings in the typical warm stone of this part of the country. It lies in a little hollow, surrounded by a charming garden. There were at least six mills in the area, and there are grounds for thinking that Sacrewell is on a very ancient site, but although Roman artefacts are still frequently turned up by ploughing in the valley of the River Nene, I think the case for a Roman mill here is not, perhaps, sustainable.

Sacrewell Mill had two wheels at one time, but only a metal, pitch-back wheel, sixteen feet in diameter, five feet wide, with fifty-six part-timber buckets, is now in position. Dating from the 1860s, it originally drove three pairs of stones, with the second, smaller wheel powering two more pairs of stones. All the internal machinery (of conventional design) and two pairs of stones remain and are in working order; there are regular demonstrations of the machinery. No flour is ground but in 1988 the mill began to grind an amount of barley for the farm pigs – rather like Maxey, a few miles away (see p.62).

Sacrewell has a growing collection of agricultural and other artefacts on the upper floors, including corn dollies, flint weapons and tools, a fearsome collection of animal traps (many of them now banned) and a large Singer treadle sewing-machine. However, the highlight is the collection of weights and measures gathered by David Powell, who is in charge here. The Roman connection is demonstrated by the display of locally ploughed Roman pottery and coins.

There is a farm trail and, in several of the fine eighteenth-century outbuildings, larger machinery is on display. A little incongruously, the trail passes the Trout Research Unit owned by the Ministry of Agriculture and placed beside one of the older barns.

The mill and collection are owned and administered by the

Avon – Priston Mill. Possibly on an Anglo-Saxon site, Priston is probably one of the oldest mills in Britain – and it is still producing flour commercially.

Avon – Claverton Pump-House. The large breastshot wheel housed in the building on the right drives pumps in the larger building, raising water forty-eight feet from the River Avon to the Kennet and Avon Canal.

Berkshire – Watermill Theatre, Bagnor, near Newbury. A long, low attractive 1830s mill on a Domesday site in a lovely garden. Now a theatre and restaurant.

Bedfordshire – Bromham Mill. An early eighteenth-century mill with an unusual half-timbered decorative section. The Victorian addition, in different brick, is on the right.

Buckinghamshire – Hambleden Mill. A beautifully restored, much photographed, white weatherboarded mill. Worked until the 1950s, it is now converted to flats.

Buckinghamshire – Pann Mill, High Wycombe. Reconstruction work in hand on the mill, demolished in 1967. The machinery has been replaced and the leat (*in the foreground*) is being repaired.

Cambridgeshire – Sacrewell Watermill, Thornhaugh, near Peterborough. A lovely, warm, group of mostly eighteenth-century buildings.

Cambridgeshire – Lode Mill. The small estate mill of Anglesey Abbey. The unusual upright weatherboarding creates an illusion of height.

Cambridgeshire – Houghton Mill. An historically important mill rebuilt in the seventeenth and eighteenth centuries. The impressive swirl of water is created as the River Great Ouse passes through the sluices!

Cheshire – Nether Alderley Mill, Alderley Edge. This remarkably well-preserved mill was built in Elizabethan times. The back of the mill forms part of the dam.

Opposite: **Cheshire – Stretton Mill, near Farndon.** A range of materials were used in the repair of this seventeenth-century mill, including slate for the original thatched roof.

Cheshire – Quarry Bank Mill, Styal. A large complex which blends surprisingly well into the valley of the River Bollin.

Cornwall – Wheal Martyn Museum, Carthew. The striking entrance to this 'museum of the china clay industry' – a fine example of how imaginatively modern museums present their subject.

Cornwall – Morden Mill, Cotehele. This well-restored group of estate buildings includes, in addition to the eighteenth-century mill (*centre*), a forge and several workshops.

Cornwall – Lanreath Mill and Farm Museum. Among the farm machinery in this museum there is internal machinery salvaged from a mill at Launceston.

Cumbria – Little Salkeld Watermill, near Penrith. Some 200 years old, this is the third mill on the same site beside Sunnygill Beck.

Cumbria – Eskdale Corn-Mill, Boot. Lying just beyond a fine packhorse bridge in the lovely village of Boot in Eskdale – few mills can have a more romantic setting.

Derbyshire – Cromford Corn-Mill. A simple late eighteenth-century mill, built to serve the rapidly growing village, at present being restored by the Arkwright Society.

Derbyshire – Alport Mill. A charming small mill on the River Lathkill. The wheel and machinery are in place but the mill is used only as a store.

Derbyshire – Longford Mill. A fine nineteenth-century mill, now a private house. There is a large millpond at the rear and the waterways are a feature of the garden.

William Scott Abbott Trust, who are now opening it every day of the year. This decision seems to me to typify the spirit of Sacrewell – it is quite one of the friendliest mills in England. We arrived (as usual) late on a Sunday evening, and Mr Powell broke off mowing the lawn to talk to us with great enthusiasm about the place in which he has lived for the past forty years.

Sacrewell lies within easy reach of the A1 and of one of the finest inns in Britain, the Haycock at Wansford. How could it fail to be on any shortlist of favourite mills?

Cheshire

The boundaries of Cheshire have undergone frequent changes since the time of Domesday – parts of Domesday Cheshire are now in Wales, and other parts have recently been lost to Greater Manchester. At the time of the Survey, Cheshire was a land in turmoil, large areas 'wasted' by William himself, others devastated by the Welsh.

Not surprisingly, relatively few mills were listed and none of the following entries is on a site associated with Domesday mills. They are, nonetheless, mills of some significance – Styal is a pivotal site in the history of cotton-milling, Nether Alderley is architecturally and historically important, while Dunham (the third National Trust mill in the county) is a good example of the increasingly rare estate saw-mill. Bunbury has been very well restored by a Water Authority (not bodies always well favoured by millers) and, for so small a mill, Stretton seems to have a positively improper number of unusual features.

Alderley Edge: Nether Alderley Mill (NT) – below.

Bunbury Mill, near Tarporley – Present mill built of local brick about 1850; worked until 1960 when water-supply was lost following a storm and flooding of River Gowey; reinstated to working order by North-West Water Authority in 1977 with advice from previous tenant; working demonstrations; some production of stone-ground flour.

Dunham Massey Saw-mill and Pump-house (NT), near Altrincham – p.67.

Stretton Mill, near Farndon – p.67.

Styal: Quarry Bank Mill (NT), near Wilmslow – p.68.

Alderley Edge: Nether Alderley Mill (NT)

Two features are immediately obvious about the mill at Nether Alderley: its unusual external appearance and the inadequate size of the stream on which it lies. The flow of water from the stream would be insufficient to drive the two wheels the mill possesses. The solution adoptd by the Elizabethan millwrights who built the mill was to construct a large dam across the valley using the back of the mill to form part of the dam wall. Water from the stream flowed continuously into the dam and was released during the course of an eight-hour working day. In the event, the reservoir proved to be inadequate in coping with lengthy periods of drought, nor could it handle the quantities of water which might usefully be stored in wet weather. Four more reservoirs were therefore built, permitting the storage of floodwater. Nowadays, with no requirement for quantities of water, three of the reservoirs have virtually dried up.

Nether Alderley mill is built of red sandstone, common in the area and used in the construction of many large houses. Soft and easily cut, the stone has exceptional weathering properties, and as a result the outside of the mill shows remarkably little wear after 400 years of life. Because of its position against the dam, the roof has only a short slope on that side, with a long sweep – broken only by four small dormer windows – almost to ground-level on the road side.

Much of the original oak woodwork fitted by the Elizabethan carpenters has survived inside the mill. The great support posts are topped by two oak roof-trusses which in turn support purlins, windbraces and rafters, secured not by iron nails but by 'trenails' (wooden pins). Only the floors and the machinery have been replaced.

The first recorded reference to a mill on the site at Nether Alderley occurs in 1290, but no description of it has survived. The present mill was worked continuously over a period of four centuries before a decline in trade beginning with the repeal of the Corn Laws in 1846 was accelerated by the development of cheap forms of transport and of roller-milling. Communities ceased to rely on local millers, but the mill at Nether Alderley struggled on until 1939, when the condition of the machinery was such that further production was impossible without extensive, and expensive, repairs. The mill was presented to the National Trust in 1950, and repairs were carried out to the structure, including the laying of a new stone flag roof.

It was not until 1967 that more money was made available, allowing Dr Cyril Boucher, assisted by his sons, to begin a lengthy series of repairs, which were not completed until 1976. Both water-wheels had to be repaired; the upper was rebuilt using new wood, the lower needed a new axle. The two pairs of French grinding-stones were re-cut, and after reassembly corn was once more placed in the hoppers, the wheel turned and flour was produced for the first time in almost forty years.

Dunham Massey Saw-mill and Pump-house (NT), near Altrincham

Built in the early seventeenth century, Dunham Massey Mill is of immediate interest to the visitor for its situation. It is perched on the side of a tiny, steep-sided valley close to the much later laundries and stable block with which it harmonizes remarkably well. It was originally a corn-mill but was refitted as the estate saw-mill in about 1860.

The mill ceased to be used by 1895 and was restored by Dr Cyril Boucher on behalf of the National Trust (see also Nether Alderley, p.65) in the 1970s. The machinery is driven by a new wooden overshot wheel, fifteen feet four inches in diameter and three feet wide. A large frame saw, a circular saw, band saw and other machinery (of the period but not original) can be seen working on certain days of the week.

Near the orangery at Dunham Massey is the pump-house. The supply of water to the house was provided by a water-wheel between 1860 and 1890, when it was replaced by an engine.

Stretton Mill, near Farndon

There was a working mill on this site from the fourteenth century until 1959; it was in the ownership of the Leche family from 1596 until the 1970s, latterly as part of the Carden Estate. The present mill is early seventeenth-century and was originally timber-framed with a thatched roof but now has a slate roof over weatherboarding.

After falling into disrepair, the mill was imaginatively restored as a working museum by Cheshire County Council, who reopened it in 1978, following a large-scale restoration programme begun in 1975. In addition to their own planners, architects and civil engineers, the Council were fortunate in securing the assistance of Dr Cyril Boucher who has been responsible for so much outstanding restoration work on mills in the north-west of England. Stretton Mill is part of a very pleasing grouping of unrelated vernacular buildings in a charming, unspoilt setting.

A major feature is the fascinating sluice mechanism, which permits water to enter at three different levels. The water turns two wheels; one overshot, the other breastshot; the external overshot wheel powers machinery dating from about 1770, while the machinery turned by the enclosed breastshot wheel is Victorian.

Styal: Quarry Bank Mill (NT), near Wilmslow

In 1783 a young man named Samuel Greg was one of the first to realize that the new cotton-spinning technology devised by Richard Arkwright had opened the way for a new system of working. By 1784 Greg had acquired a lease of land near Wilmslow in the valley of the River Bollin, where he built a small mill. Within six years his pioneering efforts (including the training of workers and the use of apprentices – preferably girls, considered to be more amenable than boys!) had established him in the forefront of the new manufacturing methods of production.

Within another ten years Greg had doubled the size of the mill, and added a second wheel. In 1819 the largest prime mover then known was installed at the mill. This 100 hp iron water-wheel, built by Thomas Hewes, was thirty-two feet in diameter and twenty-two feet wide, providing power for a total of 10,846 spindles. A prudent man, Greg also installed a steam-engine for auxiliary power. Sadly, the wheel went for scrap in 1904, and the huge wheel-chamber remained empty until very recently, when a magnificent William Fairbairn iron wheel was installed.

Quarry Bank Mill relied for its yarn on hand-loom weavers, but the arrival of power-looms produced a dramatic downturn in profits. For once Greg's breadth of vision deserted him, and he rejected the opportunity to install power-looms, which did not arrive at Quarry Bank until his son, Robert, had taken control of the mill after his father's death in 1834. With this new lease of life, the mill continued to operate until 1894. At its height, the Greg empire had several mills and warehouses in Lancashire and Cheshire, and the last mill, at Reddish, did not close until the cotton industry was in what appeared to be its death throes in the 1960s.

Like Richard Arkwright at Cromford (p.81), Samuel Greg found it necessary to employ workers from outside the immediate environs of his mill, for the village of Styal had been exclusively agricultural since medieval times and many locals found difficulty in adapting to the new factory methods. Children, often from local workhouses, were a major source of labour, and one of the earlier buildings on the site was the Apprentice House. Long before education for children employed in factories was made compulsory, Greg built a school, followed by a chapel and cottages. Oak Cottages are arguably among the most attractive estate houses ever built; it is to the credit of the National Trust, who own the mill, and the Quarry Bank Mill Trust, who run it, that they have not succumbed to pressure to release the cottages to 'incomers'.

The Quarry Bank Mill Trust has achieved its aims of resurrecting the life of the mill by employing a number of skilled textile workers to demonstrate the machines which, although not original, are representative of those used throughout the industry during the last 150 years.

He would deny it, but the unrivalled position of Quarry Bank, which has won and continues to win almost every possible major award for museums – in 1987 *The Independent* gave it its newly instituted 'Museum of the Year' award – is very much the result of the genius (I use the word deliberately) of one man, David Sekers. A world that has totally disappeared – and many, who had to endure it, would add 'Thank God' – has been brilliantly re-created by his imaginative and creative abilities. Quarry Bank epitomizes the very ethos of a 'working museum' and, although it is far from the image of the mill which is the mainspring of this book, it simply demands inclusion.

Cleveland

Guisborough is a mill of some architectural merit worth a foray into Cleveland to study.

Guisborough: Tocketts Mill

Tocketts Mill is a handsome four-storey building with an even more attractive two-storey millhouse attached to it. The bulk of the building is mid-seventeenth-century, but it was fairly extensively rebuilt in the eighteenth and nineteenth centuries. It continued to grind corn until 1960 and, as in many instances, the mill machinery was simply left in place when the mill closed.

Staff and students of South Park Sixth Form College, Middlesbrough, began the task of restoring the mill in 1976. When complete, the mill was taken over, and it is operated as a museum by the Cleveland Buildings Preservation Trust. Flour is ground once a month, and there are displays connected with milling. The large (eighteen-foot diameter) cast-iron pitch-back wheel has been restored by the original millwrighting company. There are three pairs of stones and ancillary machinery.

Cornwall

At the time of Domesday, Cornwall was a poor and relatively unpopulated county. Even allowing for this, it is remarkable that only six mills were recorded in the entire county and that two of these should have been in Launceston. Unless the Domesday scribes for the counties of the west were very lax or uninformed, it must confirm the view that water-power technology was being introduced across the country from east to west and was only just penetrating Cornwall in the eleventh century.

By contrast with 1086, a relatively high number of mills have survived in Cornwall in this century. Although not all are being used for their original purpose, a remarkably high percentage are at least being well cared for (Trethake is just one recent example of the rescue of a dilapidated mill), and Cornwall takes high rank in the list of counties where the future of the watermill seems to be assured.

The Wheal Martyn Museum at Carthew does not fall within a narrow definition of the purpose of this book but it represents an important use of the water-wheel, while Lanreath and Zennor house interesting agricultural museums. Cutcrew, Heskyn, Hessenford, Hingham and Trethake give an indication of the variety of uses to which mills are being adapted. Pont Pill awaits conversion, possibly to a dwelling-house; Morden Mill at Cotehele has been refurbished and now forms part of one of the most complete groupings of estate buildings anywhere in the country.

Carthew: Wheal Martyn Museum, near St Austell – below.
Cotehele: Morden Mill (NT) – p.71.
Egloshayles: Hingham Mill, near Wadebridge – p.72.
Hessenford Mill – Attractive stone-built two-storey mill; wide metal wheel in position; at bottom of valley beside River Seaton; converted into private residence – part used as village post office. NOT OPEN.
Lanreath Mill and Farm Museum – Machinery, but not wheel, salvaged from mill at Launceston and housed in tithe barn; also farm machinery, tractors and cider-mill.
Pont Pill Mill, near Fowey – Victorian saw-mill, built in 1872, in need of some repair; may soon be converted; wheel has unusually wide buckets; nearby is a mill converted to a dwelling-house – the wheel can be seen on the side of the building. NEITHER IS OPEN.
Tideford: Cutcrew Saw-mills, near Saltash – p.72.
Tideford: Heskyn Mill, near Saltash – p.73.
Trethake Mill, near Lanteglos – p.73.
Zennor Watermill, near St Ives – Early eighteenth-century; last worked 1900; now houses the Wayside Museum containing domestic, agricultural, tin-mining exhibits; also original machinery and millstones.

Carthew: Wheal Martyn Museum, near St Austell

The museum of the china-clay industry, Wheal Martyn has been established to preserve details of the social and industrial history of china-clay production in mid Cornwall. Although not strictly within the confines of this book, it includes two important examples of the use of water-wheels. In my view it is one of the best of the new museums using modern techniques of display – I also found the staff very considerate when I arrived late one evening.

In an industry which literally dug pits in the ground to obtain its product, the collection of water and slurry in the pit bottoms was always a major problem. Water-power was the obvious source for pumping, and at Wheal Martyn there are two working wheels with crank axles capable of pumping water at some distance from the wheels through a system of driving-rods. A thirty-five-foot pitch-back wheel (the largest working water-wheel in Cornwall) was capable of driving pumps 1,000 yards away (cf. Lady Isabella wheel, p.111); it is claimed that the eighteen-foot overshot wheel could shift twenty-five gallons of clay slurry at a stroke.

Cotehele: Morden Mill (NT)

Cotehele, which has been in the ownership of the National Trust since 1946, is one of the most complete and important medieval estates to have survived. The present mill, itself of eighteenth-century provenance, is the centre of a group of estate buildings, including a wheelwright's shop, blacksmith's forge, saddler's and carpenters' shops and a saw-pit which was once powered by one of the mill's two wheels.

Morden Mill, as it is sometimes known, was used regularly until 1964, latterly for the preparation of animal feed. The large overshot water-wheel has been restored, but the second wheel which stood behind it has totally disappeared. Water to power the mill is taken from the Morden stream, threading its way down the densely wooded valley to join the Tamar at Cotehele Quay. The water is directed along a leat from a pool a quarter of a mile upstream, flowing over the wheel from a wooden launder. The wheel worked several pairs of millstones and a low-powered electric generator, now sixty years old but in working order. The mill machinery has been recently restored and works two sets of stones on the first floor. One pair is French Burr, the other of granite of the type normally used for grist-milling. Only this floor and the ground floor containing the machinery are open to visitors to the mill.

Although Morden is an excellent specimen of a manorial corn-mill, a great deal of additional interest at Cotehele is derived from the various shops, which are displayed much as they would have been when they were a working part of the estate. One of the most fascinating parts of the complex is a traditional West Country cider-house, often found on estates like this. Power for an apple-crusher was provided by a donkey-wheel: the donkey (or horse) walked in a circle turning a large gear-wheel meshing with the crusher. The crushed apples were made into a 'cheese', consisting of apple pulp and layers of straw. When complete, this was pressed, and the resulting juices were collected for cider-making.

Egloshayles: Hingham Mill, near Wadebridge

A delightful small mill, hidden away in a shallow valley just off the main north-coast holiday routes. Hingham, like so many old mills (there was a mill on this site in 1089), has been used for fulling and grist in addition to grinding corn.

The undershot wheel is still in place, and in the latter half of the twentieth century the mill is about to acquire a new use as a feature of a group of self-catering units planned by the owners, who took on this previously tenanted mill in 1984 when it was in a very run-down condition. It is one of several mills once operating in the valley; all the others have now dried out, but, remarkably, Hingham has never experienced any major problems with its water-supply.

Viewable from the road but NOT OPEN.

Tideford: Cutcrew Saw-mills, near Saltash

Cutcrew is one of four mills which once operated along a two-mile stretch of the River Tiddy. The two highest, Tilland Mill and Criffle Mill, are on private land, visible from the public road but showing little sign of their past use as corn-mills. The lowest, Heskyn Mill (see below) is now a restaurant.

Cutcrew Mill is thought to be the oldest of the four, dating back to the late eighteenth century. It is a three-storey, stone-built building under a slate-tiled mansard roof. The other components of an interesting group of buildings around the mill cover a range of dates. Included are some tiny one-up, one-down cottages, the lower of which has deeds dating from the seventeenth century – it is now in very poor condition and is used for storage. Another cottage in the group is Victorian.

Cutcrew began life as a corn-mill but was converted to an estate saw-mill after the opening of the larger, and more efficient, Heskyn Mill with its two wheels. Using first a circular saw blade and later a bandsaw, Cutcrew continued to work until 1958, with a particularly busy period during the last war when a number of additional saws were added. The layout of the gearing in the mill is conventional. In addition to the large bandsaw, the main pulley shaft drove a small saw, machinery on the ground floor and a hoist – a fairly typical example of the versatility of the average saw-mill (cf. Foulden, p.124, and Sleningford, p.177).

The main work of the saw-mill would have been for local farmers, producing and repairing carts and wagons – when the mill was taken over in 1979 the sawyer's patterns for cart backs and shafts were recovered. Wheelwrighting would also have been carried out, along with general repairs.

After closure the mill was unoccupied for over twenty years, but a surprising amount of its contents survived in various states of repair. A great deal of repair work has now been carried out but I think it not unfair to report that more remains to be done. The cast-iron overshot water-wheel, with wooden buckets, is in a state of collapse, as is the half-mile-long leat. Most internal workings remain; one of the outstanding projects is the proposed restoration to working order of the machinery, using a pump to provide power.

Cutcrew is a working mill again in the sense that the joiner's shop on the first floor is now used as a workshop where hardwood furniture is made to order. Other wooden craft products are sold in the shop on the ground floor.

Tideford: Heskyn Mill, near Saltash

Heskyn is an attractively restored three-storey stone mill now converted to use as a restaurant. The largest mill on the Tiddy, it was powered by two water-wheels operating at either end of the building. It served as both a corn-mill and a flax-mill. The remains of one of the wood and cast-iron overshot wheels and its pentrough can be seen from the approach to the mill. The internal machinery remains.

Surrounded by a pretty garden and with a very pleasant two-storey millhouse beside it, Heskyn creates a delightful impression in the steep-sided Tiddy Valley half hidden under the main A38 road (the group is clearly visible on the left of the road travelling east towards Saltash). A slightly jarring note is introduced by a tall brick chimney behind the mill; there is no firm evidence as to its function, although it probably supplied steam-power to the mill. Heskyn is one of several mills in the Tiddy Valley (see Cutcrew Saw-mills entry, above). OPEN ONLY AS RESTAURANT.

Trethake Mill, near Lanteglos

For a peninsula with perhaps the greatest concentration of holiday traffic on the south coast of Cornwall, the area between Fowey and Looe has some remarkably remote small valleys. In one of the most remote is Trethake, a mill with a rather austere exterior; it had become very run-down before John and Mary Roberts bought it recently. Mills operated on this site from the fourteenth century until the early 1970s. Trethake was a corn-mill, originally powered by two wheels; only one remains, and it is being restored for a fresh purpose – supplying electricity for domestic heating.

Water for the overshot wheel is brought along a leat running for two-thirds of a mile through the valley. The leat needs constant attention – Mr Roberts estimates that he removes ten tons of sand from it annually, and when it was first cleaned after a ten-year period, water took four days to travel along the length of the leat! Remarkably the internal machinery is in excellent condition, with a pit-wheel estimated to be between 300 and 400 years old. Most of the stone floor machinery remains and will be used as a feature of the planned living-room. A great deal remains to be done, but the Roberts are young and, if precedent is anything to go by, they could have a long time to realize their dreams – of the thirteen children of a nineteenth-century miller, twelve lived to be over ninety and one is still alive. NOT OPEN.

Cumbria

In 1086 William the Conqueror possessed just four settlements – all near the coast – in what is now Cumbria. The Scots claimed the rest of this barren land, which did not acquire the name Cumberland until the twelfth century. Only basic details (given under Yorkshire) of the land for taxing appear in the Domesday entries. There were no mills – indeed, there is some doubt that all the settlements were inhabited.

Today Cumbria has several well-maintained mills and others which are still in existence, if adapted for new purposes. At one time the county seemed to be losing mills at a worrying rate, but a pattern appears to be developing in recent years whereby 'touristy' areas such as Cornwall and Cumbria are in the vanguard of the movement to encourage the preservation of mills. This may be coincidence but the situation is at least healthy.

The list below is by no means exhaustive and there are a few exciting 'possibles', including a superbly sited but currently near-derelict mill at the National Trust's Acorn Bank property, where it is hoped to start restoration in the next year or two. Three of the mills, Eskdale, Heron and Muncaster, are among the best examples of traditional mills to be found anywhere. By contrast, the renovation of Whitewater Hotel is almost a 'culture shock', but it has saved an important old mill from demolition and may point the way for future developments of redundant large buildings.

Ambleside: Old Mill, North Road – Good reproduction wheel dating from 1973 – sixteen-foot diameter, forty inches wide on

eighteen-inch thick oak shaft; pottery, woollens and gift shop.
Backbarrow: The Whitewater Hotel – below.
Beetham: Heron Corn-Mill, near Milnthorpe – below.
Boot: Eskdale Corn-Mill – p.77.
Embleton: Wythop Mill, near Cockermouth – Originally a corn-mill, part of a rambling collection of buildings in various materials – mostly slate; converted in 1860 for use as a saw-mill serving local estates; overshot water-wheel installed at same time; ceased to work commercially in 1969 – wheel now used to drive a collection of vintage woodworking machinery; old hand-tools also on display: coffee shop.
Little Salkeld Watermill (TCG), near Penrith – p.77.
Ravenglass: Muncaster Mill (TCG) – p.78.

Backbarrow: The Whitewater Hotel

For years the River Leven provided power for a number of industrial uses in the vicinity of Backbarrow, including corn-milling – carried out on this site since the sixteenth century. The Blue Works was established in 1890, producing ultramarine for industrial purposes. Reckitts made 'Dolly Blue' for use in laundering in the five-storey mill from 1929 until it closed in 1981.

The mill's most memorable landmark, a tall chimney, was demolished in 1983, when Backbarrow was already entering into a new era. A major time-share leisure complex was developing, and the mill has now become a hotel with all the facilities seemingly demanded by residents and casual visitors alike – bars, restaurants, conference rooms and a health centre in one of the buildings. Wheels and machinery are featured inside the hotel, and the tailrace passes under an outside terrace and back into the fast-flowing river.

I cannot say that the 'resurrection' of Backbarrow Mill is to my taste but it is undeniably professional and is attracting considerable numbers of visitors at all seasons. The work involved in the restoration of the mill must have been immense, for the walls were apparently impregnated with blue-coloured dyes. That the developers thought it worth their time and money gives some hope for the future of other large, often derelict mills.

Beetham: Heron Corn-Mill, near Milnthorpe

Heron Mill first appears in records early in the thirteenth century, when the canons of Coningshead were granted land on which to build a corn-mill. The mill stands in a sheltered spot by a waterfall on the River Bela, and the position could hardly be bettered. The name comes from a long-vanished heronry. So good was the site that other mills followed, a fulling-mill and a paper-mill – the predecessor of the large complex which dwarfs the corn-mill today. Further 'sightings' occurred in later records and then, at the Dissolution of the Monasteries, Coningshead was destroyed and the mill transferred to a certain Sir William Thorneburghe.

We may assume that the mill continued to operate successfully in the following centuries, although not until the early nineteenth century do the names of the tenants begin to appear regularly in local trade directories. In 1927 W. & J. Pye became the final tenants, using the mill for the grinding of animal feedstuffs and working it until 1955, when they transferred its activities to other mills in their ownership. In this final period the mill was producing up to eighty tons of feed a week, flour-grinding having become uneconomic as the old mills proved unable to compete with roller-milling.

The water-wheel at Heron Mill is of mid nineteenth-century design, constructed of wood and iron and powering four pairs of stones. It is an enclosed sixteen-foot breastshot wheel driven by water supplied through a launder from a weir positioned across the natural waterfall. This relatively recent addition raised the level of the water, causing the main shaft to be positioned some eighten inches higher than earlier wheels.

The basic working of machinery in most mills follows a familiar pattern, subject to minor refinements introduced by individual millers. At Heron Mill the refinement is a second wheel, outside the building, installed early this century to drive a generator providing electric light to the mill.

In a two-storey addition set at right angles to the main building, there is a corn-drying kiln – always strong evidence that a mill is sited in one of the wetter areas of Britain. At Heron Mill grain for drying was spread on the clay tiles of the first floor and heated from below. When the appropriate moisture content was reached (it varied, depending on the uses to which the grain was to be put), the grain was swept into hoppers, bagged up and sent upstairs to begin the process of milling.

The present mill was built of local limestone in the middle of the eighteenth century, fitting perfectly into its natural surroundings. The 300-yard approach to the mill from a small car-park begins well, along a grassy path, but it is necessary to pass the modern buildings comprising Waterhouse Mills (the paper-mills referred to above), and some views from Heron Mill have more of the buildings as their backdrop. Mercifully, the best view of the mill, from the footbridge over the Bela, is free of such distractions. Part of the charm in visiting Heron Mill is in reaching the bridge and seeing this very agreeable, somehow familiar, building standing reassuringly beside the river.

Boot: Eskdale Corn-Mill

In a near-perfect setting halfway along Eskdale, the mill is reached across a beautiful small seventeenth-century packhorse bridge over Whillan Beck. There has been a corn-mill here since the thirteenth century, and the present mill certainly dates to 1578 and probably earlier. It continued to serve the area until 1920. Inside are a kiln, early wooden machinery and exhibitions of milling and farming (mainly photographs and documents concentrating on local agricultural techniques and history). Outside there are twin water-wheels, all but concealed by the branches of trees. The beck pours off the side of the valley, forming a series of waterfalls. In summer the picnic area is a delight, but it can be horrendously crowded. Visitors are asked not to park in Boot village – an almost impossible achievement, even in mid-winter!

Little Salkeld Watermill, near Penrith

When Nicolas and Ana Jones began the task of restoring Little Salkeld Mill on New Year's Day 1975, the 'cottage industry' in the rescue, repair and restoration of mills was just gaining momentum. In a sense, their achievements at Little Salkeld epitomize the whole of the movement back to milling and the production of wholewheat flour.

As Mr Jones has written in his remarkably comprehensive guide, the history of the mill is very sketchy, but we do know that this is the third mill built in or near the village. For four centuries one family, the Atkinsons, were millers at Little Salkeld, building the present mill 200 years ago. The mill concentrated upon the production of oatmeal, reaching its peak in the last quarter of the nineteenth century when the Settle to Carlisle Railway opened up more distant markets. Carrs, the famous biscuit-makers of Carlisle, employed the services of the mill when their own equipment was out of action.

New cast-iron water-wheels were installed just before the First World War, but the import of Canadian wheat and the use of roller-mills were, as demonstrated in so many instances, already superseding the traditional corn-mill. Following the common pattern, Little Salkeld turned to producing animal feed, effectively ceasing work in the 1950s, although a Bamford Crusher installed on the premises continued to roll barley and oats for a small local trade.

Little Salkeld is a long, low, deep pink-washed series of buildings, standing on Sunnygill Beck, with a half-mile-long millrace. There are two overshot water-wheels, both twelve feet in diameter. The larger wheel, four feet nine inches wide, operates within the mill, driving two pairs of French Burr stones and associated machinery. An earlier pair of stones, of interest because they were made of a soft local sandstone quarried near Lazonby, proved unsatisfactory for the production of flour, although useful for coarse milling.

The Joneses have not been afraid to introduce innovations, and the second wheel is now used to drive a heat-pump. This device, best known for its use in refrigerators, transfers heat from a low-temperature source to a place of higher temperature. At Little Salkeld it provides hot air for grain-drying and space-heating in the mill.

In a sense Mr and Mrs Jones were doubly fortunate in their timing at Little Salkeld, for their determination to use only organically grown wheat coincided with the upsurge of interest in 'proper' food. Their market has expanded greatly in recent years, to the extent that Nicolas Jones can now concentrate on flour-production and on the courses in milling and baking for which he is increasingly in demand – a recent student was Trevor Ripley of Bacheldre Mill (see p.199). A further sign of change is that supplies of organically grown wheat, once almost impossible to obtain on the western side of the country, are being produced locally for use in the mill. One, to my mind, sad result of the changes is that Little Salkeld is no longer being opened to the public.

Ravenglass: Muncaster Mill

A mill was first recorded here in 1455, although the present low two-storey mill, typical of many functional buildings built on the west coast of Britain (and throughout much of Ireland) was built in the eighteenth century. Milling of flour ceased in 1918 but the mill continued producing animal feed until its closure in 1961. It was renovated in 1976-7 and, after a sixty-year gap, flour was once again milled in 1978.

Power for the thirteen-foot overshot wheel comes from the River Mite via a 1,200-yard leat. The three sets of stones in daily use cover almost all known combinations – there are French Burr, Peak and shelling stones. The traditional kiln, so necessary in this climate, has been restored using floor tiling from a disused maltings in East Anglia. There is a range of auxiliary machinery, including a flour-dresser, wire-machine and winnower. The oat-shaker is a reminder that this was an oatmeal-mill similar to Little Salkeld (p.77) at the other end of the county.

Muncaster comes as close to epitomizing the old-style estate mill as any in the country – even the trains on the Ravenglass & Eskdale Railway (the beloved 'La'al Ratty') pause on request as they pass the front of the mill, a charming detail only slightly affected by the knowledge that the company owns it!

Derbyshire

At Domesday a large percentage of Derbyshire lay 'waste' or 'partly waste'. In many northern counties this simply meant that the land had suffered under King William's earlier forays but, in this instance, it possibly referred more to the natural condition of the land. Then, as now, the county was divided geologically, and the mills were mostly in what we term its White Peak and southern areas.

The arrival of industry in the area is reflected in the mills selected – Cromford and Caudwell's were both of great significance at different periods of industrial development. In complete contrast, the external appearance of Alport Mill perfectly represents the traditional image of a small mill and, were it open, would probably have been depicted on the cover of this book! Longford is a very handsome specimen of a larger village mill. The two ruined mills, Chatsworth (often surrounded by visitors) and Ible, both have important features justifying their inclusion here.

Alport Mill – p.80.

Bakewell: Victoria Mill – Early nineteenth-century mill; operated until 1945, now a laboratory; in front of building is a large (now very rusty) iron, rim-drive, breastshot wheel, sixteen feet in diameter, thirteen feet wide – about 1850; the most complete of several mills operating on the River Wye in this century. Lumford Mill (with Arkwright connections) is a little further north. NEITHER IS OPEN.

Chatsworth Park Mill, Chatsworth – Remains of eighteenth-century estate mill badly damaged by storm in 1962; of interest, partly because of its architectural merit; designed (by James Paine) as a feature of the park, not just as a functional building; remains of lowbreast cast-iron wheel with wooden floatboards; when agent here, Joseph Paxton had problems with the weir, much of which still remains with traces of mill leat.

Cressbrook Mill, near Litton – Architecturally important 1814 cotton-mill; clock and cupola; owned by 'Poet of the Peaks' William Newton, whose enlightened treatment of apprentices was in marked contrast to that at nearby Litton Mill; attractive Georgian lines – similar to Oldmills Mill at Elgin (p.211) – somehow surmount the muddle created by present repair work; situation is highlighted because popular Monsal Trail passes beside mill. NOT OPEN.

Cromford: Corn-Mill, Arkwright Centre – p.80.

Cromford Mill – p.81.

Ible Mill, near Grangemill – Small ruined mill; fragments of machinery remain; the high-breast water-wheel (about sixteen feet in diameter) is missing; attempts are being made to repair the mill, an important example of an increasingly rare illustration of a medieval mill. NOT OPEN.

Longford Mill – A most elegant, beautifully proportioned, nineteenth-century building of red brick; interesting lattice windows under a tiled roof; lucam; very large millpond at rear, with millrace under house; wheel still in place; cast-iron internal machinery now at Cromford Corn-Mill; viewable from road. NOT OPEN.

Rowsley: Caudwell's Mill – p.82.

Alport Mill

An exceptionally pretty mill in a beautiful and largely unvisited village, Alport Mill is sadly neither in use nor open to the public. Fortunately it is possible to stand on the lovely little bridge over the Lathkill (keep an eye open for traffic) and positively drink in the scene. The mill is on the right-hand bank looking downstream, nestling under the trees which cloak the steep sides of the valley. On the left bank there is a garden, lovingly maintained and, with the mill, forming an almost perfect frame for the Lathkill, one of the gems of an area famed for its rivers. And if you think this description comes close to hyperbole, visit the spot and discover its perfection.

The frustration of those who would love to see the mill working is heightened by the knowledge that it is in remarkably good condition. It has a rim-drive water-wheel, twenty-one feet in diameter, and retains five pairs of stones. There is a long drive-shaft with bevel gearing to each set of stones. At present the mill is used for the storing of animal feedstuffs.

Cromford: Corn-Mill, Arkwright Centre

Built around 1780 as a corn-mill to serve Arkwright's factory village (see Cromford Mill, p.81), the finished mill contained a corn-drying kiln, substantial storage space and a mill cottage. At one time two wheels drove different sets of millstones at either end of the building. It ceased working in the 1930s, when the remaining wheel and machinery were removed. The mill is being restored by the Arkwright Society, who have been given two sets of replacement machinery – one of cast-iron of about 1870 from Longford Mill (see above) and a wooden set from Tideswell Mill.

A water-wheel from a mill at Darley Bridge is being renovated and will eventually drive some of the machinery. It is intended that the mill will become the headquarters of the society, containing a small museum. Architecturally lacking in importance but pleasing in scale (particularly after Cromford Mill), it is in Water Lane, and a few feet lower down the road there is an iron rim-drive wheel previously used in grinding materials for paint-manufacture.

Cromford Mill

Richard Arkwright patented his roller-spinning machine (water-frame) in 1769, setting up a horse-powered mill in Nottingham in the same year. Two years later he used water-power for his new mill at Cromford; other factories followed in both England and Scotland. For many years the industry continued to thrive in various centres, but as steam replaced water-power it began to rationalize, settling in Lancashire.

The rapid development of a previously small-scale industrial process into large-scale factory production came about because the water-frame allowed large quantities of cotton to be spun quickly by relatively unskilled labour. But Arkwright also required skilled labour at Cromford, and it was the importing of workers from outside the area that led to the extension of the village into an industrial centre. Arkwright built cottages for his workers, a hotel, a chapel and, later, a market.

The first mill on the site was a five-storey building completed within five months of the purchase of the land by Arkwright and his partners. It was extended in the 1780s, and new water-wheels were installed. They have long since gone, and the top two floors of the mill had to be removed in the 1930s after a fire. Continuing success, with the mill and his inventions, led Arkwright to build a second mill on the Cromford site. Seven storeys high, its wheels side by side in the centre of the building, it reminded one visitor (Viscount Torrington writing in 1790) 'of a first rate man of war; and when … lighted up, on a dark night, look[s] luminously beautiful'. Fire, the greatest enemy of all mills, destroyed it in 1890.

By the end of the nineteenth century the site was let, becoming in turn a brewery, a laundry and a colour works. When the colour works closed, the mills were in a poor condition, and modern additions had often obscured buildings of historical importance. The Arkwright Society bought the mill site in August 1979 and began to restore it. Progress has been slow, due to lack of funds, but young people working on Manpower Services Commission schemes have greatly assisted here and at the Society's other main centre, Cromford Corn-Mill (p.80). The modern buildings have gone and various displays and exhibitions have been mounted. A great deal remains to be done on the restoration of Cromford Mill, but its potential and historical importance make it a most exciting prospect, though I have to admit to finding it a rather bleak place.

The demands on the supply of water to the site were enormous, and the strain on the primary source, the Bonsall Brook, was lessened to an extent by the use of the Cromford Slough (a lead-mine drain) and the construction of a series of reservoirs. Nonetheless, there can be few streams which were more intensively husbanded than the Bonsall Brook at the peak of industrial development in the Cromford area. Five or six mills, including Cromford Corn-Mill and the 'dark satanic' Via Gellia (from which came the trade name 'Viyella'), relied on water from it – and all in the space of a couple of miles as it makes its way from the moorland heights above Cromford.

Rowsley: Caudwell's Mill

I have included Caudwell's Mill, a turbine-operated mill, for its historical context. For over one hundred years, at a time of rapid change, the Caudwell family showed great enterprise in their willingness to adapt the working of the mill to new technology. As a result, they were able to maintain the mill as a commercial proposition until 1978 – long after most country millers had ceased trading.

Mills have existed on the site since the sixteenth century and almost certainly earlier. A corn-mill survived until 1858, while the original fulling-mill was replaced by a saw-mill early in the nineteenth century. When John Caudwell leased the site from the Duke of Rutland in 1874, the mills had deteriorated to the stage where it was necessary to demolish them and start anew. The exterior of the complex he built (at a cost in excess of £7,000) has hardly changed; the significance of the mill is its incorporation of almost all the major developments in milling of the last century.

When first built, the mill ground both flour and animal feed and was powered by two breastshot wheels. The flour-mill almost certainly possessed eight pairs of stones, while the provender section probably had three pairs. The wheels were obviously adequate for the task but not as effective when called upon to drive the roller-mills which were installed by 1885.

The story of the growth of roller-milling is one of the most remarkable of an era noted for its dramatic developments. It wasn't until 1881 that the technique was first demonstrated in London, yet within a decade it had almost replaced traditional methods of flour-grinding. Large commercial mills, often operating near ports where imported grain was landed in increasing quantities, became the accepted means of supplying an increased demand for the new 'white' bread. The decision to re-equip Rowsley mill after only a few years operation could not have been an easy one but John Caudwell was clearly a decisive man and he invested a further £3,000 in the new system. He next replaced the wheel of the flour-mill section with a turbine to ensure a more reliable source of power. A second turbine, still in use, was installed to power the animal-feed section in 1898.

At this time the provender business was probably the main source of income, but after John Caudwell's son Edward leased the mill, also in 1898, he took the bold step of developing the flour-milling side of the business. For much of this century the company was a major supplier of flour throughout Derbyshire. That it survived long after most small companies had gone to the wall is a tribute to Edward Caudwell's readiness, like his father's, to adapt to change. The mill was modernized in 1905 and further improved in 1907. Shortly before the outbreak of war in 1914, a German company was employed to install more new plant – when hostilities opened, its entire workforce was promptly interned, almost certainly a blessing in disguise for them! Improvements to both parts of the mill continued at regular intervals until the 1950s.

The mill is now operated by Caudwell's Mill Trust Ltd, who have restored much of the machinery installed in 1905 to working order. Flour is available in small quantities. Caudwell's is not a pretty mill, and its important features may not be immediately apparent to the visitor, but it repays a little study, perhaps over a drink in the even more historic Peacock Inn across the road!

Devon

Devon is one of three counties (Cornwall and Somerset are the others) for which there are two Domesday Surveys. Information on them is included in the Exeter (Exon) Domesday, probably one of the final Circuit Summaries made before the preparation of Domesday itself. Certainly it contains a fascinating amount of information excluded from the final publication. For an area with so many small streams and settlements, Devon contained remarkably few mills at the time of Domesday: of the places in this gazetteer, only Otterton (three) and Uffculme (two) were recorded as having mills in the eleventh century. As with Cornwall, this was probably because the use of water-power was still spreading westwards.

Devon is one of my 'core' counties (those dealt with at particular length) because of the range of mills still to be found in it. Inevitably in a holiday area there are a number of craft centres – Bickleigh and Otterton are among the best-known in England. Morwellham and Sticklepath incorporate important industrial sites, while at Harbertonford and Hele Bay the enthusiast can study more traditional mills.

Bickleigh Mill Craft Centre, near Tiverton – p.84.

Chagford: Mill End Hotel – Formerly Sandy Park Corn-Mill; millrace flows under hotel.

Chudleigh: Town Mills – p.85.

Harbertonford: Crowdy Mill (TCG), near Totnes – Traditional corn-mill on old, possibly thirteenth-century site; present mill early nineteenth-century; two contra-rotating overshot water-wheels, powered by Harbourne River; three pairs of stones and ancillary machinery; returned to work in 1984 – stone-ground flour on sale; owned by Martin Watts, responsible for restoration of Worsbrough Mill (see p.180) and author of books and articles on milling, chairman of newly instituted Traditional Cornmillers Guild.

Hartland: Docton Mill – Extensive garden around working watermill; millpond and leat in 7½ acres of wooded valley; occasionally open under NGS.

Hele Bay: Hele Mill, near Ilfracombe – p.85.

Ilfracombe: Bicclescombe Watermill – Late eighteenth-century mill, owned by North Devon District Council; machinery restored by Rotary Club; large wheel, powered by River Wilder, turns single pair of stones.

Morwellham Quay: Four Waterwheels, near Gunnislake – Morwellham, once a major inland port, restored by a Dartington Hall Trust; four water-wheels on site; first, overshot, cast in Tavistock in nineteenth century, used to pump drinking-water to cottages; second, thirty-two feet in diameter, once used in grinding manganese – both these can turn; third once used to power a corn-thresher, now worked by hydraulic ram pump; fourth, eighteen feet in diameter is 400 feet underground and fed from surface; tramway ride into copper-mine; several museums and traditional workshops.

Otterton Mill (TCG), near Budleigh Salterton – p.86.

Parracombe Mill, near Barnstaple – Fifteen-foot overshot wheel still in working order; viewable only on written application; pretty village with important eighteenth-century church.

Sticklepath: Finch Brothers Foundry, near Okehampton – p.88.

Uffculme: Coldharbour Mill, near Cullompton – p.89.

Bickleigh Mill Craft Centre, near Tiverton

Bickleigh Mill stands close to the junction of the Rivers Exe and Dart at the famous beauty-spot of Bickleigh Bridge. The A396 from Exeter to Tiverton is a very busy holiday route, and it is not surprising that the craft centre opened at Bickleigh in 1972 has proved to be very successful.

Bickleigh was a working corn-mill until the 1950s, when the weir broke. At the time the mill operated with two undershot wheels which were removed, along with the internal machinery. In 1972 one wheel was replaced and repaired using machinery from the dismantled Town Mills, Dulverton. The machinery now turns for demonstration purposes only.

The complex at Bickleigh is much more than a craft centre – it contains the craft workshops which formed the core of the project, and a whole range of other features. There is a working nineteenth-century farm and farm shop, an agricultural museum, fish farm and cloth centre. The mill centre, which can be very busy, is unusual in that particular efforts have been made to accommodate wheelchair users – it is sadly true that, due to the basic design of mills, disabled visitors always face considerable problems of access when visiting them.

Chudleigh: Town Mills

The bishops of Exeter had a palace at Chudleigh, a small, agricultural village until the thirteenth century, when the growth of Plymouth and the extension of the main road from Exeter increased its importance. Its major industry was the production of limestone from the bishop's quarry, but at one time it was involved in the woollen industry, and Town Mill was converted to a fulling-mill. For most of its working life, however, the mill has produced corn.

The present iron-framed, pitch-back wheel was installed in 1860, replacing a smaller, wooden wheel. Enclosed in the twenty-foot diameter cast-iron frame are seventy elm buckets. The launder is carried between the mill and one of the converted outbuildings, and the water flowing down it and into the buckets helps the wheel develop between 15 and 30 hp. No flour is ground today, but the wheel and some of the machinery turn.

With its outbuildings, the mill is a large, not unimpressive stone complex in which several craftspeople work, producing items from the traditional to the *avant-garde*; they include a blacksmith, toymaker, stained-glass artist, leatherworker, shoemaker and printmaker. A restaurant occupies part of the ground floor of the mill – close to it is the mill machinery, well maintained and lit.

Hele Bay: Hele Mill, near Ilfracombe

In Domesday Hele is referred to as 'Hela', but by 1525 the village had become known as 'Helemyll', confirming the existence of a mill on the site in the early years of the century and possibly before. Part of the external structure of the present mill certainly dates from this period. The mill was worked until shortly after the war, when it was sold and virtually abandoned. The present owner, Mr Lovell, acquired it in 1973 and devoted five years to restoration work. He produces stone-ground flour and other items in small quantities.

Hele contains several technically interesting items of machinery. Some belong to the mill, others have been introduced. They include an early porcelain roller-mill and a complex system of flat belts powered by the wheel or by a diesel brought in to supply power when the water-flow is inadequate. This is a frequent problem in summer, as the two main water-supplies to the mill were lost during the period of neglect.

The overshot water-wheel is eighteen feet in diameter and of cast-iron construction with fifty-six wooden buckets. Manufactured in Barnstaple, it was installed when the mill underwent a major refit in the late 1920s. The internal machinery is the now common mixture of cast-iron and wood. Mr Lovell uses oak for the wheel teeth – he finds traditional apple wood in the required well-seasoned state virtually impossible to locate.

For centuries both Ilfracombe and Hele were extensively used by ships – Defoe referred to 'Ilfar-Comb ... having a very good harbour and road for ships', and it is possible, though not certain, that some of the grain used in the mill may have arrived by sea; almost certainly major items, such as new French millstones, did so.

Hele Mill stands just off the Ilfracombe to Lynton road (A329) and is now faced by a group of particularly unprepossessing holiday homes. The mill nestles into a steep, dark hill as if trying to escape from them!

Otterton Mill

The well-documented history of Otterton describes a world which remained relatively unchanged for 900 years. For all that period properties on the estate were leasehold, but the loss of farming and estate jobs and a series of Rent Acts made the cost of repairs unacceptably high to many large landowners. In little more than twenty years between the mid-1960s and mid-1980s owner occupancy rose from twenty per cent to over sixty per cent, and an irreversible trend was established.

With the progressive break-up of the estate, there was no future for a traditional community mill unequipped to operate in the modern farming climate. When sold, the mill epitomized the revolutionary nature of the changes taking place in many areas, becoming home to a craft centre, mill museum, restaurant and art gallery in addition to continuing to grind its own wholemeal flour, using only English wheat.

Seemingly even more revolutionary was the concept of a

co-operative craft shop, the very model of liberal thinking of the 1960s and 70s. Yet this idea (which for some reason manifested itself particularly in the West Country and in Wales) is hardly new. After all, the monks and priors who first administered this estate were part of a co-operative, and succeeding centuries saw the growth of a tight-knit community dependent for its survival on the inter-relationship of each member – farmer, farrier and miller.

Remarkably, Otterton estate has had only four owners in the last 900 years. At the Conquest, it was already an extensive manor held by the late King Harold's mother, Countess Gytha. King William gave it, with other lands, to the Benedictine Abbey of Mont-Saint-Michel, creating the largest and most valuable holding the abbey possessed in England. Although seized on several occasions, the manor effectively continued in monastic hands until the Dissolution, when a local man, Richard Duke, paid £1,727 42s.2d. for 5,400 acres. A contemporary report mentions 'his Mylles' which remained, with the rest of the property, in the ownership of the family until 1785. In that year Denys Rolle, of nearby Bicton, bought the estate including 'the water grist mills'. The Rolles and the Trefusis families frequently intermarried, and in 1907 Charles Trefusis, 21st Baron Clinton, inherited the estate, which still belongs to the family.

Otterton Mill is one of three shown under 'Otritona' in the Exeter Domesday Book. The Saxons conquered and peacefully settled this area in about AD 670, and the site is almost certainly Saxon in origin. Otterton has always been a corn- or grist-mill, although there have been a number of fulling-mills along the Otter. There is a reproduction of a lease of 1814 on a display panel in the mill confirming that soke rights – the requirement for tenants to have their grain ground in the estate mill – were still enforced in the nineteenth century.

The mill and outbuildings containing the individual craft shops are a pretty mixture of ages and styles around a flower-filled courtyard sometimes used as an open-air stage. The present mill is, like many others, a hybrid which was partly rebuilt (in 1850) around an older core and incorporates some older machinery. The mill was powered by two breastshot Poncelet wheels but, since the restoration carried out in 1977, only one is now in use.

Otterton is a stimulating place, never afraid to experiment, and credit for its continued success must go to its driving force, Desna Greenhow, who has so admirably maintained and developed the tradition of independent women millers (see p.53).

Sticklepath: Finch Brothers Foundry, near Okehampton

Sticklepath is the first major impediment to the River Taw as it begins its long journey from the remote north of Dartmoor to the sea. In the nineteenth century a good water-supply and a reasonable road – now the A30 – were factors leading to the rise of industrial production in this agreeable place. The Finch Foundry was one of three or possibly four watermills operating in the village; the others were corn-, grist- and cloth-mills.

The foundry (now known by an impossible variety of names – my preference is for the original) began producing agricultural and mining hand-tools in 1814 and continued until 1960, although the business was in serious decline from 1940. The value of these small businesses to villages like Sticklepath can hardly be over-emphasized. At its peak the foundry employed twenty to twenty-five men, and five generations of the Finch family worked in it. There are inevitably similarities in the histories of the foundry and Abbeydale (see p.181), since both were affected by the growth of methods of mass-producing tools and by the development of large-scale mechanical tools.

At first there were two separate mills on the site, a woollen-factory and a grist-mill. William Finch leased the woollen-factory which became known locally as 'the Foundry', although there is no evidence that iron-casting ever took place there. The building was almost certainly used from the start as a forge, with up to seven open blacksmiths' hearths. Two water-wheels were installed, one driving a pair of heavy tilt-hammers and the second the fan supplying air to the forges and furnaces. The water-wheel powering the tilt-hammers also drove a set of power-shears and two drop-forging hammers.

With the growth of the business in the middle 1800s, the grist-mill was leased and converted to a grinding-mill. A third wheel supplied power for a bandsaw in addition to the sandstone grinding-wheel which was operated by a man lying face down on a bench with his nose inches from the revolving stone! Working conditions generally were hard, the hours excessively long by present-day standards, and wages not substantially higher than those paid to the agricultural worker. Yet the evidence suggests that, throughout its working life and allowing for inevitable friction between employer and employee, morale in the foundry remained good.

Within a few years of the closure of the foundry, the complex had become derelict, and an educational and charitable trust was set up to preserve it as a Museum of Industrial History. The Trust was fortunate, as it started up at a time when interest in industrial history and vernacular buildings was increasing rapidly. The BBC, Granada and Westward Television have all made documentaries on the foundry, and the list of organizations supporting the project is impressive in both quantity and variety.

In addition to restoring all the water-wheels to their original functions, the Trust has added three galleries – two display the range of tools made and used at the foundry together with account books and catalogues of the company; the third depicts the development of water-power throughout the ages, using a range of panels and excellent models.

Uffculme: Coldharbour Mill, near Cullompton

Celia Fiennes visited Exeter in 1698 and wrote: '... the whole town and country is employ'd for at least 20 mile round in spinning, weaveing, dressing, and scouring, fulling and drying of the serges....'

The woollen industry in Devon developed during the thirteenth and fourteenth centuries but underwent a particular expansion in the seventeenth and early eighteenth centuries. A reluctance to adapt to changing technology then contributed to the decline of the industry in the West Country, leaving very few mills to continue production. Coldharbour is perhaps the most important of these; established only in 1797, it still carries out a small amount of spinning and weaving.

Domesday records two mills at 'Offecome', and it seems likely that one was on this site. The mill served as a paper-mill in the early eighteenth century but was damaged by flood in 1753 and rebuilt some time before 1788, when an advertisement offered new grist-mills at Coldharbour for sale.

The Fox family had begun developing their interests in the woollen industry with two factories at Wellington, and Thomas Fox now bought Coldharbour Mill because of the fine water-supply available from the River Culm. In 1799 he began an ambitious expansion programme at Coldharbour, intending the new mill to be used 'merely for spinning'. In this he was reversing the trend in the West Country, where many woollen-mills were already turning to flour-production.

The Fox brothers were Quakers and constantly demonstrated their social awareness. At Wellington, a shop sold food, fuel and basic clothing on a non-profit-making basis. Near their mills they built houses – including many of the existing cottages at Uffculme. They never employed children under the age of eight and, like the Gregs at Styal (see p.68), ensured that the children were educated.

Thomas Fox's entrepreneurial skills led him to develop a flannel which the East India Company wanted to buy, but his Quaker instincts caused him to reject the sale when he discovered that it was to be used for gun cartridges. When the British Army adopted khaki for its uniforms in 1881, the company justified its contract, for the manufacture of 5,000 pairs of puttees, by trusting that the camouflage would help save lives. Ironically, the spinning of yarn for Army puttees became the staple production at Coldharbour until its closure in April 1981.

When the mill closed, the Coldharbour Mill Trust was formed to save the mill buildings, textile machinery and power sources. After six months' restoration it reopened as a working mill museum of the wool and worsted industry. A breastshot suspension-wheel (installed in 1897) with gearing and line-shafting to the factory machinery can still be seen and is demonstrated on request.

Coldharbour Mill is a long, three-storey building with two chimneys rising dramatically at one end. The effect, in a largely rural area, can be disconcerting but is softened at close range by a pleasing landscaping of the Culm.

Dorset

Dorset remains today what it was in the eleventh century – with the possible exception of the busy port at Wareham – a purely agricultural county full of large estates and small settlements. The use of water-power may not have been as widespread as in some of the counties to the east, but it was considerably more developed than in its neighbours to the west.

Both Melbury Abbas and Sturminster Newton had four mills when Domesday was compiled. I find Sturminster a trifle formal but Melbury and Alderholt are delightfully informal – owner-occupied by people working hard but having fun! There can be few greater contrasts in Britain than between Cann Mill and tiny Fiddleford, the one part of a successful commercial enterprise, the other rather a sad reminder of the fate of so many mills. It would be pleasant if English Heritage, who own the remarkable medieval house on the site, could be persuaded to take on the repair of the mill.

Alderholt Mill, near Fordingbridge, (Hampshire) – p.91.

Cann Mill (TCG), near Shaftesbury – p.92.

Christchurch: Place Mill – Grade II listed building on Domesday site; unusual millrace features created by head of water and tidal conditions; water supply to undershot wheel is taken from Hampshire Avon and discharged into Dorset Stour.

Fiddleford Mill, near Sturminster Newton – Part of large complex with medieval millhouse (EH); a tiny mill, now disused and in disrepair; fascinating engraving dated 1566 over door; two pairs of Derbyshire stones. NOT OPEN, but a most romantic setting.

Melbury Abbas Mill, near Shaftesbury – p.92.
Sherborne: West Mill – Simple, three-storey, seventeenth-century mill; undershot wheel installed 1877; charming mill in secluded site by River Yeo; recently renovated by boys of Sherborne School.
Sturminster Newton Mill – p.93.

Alderholt Mill, near Fordingbridge, Hampshire

Alderholt operates as a craft shop partly in order to support the repairs which John and Ann Pye have been carrying out over the last six years. It's in a most attractive, rural setting – although the road on which it stands cannot be termed quiet: a small, red-brick house, very typical of Hampshire architecture of the eighteenth century. The mill is in Dorset only by a matter of feet, standing just on the Dorset side of the bridge spanning the Allen River which joins Ashford Water at this point. Hereabouts Ashford Water forms the boundary between the two counties – and it's worth mentioning that this Allen River is not Wimborne's River Allen.

Cranborne is not far away, and Alderholt was probably part of Cranborne Manor in medieval times. Research has shown that a mill existed on the site in the 1330s and, given that this is a very good place for a mill, the probability is that the site is even older. Domesday is not a great deal of help in this respect, for Dorset is relatively sparsely covered. The similarity in the names of many of the smaller hamlets, often including the name of the river by which they stood, appears to have confused the compilers and has certainly not assisted modern attempts at identifying sites.

Along with mills throughout the country, Alderholt stopped grinding corn commercially in the last war. Since 1980, when the Pyes took over, much of the machinery has been replaced or repaired, including the external breastshot wheel of about 1840. It's a pleasing sign of continuity that the cast-iron, six-spoke wheel is being maintained by the successors of the company which first installed it, Munden of Ringwood. The spur has had new beechwood teeth installed by a local craftsman, and other repairs are being completed as money becomes available. A milestone was reached in February 1987 with the grinding of flour for the first time in forty-five years, using the mill's pair of French Burr stones – it has a second pair of Peak stones. Commercial production is obviously not viable, but the use of home-ground flour in the making of biscuits for sale is a possibility under consideration.

I've indicated that Alderholt is a craft centre; it also has an art gallery on the lower floor, with a series of exhibitions of the work of local artists, often with a Dorset theme. The stone floor is mostly given over to craft sales, while part of the garner floor has been removed; the hoist system is still in place.

Some of the craft-shop developments in mill buildings of recent years have a commercialism quite inappropriate to their setting; even the word 'mill' in a title is no more than a good selling-point. By contrast, Alderholt Mill has a pleasant, family atmosphere akin to the many small family-run hotels now thankfully reappearing throughout the country; there is no charge to enter, and such simple touches as the availability of copies of the parish magazine serve to remind the visitor of the inter-relationship of village and mill life.

Cann Mill, near Shaftesbury

This large working mill is run by Michael Stoate, whose family began milling in Watchet in 1832 and arrived here, via Temple Meads, Bristol, in the late 1940s. Built on a Domesday site, the mill was burned down in 1954 and rebuilt a year or so later, when the line-shafting was replaced. The 10½-foot-diameter overshot wheel has wooden paddles and was made by Maggs & Hindley of Bourton in 1874, a year earlier than the wheel they supplied to Melbury Abbas Mill (below). The wheel powers five French Burr stones. Cann Mill has an unusual, and highly visible, feature – a Portuguese windmill.

The mill produces flour (using mostly Wessex-grown crops) for bakers and wholesalers and also makes a little chicken-feed. The flour is on sale to the public, but the minimum quantity one may buy is fourteen pounds.

This mill is one of three in Cann which were working earlier this century. French and Gear's mills are downstream on the River Sturkel; both have now been converted to private dwellings and are not open.

Melbury Abbas Mill, near Shaftesbury

Melbury Abbas had four mills when Domesday Book was compiled, and this small village in an enclosed valley must have been a very busy place indeed in the Middle Ages. Sited on the greensand ridge, it has always enjoyed easy access to good water and fertile land, a combination which helps to explain the number of mills once active along the tiny River Sturkel. In truth, the river is little more than a chalk stream which bumbles off Cranborne Chase through some deserted watercress beds before having its leisurely progress rudely interrupted by an obstruction in the form of the half-acre millpond.

The remaining mill at Melbury is a classically simple, old-fashioned, no-frills working mill. It ceased to operate in 1960, when the miller retired and died. The then owner virtually abandoned the mill, which suffered some deterioration but was in a reasonable condition when bought by the present owners, Mr and Mrs Giles. They have restored it, installing a small museum of country things, an attractive garden, a river walk and a few vintage cars and motorcycles.

The mill is three storeys high, built of local stone. The owners refer to it affectionately as 'just a little grist-mill' but it had a bakery until 1912 and produced, as did many others, its own cider. Mr and Mrs Giles brought their own cider-press from their old home in Devon and are once again producing a small quantity of genuine cider.

The wrought-iron water-wheel is eleven feet two inches high and almost six feet wide, producing 7 hp. Built in 1875 by Maggs & Hindley of Bourton, it was rebuilt, including forty-two new steel buckets, in 1985 by a local company.

The water-wheel at Cann Mill (p.92) was also supplied by Maggs & Hindley; it is a year older than the Melbury Abbas wheel. There are two pairs of Derbyshire Peak millstones. All the ancillary equipment and gearing (mostly by J.J. Armfield of Ringwood) is still in place. Some of the supplementary machinery and certainly the collection of millwrighting tools have been identified by no less an authority than Mr Kenneth J. Major as being of historical significance.

Sturminster Newton Mill

One of four mills on this part of the River Stour mentioned in Domesday Book, the present structure of Sturminster Mill dates, like so many others, from the seventeenth and eighteenth centuries and replaces a medieval building on the same site. The mill was worked by water-wheel until 1904, when a turbine was installed by J.J. Armfield. The mill continued working until the 1970s and was repaired and restored in the early 1980s by a Trust. It provides an interesting comparison between old and new milling methods. Certainly the present production – of wholemeal flour and animal feed – is carried out most efficiently, demonstrating that near-traditional milling can survive against the large-scale production methods which drove so many small mill-owners (or more often their tenants) to the wall in the early years of this century.

Before their replacement, Sturminster Mill employed two undershot water-wheels driving three pairs of stones. The installation of one of Armfield's own-design British Empire turbines – costing £176 17s.6d. and delivering around 24hp – meant that the capacity of the mill was greatly extended. On the ground floor are a pair of Derbyshire stones and two hammer-mills. On the first floor a combined modern plate-mill and crusher produces wholemeal flour, and there is also a winnowing-machine and oat-crusher. All these and the ancillary machinery are driven by a combination of bevel gears and flat belting.

The well-recorded history of the mill provides an excellent picture of a typical manorial mill – including a dishonest miller, one Richard Whyffin, who was fined 6d. in the sixteenth century 'for excessive toll'. The little town it serves has an equally long and fascinating history. Sturminster Newton is, with its lively livestock market, the 'capital' of Blackmore Vale, called Stourcastle by Hardy in *Tess of the D'Urbervilles*. The medieval bridge, just east of the mill, is still one of the best of its kind in the county – even though it was widened in the seventeenth century to accommodate the increased traffic flow. Deportation was once the penalty for injury to the bridge by taking an overloaded cart across it – on that scale, only hanging would seem to be appropriate for owners of the lorries which trundle over it today!

Durham

To the purist Killhope should not, perhaps, qualify for entry here but it is included for its remarkable appearance.

Killhope Waterwheel, Upper Weardale – 33½-feet-diameter overshot water-wheel, built 1877; 1,500 feet above sea-level on a lead-mining site; mine buildings and crushing-mill have been restored; exhibition on lead industry; water was supplied via eleven mile-long water-races; a spectacular sight.

Essex

Essex is included with Norfolk and Suffolk in Little Domesday, a final Circuit Summary. Although a county in the grip of change, it possessed a relatively high number of mills at the time of Domesday. In the course of the next eight centuries, many fine mills were built in Essex, often on Domesday sites. In this century a number have disappeared, and others have been converted into expensive private homes and are therefore not open to view. The same comment applies to mills in both the other counties covered by Little Domesday.

One example of the changing face of Essex must suffice. Chelmsford was said by Nikolaus Pevsner, writing in 1954, to be the place to go to when looking for mills in Essex. By 1980, Leslie Syson's tour led straight through the town and, as will be seen, I include no mills from it.

Colchester: Bourne Mill (NT) – p.95.

Colchester: Mill Hotel – p.96.

Kelvedon: Easterford Watermill – In the process of being restored; low weather-boarded mill on River Blackwater built in the eighteenth century, closed in the 1920s; restored breastshot wheel can be seen turning on certain open-days; served by a small millpond; three pairs of stones; attached two-storey millhouse is of architectural interest.

Colchester: Bourne Mill (NT)

Bourne Mill (built in 1591) stands on a twelfth-century site and incorporates material from the ruined abbey of St John. Its millpond is almost certainly the fishpond of the abbey, and opinions are divided as to the original purpose of the remarkably ornate two-storey building. It may be said that tradition and majority opinion hold that the builder, Sir Thomas Lucas, intended to use it as a fishing lodge. A very small minority, which appears to consist of Mr Kenneth Major and myself, believe that it was built as a corn-mill.

I accept that it may have been convenient to use the mill as a fishing lodge but simply do not believe that a site of historic and economic value would have been casually abandoned to sport. That the presumed stewpond was well stocked is not in dispute – as recently as the nineteenth century large fish (including a pike sent to Queen Victoria) were being taken from it – but the idea of combining business and pleasure must have appealed to Sir Thomas. After all, it was hardly a new idea, as mills had been required to provide the State with interest in the form of eels since before the mill at Bourne had existed.

And so it seems to me that the logical explanation of the delightfully inconsequential architecture of the mill is that its functional role was dressed up to amuse Sir Thomas and his guests. In a sense it was all wasted, for the Lucas family temporarily lost the mill as a result of their Royalist sympathies during the Cromwellian period – the blackest in the history of Colchester, and one from which the town never fully recovered. The mill passed briefly into the hands of Dutch refugees who converted it into a cloth-mill producing cloth for the 'Bay-trade'. This was a corruption of baize although the green cloth we know by that name did not appear until the late eighteenth century. 'Bay' was a light, natural coloured fabric, first spun and then tentered at the mill.

There is a certain irony about the Dutch connection for there can be no argument that the architecture of Bourne Mill, and in particular its large, stepped gable ends, smacks of the influence of the Flemish community who had settled in the town during the latter part of the sixteenth century.

Cloth was to bring considerable prosperity to East Anglia during the next two centuries (some fine Georgian houses remain in Colchester as tribute to the period), but its decline in the early 1800s led to Bourne Mill's returning to its function as a corn-mill in 1833. It survived until the 1930s and was presented anonymously to the National Trust in 1936.

Inside the building, open on certain days, is a very large (twenty-six-foot) wheel which turned three pairs of stones. The wheel has been restored and turns the wooden gears and shaft.

Colchester: Mill Hotel

An enormous complex beside the River Colne, once a flour-mill, but now adapted as an hotel, the mill has a long history, allegedly tracing its lineage to pre-Roman times. There is a tendency to be cynical about such claims, but Colchester itself claims to be 'the Oldest Recorded Town in Britain' (the Council's emphasis, not mine!). The building is a fascinating mix but mostly Victorian, supported by Georgian and twentieth-century architecture.

Certainly East Street, in which the mill stands, has two other buildings of historical significance. One of these, the Siege House, played an important role in the Civil War; the other, the Rose & Crown, is one of the oldest inns in Britain (although restored – as is the Siege House), and very typical of the black-and-white timbered architecture of the area. It is one of over 250 buildings in Colchester that are older than the seventeenth century, giving continued justification to Defoe's reference to the town's 'abundance of very good and well-built homes'. Bourne Mill (p.95) is another, and there are some slight resemblances between the mills at Bourne and Colchester. Both are ornate and neither would be out of place in Holland. There the resemblance ends, for Colchester Mill is very large indeed. Yet I find it has a certain insouciant charm lacking in its only comparison in this book, the Whitewater Hotel at Backbarrow, in Cumbria (p.75).

Gloucestershire

A mixture of agriculture and industry has been a feature of Gloucestershire since the Domesday Survey was compiled. The shire, first mentioned in the *Anglo-Saxon Chronicle* sixty years before Domesday, was already remarkably set in a pattern which would continue through the succeeding centuries and, indeed, still exists. It was a rural community, relying on sheep for its wealth, either directly

Devon – Coldharbour Mill, Uffculme, near Cullompton. A large complex located in a rural area, Coldharbour has been well landscaped into its setting by the River Culm.

Devon – Hele Mill, near Ilfracombe. Part of the external structure of the building dates from the sixteenth century; internally there has been a great deal of necessary restoration work.

Dorset – Alderholt Mill, near Fordingbridge. Alderholt Mill dates mainly from the eighteenth century and, though standing just in Dorset, is more typical of Hampshire architecture.

Dorset – Melbury Abbas Mill, near Shaftesbury. The mill, on the left, is actually three storeys high – sole survivor of the four mentioned in Domesday for this tiny village.

Dorset – Cann Mill, near Shaftesbury. A very unusual feature at Cann Mill is the windmill. The working mill is one of several still to be found on the tiny River Sturkel.

Dorset – Sturminster Newton Mill, near Shaftesbury. This good-looking seventeenth- and eighteenth-century mill replaced a medieval mill on a Domesday site.

Essex – Colchester Mill Hotel, Colchester. A striking combination of Georgian and Victorian architecture, overlaid with twentieth-century additions is a feature of this hotel beside the River Colne.

Essex – Bourne Mill, Colchester. A remarkably ornate mill, reflecting the Flemish influences at work in Colchester during the sixteenth century.

Gloucestershire – Egypt Mill, Nailsworth. The River Frome passes under two undershot wheels at either end of the lounge bar in this well-restored and attractive cloth mill.

Hampshire – Eling Tidemill, Totton. An important eighteenth-century tidemill now restored to fine condition after a 'nick of time' rescue in 1980.

Hampshire – Whitchurch Silk-Mill. A remarkably handsome mill of genuine architectural merit on a river, the Test, of unsurpassed beauty.

Hampshire – Headley Watermill, Borden. Displaying the classic image of mill and millhouse, Headley is part Tudor and part eighteenth century. For centuries it belonged to the bishops of Winchester.

Hampshire – City Mill, Winchester. An attractive, plain tile-hung mill over the Itchen, dating back to the fourteenth century.

Hereford and Worcester – Forge Mill Museum, Redditch. The older, two-storey, building was one of the first converted to a scouring mill when the needle-making industry was developed in the eighteenth century.

Opposite: **Hereford and Worcester – Newnham Mill, near Tenbury Wells**. Owned by the same family since the nineteenth century, this deceptively tall brick-built mill is now leased and producing flour commercially.

Hertfordshire – Moor Mill, Frogmore, near St Albans. Rural-looking mill hard beside the M25 (masked by fence visible at rear) and suffering from the effects of vibration from motorway traffic.

Hertfordshire – Mill Green Mill, Hatfield. Dated 1762 but extensively restored since 1979. Open throughout the year as both mill and local museum.

ENTRANCE
NO SMOKING

Kent – Swanton Mill, Mersham, near Ashford. Grade II listed mill and millhouse in quite delightful garden (also open to visitors). The remaining farm buildings are equally pleasing.

Opposite: **Hertfordshire – Kingsbury Watermill, St Albans.** A handsome mill – even in mid-winter when this photograph was taken.

Kent – Upper Crisbrook Mill, near Maidstone. An elegant brick-built Victorian mill. The lovely small garden has made good use of the waterways.

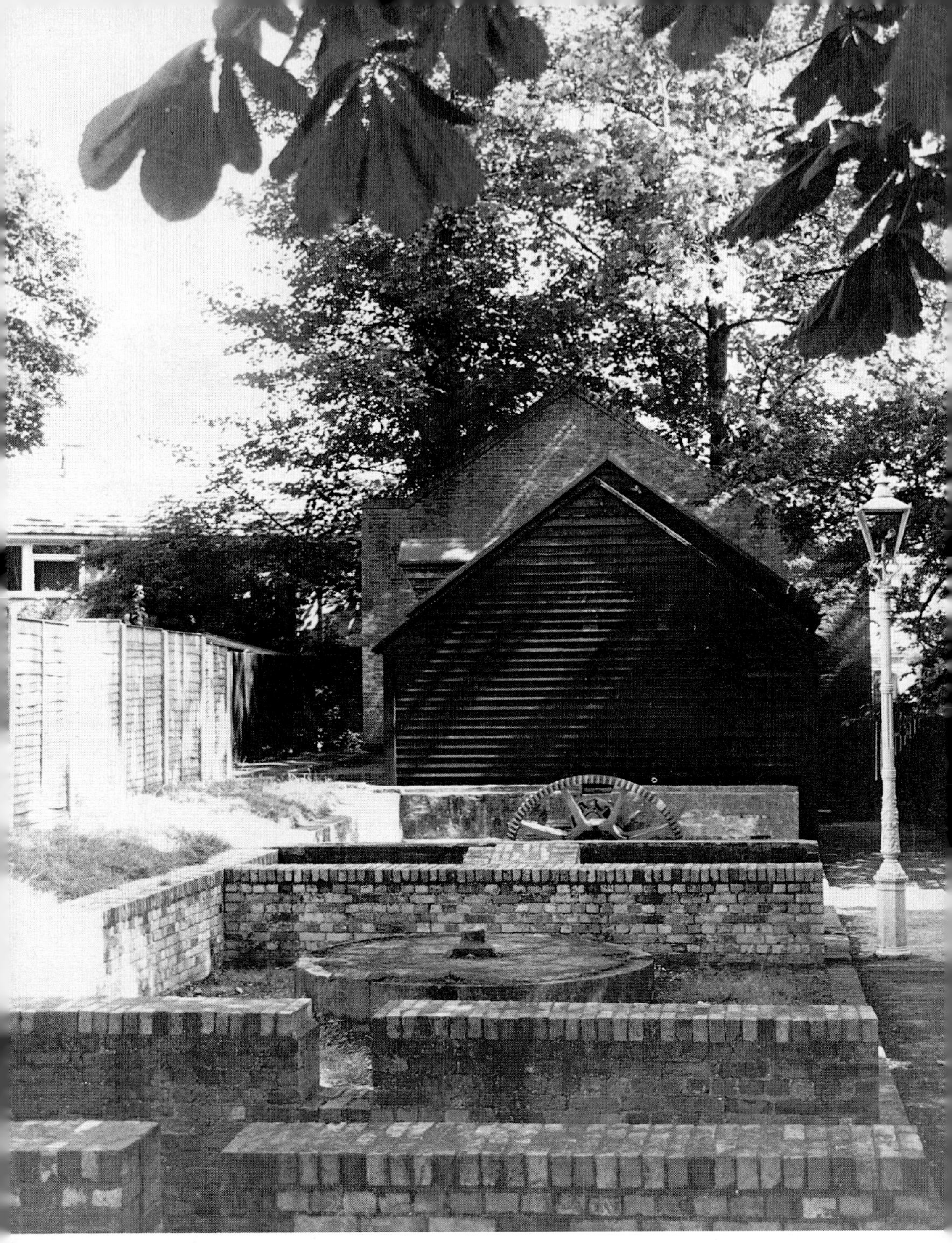

Kent – Chart Gunpowder Mills, Faversham. The stone beds of three of the original tiny mills are in the foreground. The hut (fourth mill) contains a sixteen-foot-diameter iron wheel and some machinery.

or through wool-production. In the north-west of the county the Forest of Dean provided a limited amount of heavier industry – as it did into this century.

Domesday recorded a large number of corn-mills, many later adapted to fulling-mills as wool increased in importance. Gloucestershire still contains a great range of mills, from the picture-book examples of the Cotswolds to the gaunt skeletons of the Stroud Valley. Because of the beauty of the mills in the Cotswolds, almost all have been converted into private residences, along with their ancillary buildings, while the large industrial mills have fallen into disuse or are being offered as factory units.

A perfect example of the conversion of mills can be found in the Painswick area. This once-important woollen centre has a great number of private houses with milling connections. The effect of the conversions has been to make Painswick very attractive in a sterile way. By contrast, the industrial mills of the Nailsworth area are in a generally poor condition. Even the most famous, Dunkirk Mill, is currently very run down. The conversion of Egypt Mill has restored it to a useful function as a pub, while the late David Verey's rescue of Arlington Mill saved an outstanding example of a Cotswold mill for posterity.

Bibury: Arlington Mill – below.

Withington: Mill Inn, near Cheltenham – In attractive setting at bottom of valley, by River Coln; retains wheel.

Blockley: Mills, near Chipping Campden – A hundred years ago six silk-throwing mills employed 600 people in this attractive village; all have been converted to other uses, but some (e.g. Malvern Mill and the Old Mill, sometimes open under NGS; like the Stroud Valley in miniature.

Lower Slaughter Mill – Red-brick corn-mill with tall, rather incongruous chimney in excessively pretty village, on River Eye; wide cast-iron undershot water-wheel; still functioning as village bakery.

Nailsworth: Egypt Mill – p.99.

Donnington Brewery, near Stow-on-the-Wold – A thirteenth-century site, used in the sixteenth century as a cloth-mill; in Arkell family ownership since 1827; converted to brewery in 1865; wheel still provides power for hoisting barley, etc.; millpond, formed by damming River Dikler, has ornamental waterfowl.

Bibury: Arlington Mill

Writing about Bibury in 1825, Charlotte Cornish coolly described it as 'a beautiful village ... one of the most pleasing I ever saw'. Since her time writers and artists have vied with each other in producing superlatives about the village. Much of what is written is demonstrably true but it has led to Bibury's suffering from a surfeit of visitors demanding 'attractions' which draw more visitors, creating more demand!

Arguably the most acceptable of the attractions on offer is the mill, with its Cotswold Country Museum. It has been an integral part of the village at least since King William I ordered the Domesday survey while holding his Christmas Court at Gloucester in 1085. In its time, Arlington has been a fulling-mill, a grist-mill (performing both functions at the same time for a period in the seventeenth century) and a corn-mill, finally closing in 1914. For fifty-one years after closing, it stood empty, used only for storage by families living in the attached cottages. Happily the outside structure of the seventeenth-century four-storey Cotswold stone mill was still in good condition when it was bought by David Verey, a noted writer on the Cotswolds, Gloucestershire and Herefordshire.

The machinery of the mill was removed and broken up during the Great War, but Mr Verey was fortunate in obtaining the wooden internal machinery of North Cerney Mill. The water-wheel, which does not turn, came from the Swan Hotel just down the road. A steam-engine was installed in the nineteenth century, when Arlington Mill experienced problems with its water-supply from the River Coln. Shortly before David Verey bought the mill, the water-supply rights were acquired by the neighbouring trout farm and, to simulate the corn-grinding process, the mill machinery is now powered by electricity.

The mill and cottages have a great number of small rooms, and seventeen have been adapted to house the museum, creating a series of vignettes. The ground floor contains the bulk of the mill machinery, with well laid-out blacksmith's and wheelwright's shops. Both the Arts and Crafts Movement and the Cotswold Group of Craftsmen led by Ernest Gimson, who worked in Bibury in the early years of this century, are recognized on the first floor. Examples of furniture produced by members of the Group are on display; I find technique takes precedence over design in much of this work, and the best marrying of the two occurs in some charming watercolours by Norman Jewson. A wholly delightful room on this floor is furnished with the belongings of the scholar John Keble.

On the second floor both the content and quality of the old photographs of the village are quite fascinating. The storage bins have been imaginatively converted to *tableaux vivants*. The top floors contain mill and agricultural implements – much of the latter perched on the beams of the granary floor.

It would be wrong to suggest that all the rooms at Arlington are of outstanding interest but that problem faces any museum offering 'something for everyone'; what matters is that the main theme survives – here it does.

Nailsworth: Egypt Mill

Egypt Mill is now a large pub which claims to be a sixteenth-century corn- and cloth-mill. The building, of Cotswold stone, has been well restored and has two large wheels behind glass at either end of the lounge bar, both undershot and powered by the River Frome. The wheels are cast-iron with wooden panels; one turns some ancillary machinery. The small garden beside the river is particularly attractive, with millstones as tables and tuns as seats.

The majority of mills in the Stroud valley are of seventeenth- or eighteenth-century construction, and Egypt Mill is probably no exception, regardless of what is suggested in its leaflet. It is a building of some architectural merit, distinctly more attractive than some others, including its neighbour, Dunkirk Mill, said to be the original of 'John Halifax's' mill (see p.39) and now sadly neglected.

Hampshire

Hampshire retains a considerable number of watermills – the list below, though intended to be representative, is far from exhaustive. At Domesday many settlements had several mills (nine are given for Alresford), and sites which were important then often retain mills of great historical value. In addition, some of the surviving mills are of high architectural quality – very beautiful buildings, well preserved or cleverly restored.

I cannot think of two more lovely mill buildings which stand so close to one another than Alresford and Ovington and, though neither is open, the compensation is that both are viewable at close range from public thoroughfares. Hartley represents modern conversion work – I think it succeeds here, though not at another mill only a few miles away (omitted for fear of libel action!); it can also be studied from the road. Bordon is a mill with a very long history, still working commercially, as is Wickham, a favourite with Americans for its still visible timbers taken from their historic frigate *Chesapeake*. Whitchurch and Eling are fine and exciting examples of what can be achieved by groups of enthusiasts, while the saw-mill at Ower merits mention for the careful way it has been restored – not often the case in large commercial 'parks'.

Alresford Fulling Mill, New Alresford – Fifteenth-century, beautifully restored private house in unsurpassed setting; viewable from public footpath beside River Itchen. NOT OPEN.

Bordon: Headley Mill (TCG), near Petersfield – Remarkable mill on what is claimed to be Saxon site; incorporates pre-sixteenth-century internal section – externally Tudor and eighteenth-century; owned for over 700 years by bishops of Winchester; family-owned since 1914 by J. Ellis & Sons; still working commercially producing wholewheat flour and animal feed; four-acre millpond – enlarged in 1272; breastshot wheel powering four pairs of stones – three French Burr, one Peak. OPEN BY APPOINTMENT.

Eversley: New Mill – Corn-mill, later saw-mill; claimed to date, in part, from sixteenth century; converted to riverside restaurant in 1972; large water-wheel still turns; attractive site on River Blackwater by ford; for sale May 1988, future uncertain.

Greatham Mill, near Liss – All-season garden regularly open, surrounding millhouse with mill-stream.

Hartley Mill, Hartley Wespall – Part of farm complex on Lyde river; brick and weather-boarding; two storeys and attic floor; no external machinery; mill-leat passes under house; splendid conversion to private house. NOT OPEN, viewable from lane.

Ovington Mill, near Alresford – Long, low two-storey red-brick mill on River Itchen; water passes under building; an exquisite place; by-road passes front door. NOT OPEN.

Ower: Saw-Mill, Paultons Park – below.

Sherfield-on-Lodden Mill – Rapidly deteriorating timber-framed mill under tile roof; wheel and some internal machinery; classically simple three-storey building in delightful setting – deserves to be restored.

Totton: Eling Tidemill, near Southampton – p.101.

Whitchurch Silk-Mill – p.102.

Wickham: Chesapeake Mill – p.103.

Winchester: City Mill (NT) – p.103.

Ower: Saw-Mill, Paultons Park

Tucked away in a corner of Paultons Park and Bird Gardens is an estate saw-mill, and should any visitor think this is just a gimmick, he or she would be mistaken. The estate is of great age, the saw-mill is genuine, and it has been very carefully restored in recent years.

In Saxon and Norman times the original, much larger, Paultons Estate belonged to the Abbots of Glastonbury. When 15,000 Cornishmen marched to Blackheath in 1497 in protest at being taxed for a war against the Scots, the then owner, John Touchet, was one of their leaders – he was beheaded and the estate forfeited. In 1646 it was acquired by the Stanley family, and it remained in their possession until split up in 1979.

When the Mancey family bought the land which now forms the park and decided to open it to the public, they faced a difficult task in clearing a very run-down estate. The fifteen-foot cast-iron Poncelet wheel, which had operated the saw-mill from its installation in 1860 until 1950, had to wait until 1982 for attention. The replacement of all fifty-six buckets involved the removal and refitting of over a thousand bolts. Estate hornbeam was used for the wooden teeth of the drive-wheels, and a rack bench saw for timber-cutting, similar to the original, was installed. The original rail-track and bogey for moving timber remain, and the mill now looks much as it would have done a hundred years ago.

Totton: Eling Tidemill, near Southampton

Eling Tidemill stands on a long, narrow causeway forming a dam across Bartley Water. There were two mills at Eling and one at nearby Totton when Domesday was compiled, and the river was dammed as early as the fifteenth century. But Eling Tidemill is of national importance: it is one of only three tidemills remaining from over a hundred operating as recently as the nineteenth century. Furthermore, neither of the others – Carew (p.189) and Woodbridge (p.154) – is working, although both have wheels capable of turning for demonstration purposes. Yet the position of these marvellous mills could have been infinitely worse, for both Woodbridge and Eling were in a desperate plight only a few years ago. Woodbridge was saved by the foresight and generosity of one woman, while Eling owed its rescue to the determined efforts of the Eling Tidemill Trust, who restored it as a working mill museum in 1980 at what could reasonably be said was the eleventh hour.

All tidemills work on the same principle, namely that water from the rising tide is allowed to flow through a sluice into a dam behind the mill where it is stored. Once the tide has receded, the sluice is opened again, releasing the water to turn the wheel or wheels. At Eling Tidemill the water collected provides power for about four hours work. Eling did have two wheels of the Poncelet type (an improvement on the basic undershot wheel in which water is directed into paddles which resemble buckets) but only one has survived and is used to turn two pairs of stones.

The present mill is of eighteenth-century construction, the machinery is nineteenth-century manufacture and the whole is now maintained in excellent condition – so much so that the suggestion has been made to me that Eling is a soulless place where the word 'museum' has more relevance than 'working'. Well, there is an audio-visual describing the working of the mill and a number of interpretative displays, but if there is a grain of truth in this suggestion, it would relate more to Woodbridge. At Eling it is usually possible to buy stone-ground flour, the product of the 'working' side of the mill. In any event, my great pleasure in the survival of these wonderfully evocative places probably disqualifies me from dispassionate consideration of them!

Whitchurch Silk-Mill

The saving of Whitchurch Silk-Mill in January 1986 is one of the most hopeful signs that there is a future for the watermill in Britain.

Of course Whitchurch is very important – this is the only working silk-mill in the south of England, and the history of the town is very much interwoven with its five mills. Nonetheless, it is the manner of its saving which I find significant. The preserving of a mill by individual effort is an act of faith that must be applauded, but the purchase of Whitchurch Silk-Mill by the Hampshire Buildings Preservation Trust should ensure that ambitious proposals for its future will be realized. This is not to decry individual enterprise, which in most instances is probably preferable, simply to acknowledge that there are circumstances when such a grouping as a Trust may be better placed to manage a property.

In the relatively short space of time since the mill and adjoining land were purchased and an appeal was launched, the Trust has provided, in a separate building, a small showroom to display samples of its products and has made an excellent short video on aspects of silk-production. Unlike so many mills, Whitchurch is accessible to disabled people, and an adapted lavatory has been added to the facilities. Within the mill there is a sensibly laid-out observation area where visitors can watch, through glass, three weavers and a trainee at work. Short notes describe the fifteen looms, their age and present function.

The main body of the three-storey red-brick Georgian mill dates from about 1800, and it is arguably one of the finest buildings discussed in this book, deservedly of Grade 1 listed quality. A graceful wooden cupola surmounts the slate roof of the mill, and a handsome Handley & Moore clock adds a final touch of elegance. It may also have contributed to the bankruptcy of the first owner, who departed a year after installing the clock in 1815.

The use of the mill for silk-weaving began around 1830 but water-power was not introduced for the looms until the 1890s. The wide water-wheel is of low breastshot type with elm floats, and the wheel-frame, pit-wheel, wallower and mainshaft are all iron. A complex system involving lay shafts supplied power to all floors and was replaced only after the Second World War. Nowadays the looms, whose dates of manufacture range from 1890 to 1959, are powered by electric motors. Among their products is the black silk used for the gowns of barristers 'taking silk' – quite appropriate, as a former Master of the Rolls, Lord Denning, has been closely connected with the work of the Hampshire Buildings Preservation Trust. I cannot resist adding that the looms also produce silk for the 'legitimate' theatre!

It is in all our interests that places like the Whitchurch Silk-Mill survive. And, of course, the mill is fortunate in its advantages, for not only is the site historically important but it occupies an attractive island setting on that most exquisite of rivers, the Test. How can it fail?

Wickham: Chesapeake Mill

Wickham must surely be one of the most attractive 'undiscovered' small towns (it still calls itself a village) within a hundred miles of London. Architecturally it has masses of good Georgian or neo-Georgian buildings grouped around a large, elegant square. Its church is of interest if only because it was the victim of *two* Victorian remodellings! William of Wykeham, founder of New College, Oxford, and of Winchester School, was born here in 1324, but the history of the town extends back at least a thousand years, and at the time of the Domesday survey it had two mills on the banks of the Meon.

The survivor, latest of many mills on the site, is Chesapeake Mill, a square-fronted red-brick building, adorned with tin advertisements. Built in 1820, it incorporates some impressive timbers from the US frigate *Chesapeake*, captured by HMS *Shannon* off Boston in 1813 – hence the name. The inclusion of ships' timbers into the fabric of a mill is a relatively common claim but it can rarely be confirmed; very often the shape of the beams, allied to considerable age, confuses investigators – here the recorded evidence is conclusive.

Chesapeake is a working mill, not officially open, but the owner, Mr Tappenden, whose family have worked the mill for most of this century, is happy to show it to any enthusiastic visitor – it is, perhaps predictably, a favourite with American tourists. I should add that Mr Tappenden is closely connected with the local mills group, was involved in the repair of Eling Tidemill and is a mine of information on developments in the county.

Winchester: City Mill (NT)

The Itchen is a fascinating river, rising sluggishly some miles east of Winchester and gathering volume and speed as it approaches the city. On its way it passes two of the most beautiful mill buildings in

England, privately owned but visible from public rights of way. The beauty of Alresford Fulling-Mill has been celebrated in almost every book on Hampshire ever published, and Ovington Mill is a gem made even more exciting because the little by-road from Ovington to Itchen Abbas seems to pass through its garden. In addition to mills like these, the Itchen once powered eleven or twelve mills within the boundaries of Winchester. Several remain in various guises (the most recent conversion is into a block of flats) but City Mill is the sole survivor, though even it possesses no machinery other than a wheel.

The history of Winchester is well recorded, although not in Domesday, an omission which probably has to do with royal exemptions from tax-paying. Nonetheless, the Eastgate Mill (as it was known) was in existence in 1086 and is recorded as part of the property of the abbess of Wherwell, a Benedictine nunnery near Andover. The Charter Book of Wherwell Abbey, now in the British Museum, records details of the medieval tenants of the mill. One reference is to two mills at Eastgate, perhaps operating on separate branches of the Itchen, a river known for its habit of changing channels, although the use of 'mills' commonly referred to pairs of stones (see Glossary, p.230). In 1347 a prominent local family, the Fondes, leased the mill but great changes were about to engulf Europe – and Winchester in particular. The Black Death was followed by the removal of the wool staple to Calais, and the city entered into a long period of decline.

Within sixty years the mill was derelict, and it remained so for a century – 'a tenement which was once a mill', said a lease of 1513. The mill acquired its present name when it formed part of a gift to the city by Mary I shortly after her marriage in the cathedral to Philip of Spain in 1554. Evidence suggests that it remained derelict through a further series of tenants.

In 1743 a tanner, James Cooke, began to rebuild the mill, incorporating fabric from the earlier building; fourteenth- and fifteenth-century materials have been identified in the structure. Built of brick with delightful tile-hung gables, the mill had three storeys, but the floor of the grain-storage attic has been removed, revealing the magnificent roofing structure. The Itchen flows beneath the mill, which is sandwiched between other, taller houses.

Cooke almost certainly used the mill in his tanning business, but by the time the Corporation sold it, in 1820, it was operating as a corn-mill; it finally closed in 1928, and to save it from possible demolition a local group bought the mill and gave it to the National Trust. After restoration it was leased to the Youth Hostels Association. The lovely enclosed garden at the rear was replanted in 1982 and is a remarkable area of shaded calm not seventy feet from the traffic pounding along the A272, the old drovers' way from Kent to Salisbury.

Hereford & Worcester

The contrast between what are now, for administrative purposes, linked counties was very marked at the time of the Domesday survey. Herefordshire was frequently under attack from the Welsh (the town of Hereford had been sacked in 1055), and the death in 1071 of William FitzOsbern, one of King William's most able lieutenants, had created more problems. Archenfield, that fascinating land between the Monnow and the Wye in which Llangarron lies, was treated in the Survey as Welsh, a situation that was to remain unaltered for several centuries.

By contrast, Worcestershire was remarkably settled for the time because it was largely in the hands of the Church through the great Benedictine houses of the area (Pershore, Evesham and Worcester) and St Peter's, Westminster. Redditch hardly existed at Domesday, and it was to owe its growth to the Cistercian abbey of Bordesley. Much later, the town showed a willingness to adapt and developed into an important industrial centre through its pre-eminence in the needle-making industry.

Avoncroft Museum of Buildings, near Bromsgrove – A museum of vernacular buildings containing a saw-mill and windmill; when funds permit, a watermill, already in store, will be erected on site.

Llangarron: Trereece Mill – Part of complex used as canoeing and adventure centre; interesting large barn conversion to accommodation; mill (NOT OPEN) is dwelling-place; good farm buildings in delightful steep-sided valley.

Lucton: Mortimers Cross Mill (EH), near Leominster – Eighteenth-century sandstone building with undershot wheel; last worked commercially, grinding animal feed, in 1940s; pleasant site beside River Lugg.

Newnham Mill (TCG), near Tenbury Wells – below.

Redditch: Forge Mill Museum – p.106.

Newnham Mill, near Tenbury Wells

Newnham Mill is a tall building for an early eighteenth-century mill, although the impression gained from the approach to it is of a small mill set deep in the valley of the River Rea. Brick-built, it is one of a number of interesting vernacular buildings, including a superb barn, lying along Mill Lane, just off the busy A49.

Like many estate mills, Newnham had a fairly quiet history, continuing to work commercially until the 1950s. It has been in the ownership of the same family, the Lears, since the nineteenth century. The machinery was renovated in 1928, when the fifteen-foot undershot wheel by Turton of Kidderminster was installed. The wheel has cast-iron shaft rings and spokes, with wooden starts and paddles.

Dr Roger Lear undertook a partial restoration of the mill in 1978, and it is now leased to Jim Bartlett, who has set up a company, Rea Valley Mills, to develop this and Claybury Mill, also on the Rea, at Cleobury Mortimer in Shropshire (p.135). Mr Bartlett is using Newnham to produce a commercially viable quantity of flour – forty bags a day or some six tons a week, which he is already selling in a wide catchment area. The mill is now open only for flour sales when operating, or to pre-booked parties.

Redditch: Forge Mill Museum

The history of Redditch virtually begins with the founding and development of the Cistercian abbey of Bordesley in 1138. Established on meadowland beside the River Arrow, a largely agricultural community was created and wool from estates in Herefordshire and Worcestershire was sold throughout Europe.

Within the seventy-five-acre site, the monks used water-power for a range of functions, and few of the many significant finds made during the excavation of the abbey, in progress since 1968, are more exciting than the remains of what may be the earliest known post-Norman watermill. When a new museum planned for the abbey site is completed, it will include various items from this mill, including the timbers of the millrace, parts of a wooden gear-wheel and a claw hammer dating from the thirteenth century.

There is already one fine museum on the site, at Forge Mill, home of the National Needle Museum. Forge Mill is one of the earliest examples of an adaptation of an existing mill to fulfil changing industrial demands, in this case the rapid development of needle-making from a true 'cottage' industry to a factory-based manufacturing process. Local firms quickly appreciated the need to specialize and modernize for increased efficiency, and individual mills took on different elements of production, although at least one (Hoo Mill) worked a shift system for a while, grinding corn by day and pointing needles by night! This specialization, and factors such as the expansion of overseas markets in the colonies and elsewhere, helped make Redditch the world centre of the needle industry.

Forge Mill was converted from a forge to a scouring-mill in the 1730s; it is the oldest surviving water-powered scouring-mill in the world. The scouring process, cleaning the finished needles, is fully described in the excellent guidebook and in photographs and videos made for the museum. Indeed, a remarkable range of instruction methods, including models, old machinery and short tape presentations of reminiscences by workers, are used to demonstrate and explain the processes involved in needle-making. Wire-drawing, rubbing, pointing, stamping and eyeing, hardening – all are made clear, even to the least technically minded visitor.

The mill consists of two red-brick buildings, linked by an overshot wheel 14½ feet in diameter and ten feet wide with eighty buckets. Installed in 1912, the wheel develops up to 37 hp – sufficient to provide the motive power for the needle machinery in the east wing and the scouring-beds in the west wing. The development of Redditch and the needle industry, explanations of the various processes (except scouring) and a comprehensive display of 'thousands of uses for millions of needles' are the main features of the east wing, the more modern part of the museum. In the older, two-storey west wing, the layout and machinery have been retained as they were when scouring ceased in 1958.

Opened by the Queen in 1983, Forge Mill Museum graphically illustrates a vitally important aspect of local history. But its wider significance is to remind visitors of a vanished manufacturing industry. How fortunate that the history of the needle industry – like that of several others – has been so brilliantly encapsulated for future generations.

Hertfordshire

Hertford was considerably more important than St Albans at the time of the Domesday survey. There were historic reasons for this – Verulamium (modern St Albans) seems to have been unpopular even before Boudicca burned it in AD 61, and the Saxons never colonized the area to any extent, possibly because of local resistance. Hertford, capital of the county and the site of the first national Synod, was supported, and rebuilt, by both Saxons and Normans.

Even at the start of this century, Hertfordshire had many mills, often grouped along certain rivers. The Ver and the Lea both supported several and still retain some. Unfortunately for our purposes, they are now either privately owned, and have been converted to other uses, or are currently in a poor state of repair. I say 'currently' advisedly, for there are hopeful signs of a revival of interest in saving and repairing more than one mill in the county. Corvill Mill is a good recent example of sensible conversion, while Mill Green and Kingsbury have both been restored in a manner which does not diminish their historical importance.

Frogmore: Moor Mill, near St Albans – Pleasant white weather-boarded, two-storey mill in poor state of repair; lucam with tile extension to protect carts; small attached millhouse; machinery said to be in place; hard by M25 and suffered badly from vibration when M-way was constructed; remarkably rural setting with ducks on River Ver. NOT OPEN.

Hatfield: Mill Green Mill – below.

Park Street, Frogmore: Corvill Mill, near St Albans – Excellent conversion and extension, to offices, of already large four-storey, brick-built mill; burnt down in early part of century, repaired and later used as glueworks and for storage; three modern wooden lucams with windows; cast-iron pit-wheel in car-park by main entrance; two water-wheels – larger cemented into pit, smaller has been freed and can turn; no machinery above ground floor; sluices still in place, modern leat, wooden pentrough; renovation by Millwrights International Ltd (see Mill Green Mill). NOT OPEN.

St Albans: Kingsbury Watermill Museum – p.109.

Hatfield: Mill Green Mill

Mill Green was almost certainly one of the four mills operating at Hatfield when Domesday was completed, and the site, on the River Lea, is probably a thousand years old.

The mill carries the date 1762 and was probably extensively repaired at that time, the mill and millhouse being joined with the enclosure of the wheel. More major changes, to the internal machinery, took place in 1824 – the hurst frame has the date 'Aug 4 1824'. In 1894 Thomas Lawrence, mill foreman for the previous eighteen years, acquired the lease, but his expertise was of little help during the rapid changes which affected milling in the last years of the century. Mill Green became increasingly uneconomic to run and survived as a working corn-mill only until 1911.

The millhouse continued to be tenanted, but the mill was neglected, the stones and some ancillary machinery were removed, and the outlook was poor until the local council stepped in, buying both mill and millhouse with other buildings, including two cottages beside the mill-leat. These outwardly unremarkable buildings (not open) have been dated as being among the oldest surviving in Hertfordshire.

In 1973 the Council leased the millhouse to the Hatfield and District Archaeological Society, who established a small museum on the ground floor of the millhouse and then turned their attentions to the restoration of the mill. Preliminary work was completed but full-scale restoration was beyond the unaided capabilities of the Society. In 1978 Welwyn Hatfield District Council acquired responsibility for local museums, establishing the millhouse as their headquarters. The Mill Green Restoration Trust was set up in the following year with grants from the District Council and the Historic

Buildings Commission.

Millwrights International Ltd were employed to carry out repair work, including the replacement of much of the interior woodwork, restoration of the leat and sluices and, most important, the construction and fitting of a completely new wheel to replace the old one, rotted beyond repair. Elm was used for the paddles on the overshot oak wheel. It was not until the early hours of 8 August 1986, following a great final burst of activity, that a near-exhausted Mike King of Millwrights International operated the machinery for the first time in seventy-five years. A commemorative loaf was baked and a few hours later the mill was officially reopened.

Was it worth seven years hard work and nearly £100,000? The answer must be a resounding 'Yes!' Beautifully restored, well lit, with a museum operating as a year-round service (they even open on Boxing Day and are well patronized), Mill Green has been attracting up to 900 visitors on summer Sundays and a steady stream even on wet winter days. Some of the flour produced is sold to a local baker, Simmons, re-establishing a link forged over 120 years ago when Mill Green first supplied flour to the company.

The recent successes at Mill Green and Whitchurch Silk-Mill (p.102) – another combination of inspired amateurs prepared to engage professional help – must contain useful lessons for others looking to preserve mills or, indeed, other parts of our vanishing heritage.

St Albans: Kingsbury Watermill Museum

The exact age of the mill site is in doubt but Kingsbury was a fortified royal settlement in Saxon times. Archbishop Aelfric is thought to have presented it to the abbey of St Albans in the early years of the eleventh century – he died in either 1005 or 1006. Ownership by the abbey was confirmed by King John in 1199, by which time it had ceased to be a defensive site. I think it is possible that any mill here would have been one of three recorded for St Albans – one was certainly the Abbey Mill. Nonetheless, the first positive reference to a mill at Kingsbury comes in 1568, with the conveyance of 'a watermill and free fishery in St Michaels' to Sir Nicholas Bacon, Keeper of the Great Seal to Elizabeth I and owner of Gorhambury House.

Gorhambury has a fascinating history: the first house was built in the twelfth century, the second in Elizabethan times, and a third in the eighteenth century, with alterations in the nineteenth century. A door incorporated into the charming eighteenth-century Kingsbury Manor-House, next to the mill, is almost all that remains of the great Elizabethan house at Gorhambury.

Even if the mill mentioned in the conveyance of 1568 was newly built, the date takes on considerable significance, because the present Kingsbury Mill contains sufficient material to suggest that its basic structure is Elizabethan. Allowing for such additions as the attractive Georgian façade with its weather-boarded gables, parts of the mill must be at least 420 years old.

Gorhambury Estate retained the mill through several changes of owner (including Sir Francis Bacon) and many tenancies. Kingsbury finally ceased grinding corn for the estate in the 1920s, although it continued producing flour until 1936, when it became a grist-mill and a store. Work on restoring the mill began in 1970 and took some three years to complete.

Kingsbury Mill is now used as a museum, with a good selection of simply labelled farming and dairying equipment in addition to its well-restored conventional mill machinery. The wood and metal wheel is said to be 200 years old (the lime-covered cast-iron spokes certainly look impressively aged, but the floats are modern sheet-iron), with one of the three bed stones visible from the walk-way beside the wheel. The excellent leaflet says the wheel is undershot – my notes and those in the mill say it is low-breast!

The museum has a small gift shop and, since 1982, a restaurant in what was once the miller's parlour, specializing in delicious waffles (in the interests of research we ate four!), both sweet and savoury. The staff, whether in the mill or the restaurant, are uniformly charming, and their potentially risky motto, 'Service is our pleasure', is, for once, fully justified. There is, of course, always a danger in what is unreservedly a commercial venture that the prime aim – to display the mill – will be lost. At this beautiful, classically simple mill, cleanly laid out and well lit, the danger has been most successfully avoided.

Isle of Man

I believe there are compelling reasons for including Laxey in this book – and not just because of its size. It is virtually unique, demonstrating a use for water-power which, I suspect, only the Victorians would have considered – granted the problems to be overcome in implementing the scheme. The three little corn-mills serve as reminder of the more humble uses in which water has traditionally been employed.

Castletown: Golden Meadow Mill – Eighteenth-century, corn-mill (occasionally snuff-grinding) on early sixteenth-century site; breastshot wheel, four pairs of stones and remains of overshot wheel; electrically powered.

Colby: Kentraugh Mill, near Port St Mary – Corn-mill, last worked

1943; retains restored original internal machinery, *c.* 1832; breastshot wheel, *c.* 1888; electrically powered.

Laxey: Lady Isabella Water-wheel – see below.

Silverdale: Cregg Watermill, near Ballasalla – Corn-mill, last working 1940s; recently renovated wheel – little machinery; on café and leisure centre site; ruins of Rushen Abbey are nearby (see Laxey, below).

Laxey: Lady Isabella Water-wheel

Strictly speaking, the largest water-wheel in the world doesn't fall into the scope of this book, but it demonstrates a fascinating use for water-power. Laxey is probably visited by more people every year than any mill on the mainland – even if some regret it after climbing ninety-five spiral steps to the viewing-platform.

Mining was, until the advent of tourism, the prime source of the island's wealth and may have been started by the Romans. The evidence for this is, shall we say, slender, but it does seem certain that the industry was established before 1246 when Harald Olafsson, one of the Viking kings who ruled the Isle of Man from the eleventh to the thirteenth century, granted a charter to the monks of Furness allowing them to use 'all kinds of mines ... for their full profit'. The monks had previously established Rushen Abbey at Ballasalla in 1134 and had begun to improve agricultural standards on the island. By the Middle Ages lead from the island was appearing on abbey and cathedral roofs throughout northern England, and by the end of the seventeenth century iron ore was regularly exported.

The advent of the Industrial Revolution led to a major expansion of the industry, producing the problem of pumping water from increasingly deep shafts. The mines engineer Robert Casement designed and built the wheel, using local materials and labour for all but the axle, which was manufactured in Liverpool. The wheel commenced working in 1854 and was named after the wife of the island's Governor, who performed the opening ceremony.

It is possible that there were larger fairground mills in the Victorian era, but today the next largest wheel is at Llanberis (p.195) and that is only two-thirds of the size of the Lady Isabella. A list of statistics is now unavoidable: the pitch-back wheel has a circumference of 228 feet and is 72½ feet in diameter, six feet wide; each of its 168 buckets holds up to twenty-four gallons; the axle is seventeen feet long and twenty-one inches in diameter and weighs nine tonnes; the wheel originally revolved 2½ times a minute, generating 185 hp and pumping 250 gallons of water a minute.

Laxey Wheel is a lasting tribute to Victorian engineering ingenuity and thoroughness. The use of water had never before been considered for a scheme of this size and, in any event, the little Mooar Stream which flows down the valley was totally inadequate to provide the necessary volume of water. As an additional complication, the new wheel could not be positioned near the pump site. Casement constructed a complex system of water-lades (channels) to gather rainwater from the surrounding hills and lead it into a stone cistern just higher than the wheel. Gravity carried the water underground and then up the centre of the stair tower to flow into the buckets. Push-rods were activated by the turning wheel, and they in turn operated a 'T'-rocker at the top of a shaft 200 yards away, pumping the water from a depth of 1,200 feet.

The mines closed in 1929, and by 1937 the wheel was in poor condition. It was bought and repaired by a local businessman and passed to the Manx Government in 1965. Major repairs lasting five years were undertaken, and the wheel was eventually re-started in 1970. An important stage in an ambitious development scheme planned by the Government was reached in 1986 with the completion of work on reconstructing the push-rods.

Isle of Wight

The Isle of Wight was separated from Hampshire in Domesday, although most of the land held by the King is listed in the Hampshire section. Calbourne had three mills, Yafford none. Even so, both have a long history as working mills and now serve a wider public through their various attractions. Both demonstrate, as does Paulton's on the mainland, that mills run as modern commercial enterprises need not be the disaster some enthusiasts may have feared.

Calbourne: Upper Watermill and Museum of Rural Life – below.
Yafford Mill and Farm Park – p.113.

Calbourne: Upper Watermill and Museum of Rural Life

Calbourne Mill is one of a very small number of mills to have made the conversion to the production of flour by the roller-mill process. Where most small mills struggled on, often grinding only animal feed and eventually losing the battle with the roller process, Calbourne's owners installed roller plant in 1894 (nine years after John Caudwell at Rowsley; see p.82), powering it by steam. The mill was enlarged to incorporate this new machinery but the old bakery was closed and the new 'white' flour was sold to bakers. The steam-engine lasted until 1920, when it was replaced by a 30 hp suction gas-engine. The plant and the gas-engine continued to work efficiently until roller-milling ceased in 1955. The mill retains sets of 'break' and 'reduction' rollers and, as a complete contrast, there is, in the museum, a rare wooden hand-mill intended for operation by two people.

Calbourne's long history begins with a reference in Domesday to three mills in the parish among the thirty-four mills listed on the island. At one time the Caul Bourne powered five mills, including a fulling- and a paper-mill. Later records are a little confused because the mills fell into different holdings: two in the manor of Swainston were held from the bishop of Winchester; the third, Calbourne, was part of the holding of William FitzStur. To add to the confusion, Mylplace Mill, as it was then known, was later incorporated into the larger manor of Gatcombe. It also produced both grain and malt, resulting in references to two mills! From the early seventeenth century the history of the mill is well documented, leading to its purchase by George Weeks in 1878.

The Weeks family still own the mill and have developed it as a museum. The thoroughly professional approach they adopted in the nineteenth century when faced with change is still in evidence, and the exhibits, distributed throughout the mill and in a separate Museum of Rural Life, are very well presented. Attention to detail ranges from clear notes, including an excellent leaflet (a model of its kind, neither too technical nor too patronizing), to the purchase of a redundant farm building and its rebuilding on the Calbourne site to house the expanding museum and gift shop.

Calbourne Mill and millhouse form a pleasing group in a most attractive garden. Entrance to the seventeenth-century mill is beside the millpond on the stone floor level where, in addition to two pairs of Derbyshire Peak stones, there is a display of agricultural implements. The granary's roof timbers are said to be from a ship wrecked at nearby Brook – a claim often made but rarely confirmed (Chesapeake Mill, p.103, is the exception), and Calbourne sensibly makes no extravagant claims. If the geological finds on the screen floor are not entirely appropriate, they were at least collected on the island.

The twenty-foot-diameter overshot iron wheel is demonstrated daily. The mill leaflet includes a remarkable calculation of 252,000 gallons of water an hour flowing over the wheel when working at full power – I have a suspicion there may be a mathematical error here. However, should the wheel succumb to this watery 'bombardment', it can easily be replaced, for, uniquely, there is a 'spare' in the grounds!

Yafford Mill and Farm Park

As a name, 'Yafford' is relatively recent – it first appears in 1637, but

'Heceford', held from the King by Aelfric and Wihtlac, occurs in the Domesday entries for the Isle of Wight. There is no mention of a mill and no certainty that the site is older than the middle of the eighteenth century, when the first record of a working mill appears. Nonetheless there are signs that the present building, of nineteenth-century construction, incorporates parts of a much older building, possibly even fifteenth-century.

Yafford was a successful mill, functioning profitably until the 1960s. That it lasted so long at a time of almost unrelieved difficulty for mills and millers was due largely to its long-term concentration upon grist-milling – producing animal feed for local farmers and, in particular, for the Bowcombe Estate. The mill has now made an equally successful transition to present-day demands by providing a variety of alternatives in support of the fully restored working wheel. These include a nature trail, a collection of waterfowl, several grey seals, some rare breeds including Portland sheep (forerunner of such modern breeds as the Dorset Horn) and a large number of agricultural tools, many used on the farm until comparatively recently.

The overshot wheel (13½ feet in diameter and 4½ feet wide) was repaired in 1947 after collapsing. The forty-two original wooden buckets were replaced by iron; fitted to a wooden frame, they have not been a success. The fitting of wooden paddles or buckets to iron wheels is commonplace and works well; I suspect that loading and stress factors are involved in the problems of Yafford.

The availability of water has always been of prime importance to the miller, and Yafford is fortunate in that its supply to the artificially constructed millpond – very similar to that at Park Mill, Bateman's (p.162) – is from a stream with a reputation for never drying up. On its route to Yafford the stream passes Brighstone Mill, water-powered for centuries but now driven by turbine.

The gearing and, indeed, all the well-restored machinery displayed in the mill are typical of those once found in hundreds of mills throughout the island and the mainland. But then, the success of Yafford Mill has always been based on a sensible appreciation and application of the resources at its disposal – which may seem obvious but hasn't always obtained either in milling or in a variety of other fields.

Kent

Kent has some exceptionally attractive mills, many of them clad in the traditional white-painted weather-board of the county. It has to be said that Kent has, in the recent past, been remarkably cavalier in its attitude towards mills, and not least towards Crabble Mill, which has deteriorated so badly in recent years that it is now barely standing.

Many of the best and historically most important mills have passed into private hands and are neither open nor visible to visitors. Frustrating though this is, a few are still open or may be viewed without disturbing the owners. Perhaps significantly, one or two mills which were almost lost (Brattle's is a good example) are now being restored by enthusiasts.

Chilham, Farningham and Wickhambreaux are all handsome and aesthetically pleasing mills, matching any in Norfolk, while Upper Crisbrook is a fine specimen of a brick-built mill in a valley full of interest for the mill buff. Swanton Mill is surrounded by a beautiful garden which adds to its already attractive appearance.

Buckland: Crabble Watermill, near Dover – Important and once impressive six-storey brick and weather-boarded mill; one of five built in 1812 to supply local garrison during time of Napoleonic Wars; ceased to work in late 1890s; high-breast wheel and original machinery; presently held up by scaffolding and considered unfit for visitors.

Chilham Mill – A most elegant five-storey building on the River Great Stour, some way from the picture-book village; brick and white weather-boarding; nineteenth-century, ceased working 1933; owned by water authority and leased (NOT OPEN); awkward to reach over unmanned railway level-crossing but repays effort.

Edenbridge: Honours Mill – brick and weather-boarded eighteenth-century mill; worked until 1968 flooding of River Eden fractured pit-wheel – on that day I saw a 'rescuing' Land Rover create a bow-wave sufficient to break shop-front windows near the mill; internal breastshot wheel drove three pairs of stones (latterly one pair were electrically driven); now converted by international swimmer Duncan Goodhew into restaurant – ground-floor area features old mill machinery.

Farningham Mill – Outstandingly handsome and beautifully maintained three-bay, four-storey weather-boarded eighteenth-century building; set at right-angles to Georgian millhouse with delightful Gothic cottage and half-timbered house forming perfect frame; mansard roof; particularly impressive lucam with windows, one with 'Gothick' tracery; nice example of unchanging human behaviour – expensive grey bricks were used for chimneystacks facing road, cheaper red brick for sides; private dwelling. NOT OPEN.

Faversham: Chart Gunpowder Mills – p.116.

Goudhurst: Hope Mill – Well-restored mill on River Teise, west of village; typical architecture of area – one-storey red brick, three-storey white weather-boarded; sluices in position, no wheel; pretty tile-hung Kentish house and oast complete fine vernacular group. NOT OPEN. NB: A262 is very busy and narrows by bridge beside mill – great care is needed if crossing road here: do not park on road.

Loose: Old Mill House – Attractive building, one of many in Loose valley (see below); millrace converted to waterfall. NOT OPEN.

Maidstone: Hayle Paper-Mill – One of more than a dozen mills once operating in historic Loose valley south of Maidstone; all either gone or private properties – see Upper Crisbrook below; Hayle has long history of producing handmade paper; was powered by eighteen-foot iron wheel with provision for pitch-back and overshot working; latterly electric-powered; large complex – not pretty and currently run down – mostly of brick; Hayle Millhouse best building architecturally – restored 1978 and now used as offices; refurbished Hayle Mill cottages (upstream) are very pretty. NOT OPEN.

Maidstone: Upper Crisbrook Mill – Fine Victorian three-storey brick and timber building; double weather-boarded lucam over lane; sixteen-foot diameter by eight-foot wide iron overshot wheel, wooden paddles; pretty garden – interesting marble memorial to two Scout Leaders of 1914-18 War; tailrace feature of garden; see Old Mill House and Hayle Paper-Mill above. NOT OPEN.

Mersham: Swanton Mill, near Ashford – p.117.

Smeeth: Evegate Mill – Four-storey, brick and timber building *c.* 1750; used for antique furniture-restoring workshop; millhouse is older (1650); some nineteenth-century additions; attached stables used as showroom; setting , by East Stour, is delightful – very pleasant private garden; water-wheel mechanism remains – wheel has gone. OPEN ONLY FOR BUSINESS.

Tonge: The Old Mill – p.118.

Wateringbury: Brattles Mill – p.119.

Wickhambreaux Mill – Large, handsome late-eighteenth- or early nineteenth-century six-storey white weather-boarded mill on River Nailbourne in attractive village; breastshot wheel on slatted case; currently rather rundown; privately owned. NOT OPEN.

Faversham: Chart Gunpowder Mills

Historically of great importance – visually an enormous disappointment! The site consists of a series of rainwater-filled pits flanked by a wooden structure looking like the sort of municipal park hut which dispenses watery tea and ice creams.

The pits are actually the stone beds of three of the original tiny mills. The hut is the fourth mill and contains some nineteenth-century machinery including a sixteen-foot-diameter breastshot iron wheel connected by gears to a pair of three-ton edge-runner stones. These turned on the bed stone, mixing sulphur, saltpetre and charcoal in a very slow, dangerous process, now simulated in demonstrations using an inert compound.

With unusually heavy humour, Defoe says of Feversham: 'While I was near this town some years ago, a most surprising accident happened, namely, the blowing up of a powder-mill ...; the blast was not only frightful, but it shattered the whole town ...; also several people were killed at the powder-house it self....' The exact date of this explosion is difficult to pin-point (it could have been as early as the 1680s) but other serious explosions occurred in Faversham in 1767, 1781 and 1847. To minimize damage, the works were invariably screened from the public by banks and walls – how ironic that the surviving mill is now surrounded by a large modern housing estate!

Chart Mills were part of Home Works, known to have been in existence by 1653 and believed to have been established some ninety years earlier. The mills were nationalized in 1759 because, it was said, private suppliers were producing poor-quality gunpowder. Modernized in the following year, the mills became part of the Royal Gunpowder Factory which reverted to private ownership at the end of the Napoleonic Wars. The mills underwent several changes of ownership at the end of the nineteenth and early in the twentieth century, finally closing down in 1934. The remaining mill was restored, by the Faversham Society, between 1968 and 1970.

Mersham: Swanton Mill, near Ashford

Swanton is a most attractive Grade II listed building, surrounded by a garden of great charm in which visitors are free to wander. It is one of two mills recorded for Mersham in Domesday Book. The ground floor is in splendid condition, the machinery beautifully maintained and labelled, as befits a winner of a European Architectural Award and a Civic Trust Award. The upper floor, with its exhibition of photographs and records, is perhaps less effective – many items appear to have little connection with each other. The most important section is that showing records of Swanton Mill and of the history of Mersham.

There is little doubt that many, if not most, surviving mills are on sites close to, or identical to, the position they occupied at the time of the Domesday Survey. All the evidence suggests an unwillingness on the part of the yeomanry to move except under military or strong economic pressure – and, as mills have little strategic importance and were, until the last century, largely economically viable due to their captive market, it seems reasonable to make this assumption. Conclusive proof is, of course, virtually impossible to obtain but any mill which can show continuous occupancy of a site for four or five centuries can hardly be challenged on its claim to 900 years of milling. The evidence adduced from a marriage settlement of 1610 in the records at Swanton confirms the existence of a mill here at that time, and the presumption must be that the site has been occupied since Domesday.

The bulk of the complex, consisting of the mill, millhouse and additional buildings for storage or to house a beam-engine, is seventeenth-century. Parts, including the engine-house and lucam, were added in the nineteenth century. The enclosed overshot waterwheel has unusual dimensions: 7½ feet in diameter and eight feet wide. Both it and the pit-wheel are metal – the rest of the mill machinery is apple or hornbeam.

At the turn of the century Swanton was operating four pairs of stones, although the water-supply then, as now, was not always reliable. A beam-engine was installed in 1841 but was dismantled and sold to America in 1920, when the mill ceased grinding corn, although it continued to be used for animal feed for some years. The present owner, Mrs Gay Christiansen, bought the mill, by then in a derelict state, in 1969, taking six years to restore it. Two pairs of stones are now in use, and the mill is capable of producing three hundredweight of flour an hour.

Swanton is of particular interest in demonstrating how a small farming complex grows and develops. Its practical but aesthetically satisfying buildings create a very pleasing 'picture' – and the setting, in the garden Mrs Christiansen has created, is not bettered by any other working mill.

Tonge: The Old Mill

Only the beautifully maintained garden has been open to visitors and, at the time of writing, with the sale of the house and attached craft centre about to take place, even that is in doubt. A pity, for the back of the combined mill and millhouse is a charming jumble, and the various waterways flowing under and around the house have been cleverly absorbed into the planning of the garden.

Tonge had a mill in 1086 but the present buildings are a mixture – possibly seventeenth-century in part but mostly mid-eighteenth-century. The wheel was installed across the road in the far less attractive 'New Mill' when it was built, complete with ugly chimney, in 1837.

Wateringbury: Brattle's Mill

An eighteenth-century mill, one of three working at Wateringbury when Domesday was compiled. After years of neglect, Mr and Mrs Bruce, the new owners, are restoring this delightful mill themselves, with local help, and converting part of it to a private dwelling. There is a sixteen-foot-diameter overshot wheel which should be turning soon.

The millpond is in good condition, as are the sluices, and the mill is part of a complex of buildings, some a touch over-restored, which are, nonetheless, a visual delight to discover at the end of a narrow lane leading from the main Tonbridge to Maidstone road.

Lancashire

Lancashire did not exist when Domesday was compiled, and its settlements, listed under Yorkshire and Cheshire, were poorly recorded – there is no information on mills in the Survey.

In the intervening centuries the position has changed several times. Corn-mills played an early part in the history of the county, and two centuries ago water-power was responsible for the initial creation of much of Lancashire's prosperity. The main contributor was the cotton industry, with its enormous appetite for water to power the looms of the great mills. Other industrial processes took advantage of the plentiful supply of water in the county – paper-making, forge-mills, dyestuffs.

What then has happened to the mills, for it is certain that the majority have disappeared? First, the corn-mills were replaced either by larger industrial mills or disappeared after failing to survive the roller-milling revolution. Then steam and the turbine replaced the water-wheel before the cotton industry itself went into an abrupt decline. As for the other processes, they have been overtaken by or have adopted modern technology. I have listed three examples of the type of complex traditionally associated with the textile industry. All were once powered by water and include, at Calder Vale, housing for workers similar to the style pioneered by Arkwright at Cromford (p.81).

Burnley: The Weaver's Triangle – a group of textile mills and allied factories along the Leeds & Liverpool Canal.

Calder Vale: Mill and village – Nineteenth-century formerly water-powered textile-mill; opened in 1835 with housing for key workers (cf. Styal, p.68); woodland walk takes in pond and millrace; arguably best surviving example of such a complex in county.

Chipping: Waterwheel Restaurant – Former corn-mill on Chipping Brook; recently converted to restaurant; external working breastshot wheel.
Galgate: Silk-Mills – Stone-built group of mills dating from late eighteenth century; originally water-powered – later steam.
Helmshore: Higher Mill and Museum – below.

Helmshore: Higher Mill and Museum

Higher Mill, a three-storey late-eighteenth-century woollen fulling-mill which last worked in 1967, has been adapted to serve as part of the Museum of the Lancashire Textile Industry. Built by the Turner family and operated first by them and later by the Whitaker family, the mill has survived almost unchanged through the upheavals in the industry over the last century.

The mill was water-powered until 1954, and the present wheel is the third on the site. The water-supply to the wheel was supplemented by the reservoir immediately above the mill. The high breastshot wheel (installed *c.* 1850) is approximately eighteen feet in diameter and eleven feet wide and originally transmitted power to five pairs of fulling-stocks by two pairs of rim-gears and a large spur-gear. It was the failure of this gear which ended the use of the water-wheel for commercial powering of the stocks.

The wheel was repaired and substantially rebuilt in 1978. All the original ironwork was retained but the timber was replaced. English oak was used for the arms, with pitch pine (reclaimed from mill beams) used in all the remaining repairs, including the buckets. The rim-gearing and spur-gear are still to be repaired, and the wheel is not currently connected to the fulling-stocks. However, the enthusiastic team at the museum, led by Robin Green, have plans to ensure that this work is completed by 1989, the bicentenary year of the building.

The Museum of the Lancashire Textile Industry provides working demonstrations of the wheel and of the fulling-stocks (used for shrinking and matting cloth to produce a heavy, dense fabric) which are contemporary with the wheel. A particularly attractive beam-engine, built in 1846, is housed in Higher Mill with an internationally important collection of Arkwright machinery, some of which, including a water frame, comes from Cromford (p.81).

Whitakers Mill, the adjacent nineteenth-century steam-powered condenser cotton-spinning mill which worked until 1978, has an exhibition containing early twentieth-century machinery used in the mill, an audio-visual and a textile exhibition gallery. Condenser cotton plants were employed to process cotton waste, making such useable fabrics as flannelette.

There is a disused railway viaduct beside the mills which has a part in a story about William Turner, one of the characters of the family and responsible for many developments at Higher Mill. It indicates entrepreneurial flair at work in the nineteenth century for, when the viaduct was built, William, a shareholder in the railway, obtained compensation for the inconvenience, then proceeded to build under the viaduct arches!

Leicestershire

When Norman Ashton published *Leicestershire Water-mills* in 1977, he was able to include a total of forty-three surviving mill buildings. He regretted then that none was in public hands and, in view of what has happened in the interim, I can only agree. This large county, with a long tradition of small corn-mills (123 at Domesday) now offers only a few converted to public houses and private dwellings. The list below is a representative selection, but there is little else for any but the most dedicated seeker of half-hidden mill-leats and rusting sluices.

Cossington Mill, near Leicester – Long history, now a smart-looking restaurant; millpond converted to car-park.

Cotes Mill, near Loughborough – Potentially handsome, large black-and-white building, one of many mills once operating on River Soar; long converted to pub; pleasant setting by pond but currently run down; corroded wheel inside; pub closed suddenly in late 1986 – there are reports it may have been sold as this gazetteer was being prepared; connection with family of comedian Spike Milligan.

Ratcliffe-on-the-Wreake Mill – Most attractive building on lovely site; can be viewed from bridge on public road; machinery and wheel visible; beautifully maintained. NOT OPEN.

Rearsby Mill – Retains iron wheel and small pond; part local Switherland slate; viewable from public footpath running between pond and house. NOT OPEN.

Sibson: Millers – Conversion to pub; internal water-wheel.

Sutton in the Elms: Mill on the Soar – Good recent conversion of large brick mill building; external wheel restored and turning; glass panel in conservatory bar floor showing mill-stream; collection of rare farm breeds including waterfowl on millpond.

Lincolnshire

At Domesday Lincolnshire had a relatively large population, with a great number of settlements. Not surprisingly, the county also possessed many mills, although they were often in groups – for example, Tealby had twelve. Most of these mills were in the Wolds, more suitable for water-power than the then virtually undeveloped Fenlands.

The county now has remarkably few mills, but those listed reflect the situation over most of England. A mill that grinds for demonstration, a museum, a restaurant, a craft centre and a conversion to a private house – how often is this repeated with minor variations around the country?

Alvingham Watermill, near Louth – Late eighteenth-century mill on River Lud – one of thirteen once working on river; site of mill for 900 years; rather plain red-brick three-storey mill under pantile roof; modern two-storey house attached; worked commercially until 1950; eleven-foot-diameter, eight-foot-wide cast-iron breastshot wheel, elm boards, following restoration now grinding corn again; uses Derbyshire Peak stones.

Bourne: Baldocks Mill Heritage Centre – Former mill now converted into centre for local history; also houses motor-racing display provided by Raymond Mays Memorial Fund.

Claythorpe Mill, near Aby – Attractive 1720 mill in small valley setting; working wheel; millpond; fish smokery and restaurant.

Stockworth Mill, near Somersby – Associated with Tennyson's 'The Miller's Daughter'; wheel a mixture of iron and wood; now a craft centre.

Tealby Thorpe: Thorpe Mill – Pleasant three-storey corn-mill in attractive setting; dates from 1790s; combination wheel – high-breast/undershot (cf. Letheringsett Mill p.125); now a private residence. NOT OPEN.

Norfolk

Few counties have as many beautiful mills as Norfolk, and many are still viewable from public roads and paths. By contrast, there are few other counties where so many blunt notices appear, warning off the public. One of the mills listed below (fortunately easily studied from the road) adds a further warning about an alsatian which, when I passed, was sitting in the drive close to an open gate and so was, presumably, a hazard to passers-by.

The problem is that many of these mills, which are large and must be horrendously expensive to run, can survive only if converted to homes for the wealthy. Not unnaturally, these owners wish to preserve their privacy and have the wherewithal to do so. It is no coincidence that the four mills I have highlighted are neither suitable for use as private dwellings nor (begging their owners' pardon!) architecturally or aesthetically outstanding.

Nonetheless, the range of mills available for studying in this lovely county must satisfy any visitor, and the historical context (at Domesday, Norfolk had far more mills and fisheries than any other part of East Anglia) simply adds to the interest, for so many of the sites extend back to at least the eleventh century and have a real 'feel' of history.

Bintree Mill – Four-storey building on River Wensum; pantile roof; attractive bridge over millpond; interesting gearing of sluice gates. NOT OPEN.

Burgh-next-Aylsham Mill – Large and attractive mill; six-pointed gable ends; worked until last few years; converted to flats. NOT OPEN.

Burnham Overy Mill (NT) – Pleasing eighteenth-century three-storey brick-built building; weather-boarded lucam; part of large complex including millhouse, cottages, maltings and windmill; well-known bottleneck on A149. TENANTED – NOT OPEN.

Corpusty Mill – Outstandingly beautiful conversion to private house of 'classic' part-weather-boarded mill; fine dormer windows; weather-boarded lucam; stands over River Bure on very awkward bend on B1354. NOT OPEN.

Elsing Mill – Architecturally a building of considerable interest – half brick, half weather-boarding with decorated bargeboards; on edge of pretty village beside River Wensum; another outstanding example of a large East Anglian mill. NOT OPEN.

Foulden Mill – p.124.

Gunton Park Saw-Mill, near Cromer – p.125.

Holt: Letheringsett Mill – p.125.

Lenwade Mill – Worked until recent years by Sayer Bros Ltd – name still appears, faintly, on front of large and handsome weather-boarded building; attractive gardens beside River Wensum. NOT OPEN.

Little Cressingham Mill – p.127.

Narborough Mill – Beautifully proportioned, well-preserved mill; River Nar still races beneath twin-arched bridge on which three-storeyed brick building stands; fine weather-boarded lucam projects from tiled roof; site is home to trout farm shop; angling competitions a regular feature in 'Miller's Lake' behind mill; machinery is in place but mill is NOT OPEN.

Stoke Holy Cross Mill, near Norwich – Recently a restaurant, this large white weather-boarded mill complex is now in run-down condition; historic mill where Jeremiah Colman first made his mustard in early years of nineteenth century, before moving to Carrow in 1856; mill worked until 1962, producing animal feed. NOT OPEN.

Foulden Mill

Foulden Mill has a number of claims to interest, not least for its long history: there were two mills and two fisheries in the area when the Domesday Survey was compiled, one almost certainly on this site. Foulden is a fine example of an estate mill, an important feature of many large Victorian estates. Often referred to as saw-mills, they invariably performed a variety of other functions.

The mill had fallen into disuse when the future Lord Amherst bought the estate in 1868, repairing the mill the following year. Among the achievements of the family was the introduction of the pheasant named after Lady Amherst – this colourful Oriental import now occurs regularly in collections and occasionally in the wild.

The current re-development of Foulden Mill owes much to the determination of one man and his wife to achieve a goal set many years ago. A passionate interest in the history of watermills and an increasing concern about their virtual disappearance (particularly in East Anglia) led to several attempts on the part of Graham Martin to acquire one. After a series of frustrations, Foulden was secured and restoration began, encouraged by Anglia Television and their presenter, Dick Joice, who has already made a documentary on the project. Anglia TV was always a leader in supporting and featuring major local initiatives, such as the one at Foulden, and it's good to see that the spirit Aubrey Buxton created lives on.

The major aim at Foulden is to emphasize how the burgeoning use of machinery during the nineteenth century was facilitated by 'rediscovering' and harnessing the power of the water-wheel – and not only on such industrial sites as Abbeydale (p.181). On many relatively remote estates, such as Foulden, the wheel, which for centuries had helped to sustain the community became, for a brief period, quite literally pivotal in schemes involving the introduction of powered tools, as landowners attempted to maintain economic viability and independence. Even more ambitiously, the Martins hope to draw attention to the continuing value of the wheel in the twentieth century – particularly in Third World countries.

The mill machinery is contained in a wooden shed attached to a threshing-barn built of clay lump under a slate roof. The shallow cast-iron overshot metal wheel has elm buckets repaired and replaced, like the bulk of the machinery, by Mr Martin. Further interest is added by the presence, in the barn, of a number of the original machines, including a corn-roller, cake-crusher, chaff-cutter and water-pump. All are belt-driven from a transmission shaft running the length of the barn. Power is provided through a belt drum driven by an unusual cog-drive system operating through a seven-foot cog beside the wheel. Some of the machines which would undoubtedly have stood in this type of mill (a threshing-machine, for example) will be reconstructed and added later.

Graham Martin has a background in model-making and intends to make Foulden a centre where enthusiasts can meet and work – he organized a gathering in mid-1988. The milling of flour has already begun, using the four-foot French Burr stones installed by Lord Amherst. As more of the machinery 'comes on stream', the educational value of Foulden will increase – in racing parlance, this is definitely 'one for the notebook'.

Gunton Park Saw-Mill, near Cromer

A timber-framed one-storey building of no particular architectural merit. Technically, however, the mill is of outstanding importance. Built around 1775, it was, for a long time, the only water-powered saw-mill known to be in existence in the country, and certainly the only one in Norfolk. The restoration of Foulden (above) has removed both claims at a stroke.

The water-supply itself comes from the ornamental lake in the park, and it powers the one surviving water-wheel. The most important mechanism in the mill is the vintage reciprocating saw (probably installed in the early years of the nineteenth century) mounted in a heavy wooden framework. A variety of blades can be employed in the saw frame, allowing variations in the thickness of timber being cut. The saw is operated through a large flywheel, crankshaft and connecting-rod while the timber is placed on a rail-mounted carriage connected to the saw. The carriage moves the timber forward at each stroke of the saw.

The Norfolk Windmills Trust has a long lease on Gunton and, as at Little Cressingham Mill (p.127), is hoping eventually to restore both the wheel and the machinery to full working order.

There is a place to park a few yards from the mill, and a footpath past it leads to the pretty lake now in regular use by fishermen; a notice by the mill restricts the use of certain baits as being unnecessary – obviously the lake is well stocked with accommodating fish. The great storm of October 1987 affected this part of Norfolk badly, and Gunton Park did not escape, but fortunately none of the many uprooted trees in the vicinity of the mill fell onto its reed-thatched roof.

Holt: Letheringsett Mill

'Leringaseta' had its Domesday mill beside the River Glaven, a relatively swift-flowing river in an area where many streams meander. There are sufficient references in the succeeding centuries to make it probable that the latest tenant, Mike Thurlow, is simply renewing an almost continuous process. A mill was included in a sale of land in 1384, and the Buckenham family were tenants in the hundred of so years leading to the Restoration of the Monarchy in 1660. Some time before 1744 the mill burned down (a common occurrence) but it was rebuilt and operating by 1754. The owner, a Sheringham miller, added a wind-powered grist-mill to the property but then went bankrupt – another regular happening (see Sarehole Mill, p.172, for a very similar story some twenty years later). A second fire in 1800 led to the building of the present solid four-storey red-brick mill in 1802. The Hardy family of Letheringsett Hall bought the mill in 1826 and it is still in the possession of the Cozens-Hardy family, the name they took in 1842. The mill was producing animal feed in the last years of its working life, ceasing to operate in 1945.

I doubt that anyone will dispute too strongly that, in an area where the majority of mills rank among the most beautiful anywhere in the country, this mill is perhaps the least stimulating architecturally. The fascination of Letheringsett is that its machinery can be powered in any one of three ways. The water-wheel was assumed to be a breastshot wheel until restoration work carried out on it and the sluices in 1983 revealed that it had been installed as an undershot wheel. There is no evidence that it ever operated in this fashion but the removal of timber from the flow area means that the wheel may be used in either breast- or undershot mode depending on the current water-supply situation. If both methods should fail, a Ruston Hornsby oil-engine could be called into use. This diesel-engine replaced the water-wheel as the power-source in 1945 and is in excellent working order. The interior of the mill and the machinery contain little that is unusual – indeed, 'normalcy' extends to still using traditional apple-wood teeth in the great spur-wheel.

Mr Thurlow served in the Royal Navy for many years, leaving with a disability pension in 1981. By sheer determination he now walks without support and showed greater mobility in climbing to the fourth floor than I did! His willingness to tackle any job has already led him to make a start on dressing one of the two pairs of stones and, when I called, he was joyfully contemplating the task of essential, and very wet, maintenance work to the water-wheel pit. For the immediate future he will be concentrating on the sale of animal feed but he aims eventually to start producing flour commercially again – and I wouldn't bet against him.

When we met, the results of the desperate storm of 16 October 1987 were all around us: a few miles south the classic garden and park of Blickling had been irrevocably changed, Gunton Park Saw-Mill (see above) was reachable only via an obstacle course of fallen trees, and the Glaven had been level with the ground floor of the mill when Mr Thurlow arrived on the morning of the 17th. But happily, and not for the first time, Letheringsett had survived and its future now looks bright.

Little Cressingham Mill

There seem to have been two mills in the parish of Little Cressingham when Little Domesday was compiled. As so often happens, there are few records of the mill or mills in succeeding centuries, but there was certainly a water-mill on this site in 1780. Nearby, a smock windmill had apparently been built, and both were advertised for sale in 1795. The present combination mill, built around 1821, looks like a windmill; it is unique, not because it uses both forms of power but because each services two pairs of stones. The probability is that the wind-driven machinery was taken from the smock-mill, but the water-driven machinery is of iron and therefore almost certainly contemporary.

The breastshot iron wheel, twelve feet in diameter and six feet wide, drives one pair of French Burr and one pair of Peak stones on the first floor. On the fourth floor two pairs of French Burr stones were underdriven by sails. The mill was tail-winded in 1916 and never again worked by wind-power.

The watermill continued to operate until 1952, latterly producing grist for feeding pheasants on the Clermont Estate, which owned it until 1980. In 1981 the mill was leased to Norfolk County Council for twenty years at a peppercorn rent subject to restoration by the Norfolk Windmills Trust. Work on the project is currently rather bogged down – a polite way of saying that nothing much is happening, probably through lack of funds! Norfolk possesses one or two mills with unique features, and it must be hoped that Little Cressingham and others do not end up as footnotes in future books.

Northamptonshire

Northamptonshire was a difficult county for the Domesday scribes to survey, for it was part English and part Danish. Another major problem was the amount of 'waste' created (if that is the right word) by Morcar, Earl of Northumbria, in 1085.

It is unlikely that Morcar did more than present-day planners have achieved in the centre and environs of the county town of this loveliest of English Shire Counties. If you doubt me, visit Upton, one of several mills in and around Northampton currently in very poor condition. But it is not just the mill: a whole triangle between the A45 and the M1 appears to have been abandoned, resembling one of those sites surrendered by Government ministries at the end of the Second World War. Almost certainly there is a master-plan for a bigger and better industrial estate, but as long as this sort of eyesore is permitted, 'planners' can have no complaints if the Prince of Wales (and we lesser mortals) continue to lambast them.

It is still a little surprising that the remaining Northamptonshire mills are, by and large, rather unattractive. Duddington is pretty but the rest are hardly memorable, and Bugbrooke is without doubt the ugliest mill on any Domesday site.

Ashton Wold: Ashton Mill, near Oundle – Estate mill rebuilt by Lord Rothschild on site of corn- and fulling-mill; late nineteenth-century machinery – turbines and Blackstone diesel-engine; supplied electricity and water to estate and estate houses; fish museum, antique farm machinery; forge.

Billing Mill, near Northampton – Early nineteenth-century corn-mill; working until early 1960s; restored 1965-8 as a milling museum; large working Poncelet iron wheel with open paddles; ancillary machinery; part of Billing Aquadrome – sited in caravan park.

Bugbrooke Mill – Of interest only in that it is on site of mill with highest value of any in county at Domesday – one of two at Bugbrooke; vast, unattractive commercial complex with interesting 1866 yellow stone cottage, built over river; other buildings of similar age.

Dodford Mill – Interesting collection of old buildings including mill, beside infant River Nene; latterly in very poor repair; signs, in early 1987, that restoration work was being carried out on nearby buildings. NOT OPEN,

Duddington Mill – Picturesque, dates from 1664, though much altered; stands by fourteenth-century bridge; now used as offices. NOT OPEN.

Upton Mill, near Northampton – Three-storey red-brick mill and millhouse on River Nene; boarded up and in poor condition on outskirts of Northampton in area which is seemingly being deliberately rundown; see above.

Waterways Museum, Stoke Bruerne – Converted corn-mill, housing a museum on history of canals.

Northumberland

A county which has fared badly in recent years with the loss through neglect, sometimes deliberate, of several valuable and interesting mills. Many of these mills are, or were, on dramatic sites similar to that at Thrum, making their loss the harder to explain. [These

Lancashire – Higher Mill and Museum, Helmshore. Carefully landscaped, this large fulling-mill is now the Museum of the Lancashire Textile Industry.

Leicestershire – Cotes Mill, near Loughborough. A large white-painted brick building of different periods. Cotes Mill was a public house for a long time and may soon reopen.

Opposite: **Lincolnshire – Claythorpe Mill, near Aby**. Now a restaurant and fish smokery, the eighteenth-century Claythorpe Mill retains its working wheel.

Lincolnshire – Alvingham Watermill, near Louth. Thirteen mills once operated on the River Lud. Only one, this good, solid, eighteenth-century building, still grinds flour.

Claythorpe
Mill

Norfolk – Burgh-next-Aylsham Mill. This very large mill – with its six pointed gable ends at the left – has recently been converted to flats.

Norfolk – Corpusty Mill. Straddling the River Bure, and one of the finest of the many handsome weatherboard mills in Norfolk, Corpusty is now a private house.

Norfolk – Foulden Mill. An unpretentious Victorian estate mill, Foulden is being steadily restored to its nineteenth-century condition using original machinery wherever possible.

Norfolk – Little Cressingham Mill. Built in the early 1820s and unique – not because it had a windmill, but because the wind- and water-powered wheels both turned two pairs of stones.

SPUR WHEEL
SPINDLE
FLOW CONTROL
STONE NUT

Northumberland – Heatherslaw Mill, Ford Forge, near Cornhill on Tweed. A square, imposing building standing high above the River Till yet, surprisingly, prone to flooding.

Opposite: **Northumberland – Heatherslaw Mill, Ford Forge, near Cornhill on Tweed.** Well-labelled internal machinery at Heatherslaw Mill – typical of the care taken with exhibits at many mills.

Oxfordshire – Mapledurham Mill, near Reading. This eighteenth-century brick-and-weatherboarded mill in a tiny village has a marvellous timeless quality.

Shropshire – Claybury Mill, Cleobury Wells. Claybury under repair in early 1988. It last worked in 1933 and attempts to use it during the last war were thwarted by the collapse of the weir (on the right).

Somerset – Combe House Hotel, Holford. An unusual feature of this hotel, beautifully situated in a valley under the Quantocks, is the twenty-six-foot wheel, once used to power the tannery pump.

Somerset – Orchard Mill, Williton. Built during the seventeenth century, at a time of prosperity for milling, Orchard Mill has more than a touch of elegance about it.

Somerset – Mill Pottery, Wootton Courtenay. No ordinary wheel, this is believed to be the only one in the country to be made entirely of fibreglass.

Somerset – Piles Mill, Allerford. 'Rural' in the highest degree, said an eighteenth-century visitor to this delightfully unspoilt mill. Little has changed in the intervening centuries.

Staffordshire – Brindley Mill. Now dwarfed by a modern textile mill, the mill retains windows with arches and keystones of a design linked with James Brindley.

Staffordshire – Cheddleton Flint Mills. The north mill at Cheddleton was built to grind flint for the expanding pottery industry in the mid-eighteenth century; the older south mill was converted later.

Suffolk – Little Glemham Mill, near Wickham Market. The unattractive corrugated mansard roof probably saved the internal machinery, during years of neglect – the mill is now being restored.

Suffolk – Pakenham Watermill. A view across the millpond of an architecturally and aesthetically pleasing mill – almost lost after it ceased to operate in 1974, but restored by volunteers.

Suffolk – Flatford Mill, East Bergholt. A pleasant group, including the small brick building which once contained an undershot wheel.

Suffolk – Letheringham Mill. A lovely mill in a very beautiful and peaceful setting by the River Deben.

Suffolk – Woodbridge Tidemill. The old tidemill standing proudly in front of the busy shipyards of Woodbridge.

comments were written before I discovered early in 1988 that Felton (one of the mills I had in mind) had been converted to four houses!] Heatherslaw Mill is now the only important working mill surviving in Northumberland.

Cornhill on Tweed: Twizel Mill – Mill is in poor condition; millhouse being used as fishing lodge; attractive setting – reached along public footpath beside river. NOT OPEN.

Felton Mill – Large, three- and four-storey stone mill which was unoccupied for some time, although much internal machinery remained in late 1986 when I visited it; part of attractive group in beautiful setting by River Coquet; now converted to four houses. NOT OPEN.

Ford Forge: Heatherslaw Mill, near Cornhill on Tweed – below.

Newton: Hunday National Tractor and Farm Museum, Westside, Stocksfield – Bardon Mill, built 1717, reconstructed on site; twenty-foot wheel powering two pairs of stones; fine display of vintage tractors and other agricultural machinery.

Otterburn Mill – p.130.

Rothbury: Thrum Mill – Dramatic setting in deep valley of River Coquet; beautiful small mill building; no machinery apparent; one of group of restored houses; reached along public footpath south from bridge in town. NOT OPEN.

Weldon Mill, near Rothbury – Attractive mill by Weldon Bridge on A697; possible connections with Brinkburn Priory; wheel being restored. NOT OPEN.

Ford Forge: Heatherslaw Mill, near Cornhill on Tweed

The model village of Ford was created by Louisa, Marchioness of Waterford, in the last century. It forms, with nearby Etal, part of the attractive estate of Lord and Lady Joicey – one of the most interesting in England. The Joiceys were among the first to recognize the gathering renewal of interest in traditional crafts, and there are a number of craft centres, including one at Heatherslaw Mill, in the thriving community which has been built up around their home, Etal Manor.

There have been mills on the Heatherslaw site since the thirteenth century, although the present building dates largely from the 1830s. The difficulty of accurately dating old vernacular buildings which have probably been cannibalized is well demonstrated at Heatherslaw. During renovation work a beam, known to have been removed from a farm built in 1790, was studied and found to be at least a century older than the farm.

Heatherslaw Mill contains two mills under the one roof, a common arrangement at one time. Two wheels produced oat and barley meal, flour and pearl barley, but only one remains – a reconstruction of an undershot wheel 16½ feet in diameter and five feet wide. It powers the stones in the restored upstream mill – the most northerly working mill in England.

Heatherslaw has always been vulnerable to flooding – difficult to appreciate at first glance, for the mill stands well above the normal level of the River Till; indeed, access to it is across a high bridge. The narrowness of the valley, together with the amount of water flowing from the hills into the river, produces the sort of floods that caused near disaster in 1948, when 500 sacks of barley had to be hastily removed from the basement of the lower mill; a mark on one of the pillars indicates the level the flood-water reached.

This section of the mill houses a collection of troughs, covering a period from medieval times to the eighteenth century, and part of a saddle quern believed to be nearly 4,000 years old. The troughs were probably used to grind grain or bruise barley or oats, the most common crop in this area.

The low kiln in the basement of the upper mill was rescued from the now-demolished mill at Guyzance on the River Coquet and is an example of a type still in regular use in the Orkneys. There it is known as a 'pease girdle', drying peas in preparation for grinding into meal; here it dries oats for oatmeal production. On the stone floor there is a pearl-barley mill where a vertically mounted stone revolves inside a 'box' (in reality a wire-mesh cage) to remove the husk and polish the barley. The top floor runs the length of the building and contains various ancillary machines including a barley-dresser and a kibbler.

It happens that Heatherslaw Mill was the first mill I visited in the course of my 'odyssey' around the mills of Britain, and the helpful welcome I received from the Stobbs family, who manage this homely place, was typical of what I have come to expect and appreciate from everyone connected with mills.

Otterburn Mill

The Battle of Otterburn (or Chevy Chase) was fought less than a mile away from this historic mill, known to have been in existence in 1245, almost 150 years before the moonlight clash between the Douglases and the Percys ended with the death of the 2nd Earl of Douglas and the capture of Harry Hotspur by the Scots.

In this part of Redesdale all the villages had their own mills, usually grinding corn but sometimes, as at Otterburn Mill, extending the use of the mill to fulling and even washing and dyeing wool. The Waddell family have owned the mill since 1821, shortly after seventeen-year-old Charlotte Ferrier eloped from school with William Waddell of Jedburgh.

In the course of six generations there have been many developments in the operations of the mill, with spinning, weaving and finishing added to the traditional processes. Otterburn Mill continued to produce its own tweeds and woollens until a few years ago, using the fleece of local sheep which still contribute to the very rural scene as they feed in the fields surrounding the mill.

Nottinghamshire

Nottinghamshire has very little remaining in respect of watermills. With Leicestershire, it constitutes one of the poorest areas in the whole of England – and there is no evidence to suggest the position will be changed. There are some industrial sites, but they have no close connection with water-power – even Arkwright's first plant using spinning-machines was horse-powered! Buildings haven't been converted to pubs, craft centres or even houses in the way they have elsewhere.

Carlton-in-Lindrick: Old Mill Museum, Carlton Mill – Museum with mill machinery; undershot water-wheel; rural tools; country crafts.

Cuckney: Old Mill House – Old mill site; millpond; emphasis in garden on wild planting; house not open – garden sometimes under NGS.

Langwith Mill House – Stands beside old cotton-mill; small garden featuring millrace; house not open – garden sometimes under NGS.

Ollerton Mill – Still produces animal feed; low-breast wheel; overdriven stones; commercially run. NOT OPEN.

Oxfordshire

Oxfordshire had a relatively large spread of mills at Domesday, befitting a county with a series of well-established settlements. Local government re-organization in the early 1970s has left the modern county bearing little resemblance to that of the eleventh century. For example, four of the mills listed below were in Berkshire in 1086.

Like most of the wealthier counties now within reach of London, Oxfordshire has lost many of its historic buildings to private dwellings, which may be neither open nor easy to view from public land. As a result several mills which might have qualified for this gazetteer have been omitted. Attractively modernized mills such as those at East and West Hendred have been left out, while East Hannay Mill, which can at least be studied from the road, is included. As in Wiltshire (see p.173), several of the mills selected are in a relatively small area, making visits to them easy – they are also quite different architecturally.

Charney Bassett Mill – On River Ock close to Venn Mill; small, brick and timber mill with attached mill cottage on edge of village; restored and used as private dwelling. NOT OPEN.

Cothill Mill, near Abingdon – Victorian mill, brick and tile; weather-boarded lucam; ceased operating in late 1920s; wheel removed in Second World War; mill house is earlier; quite close to Venn Mill and of interest for contrast between styles of mills. NOT OPEN.

East Hagbourne Mill – Fine, large brick and white weather-boarded mill; on Domesday site south of pretty village; interesting architecturally – well maintained; once powered three pairs of stones; now a farm catering for PYO. OPEN ONLY FOR SALES.

East Hannay Mill – Large, red-brick ex-commercial mill – probably on Domesday site; one of two in village; now part used as studio. NOT OPEN.

Epwell Mill – Historic mill (connections with Bruern Abbey) no longer used; well-landscaped garden makes clever use of water taken from millpond; open occasionally under NGS and for annual floodlit Midsummer Night Wine and Cheese Party.

Garford: Venn Mill – Very traditional style mill, horizontal weather-boarding under tile roof; built around 1800 – millhouse on opposite side of A338 looks newer; ceased milling in about 1940; undershot wheel drove two pairs of stones; mill machinery mostly timber; being restored; owner Alan Stoyel has fine collection of mill photographs.

Mapledurham Mill (TCG) – below.

Standlake: Gaunt Mill – said to be thousand-year-old mill site on River Windrush, a river with many mills, almost none now open to view; island garden between the two branches of river; sometimes open under NGS.

Weston-on-the-Green: The Mill House – small garden grouped around mill and pool; mill may be one of two recorded in Domesday; open occasionally under NGS.

Mapledurham Mill

On quiet evenings there is a quality about Mapledurham Mill which transports the visitor instantly to an earlier age. It's a quality emphasized by its surprising remoteness, and that of the village of which it forms so harmonious a part. Beside the Thames, yet somehow not part of it, the village, little more than a hamlet, seems to be caught in a spell. Not quite *Brigadoon* in Oxfordshire but close enough.

A narrow lane leads past some almshouses of 1613, now converted to cottages, before revealing a classical grouping of manor-house, church and mill. It needs no adaptation to qualify as a film set, although when it was used, for the making of *The Eagle Has Landed*, the film-makers, typically, changed it beyond recognition.

Mapledurham House is Elizabethan, warm and mellow red brick. Seen from the side, it has a rambling appearance with jumbled chimneys; from the front it is more formal but equally pleasing. The Roman Catholic Blount family, local landowners since the 1490s, began the building of the present house in 1588.

In the early eighteenth century Alexander Pope was a frequent visitor, corresponding regularly with two of the Blount daughters, Martha (his heir and possibly his mistress) and Teresa; he wrote some far from deathless lines to 'Miss Blount, On Her Leaving the Town after the Coronation'. Later John Galsworthy set his fictional 'Forsyte Saga' at Mapledurham, where Soames Forsyte lived in a house called 'The Shelter' and where he is 'buried'.

Next to the house is St Margaret's Church, with memorials to members of the family, and one very rare feature: the keys to the Blount chapel are held only by the family and so part of this Protestant church is retained for the personal use of a Catholic family. I know of only one other such instance – at Arundel, where the Howard family chapel is similarly separated.

A few yards away is the mill, sitting quietly, almost meekly, behind a small millpond on which coots squabble and shadow-box. The Thames is hidden beyond trees and across a series of mini-backwaters but its presence is not missed in this setting. The mill is a combination of periods on a Domesday site, mostly eighteenth-century brick and weather-boarding, slightly battered, a little dusty in appearance but full of charm. Parts of the fifteenth-century mill can still be identified, together with later, seventeenth-century additions.

The remarkably wide external undershot wheel is used to drive two pairs of French Burr stones; there are a further two pairs for demonstration purposes. All the machinery, including the wheel, is wooden. The mill was restored in the 1970s and is now the oldest working mill on the Thames, producing wholemeal flour for sale to visitors.

To me, Mapledurham is one of the loveliest mills to be found; certainly the most beautiful on the river, and I was pleased to see that J.H.B. Peel, in his *Portrait of the Thames*, written twenty years ago, says exactly the same. Peel was afraid that the inevitable opening up to the public of places like Mapledurham would reduce their long-term prospects of conservation. In the event I believe that Mapledurham has adapted well to the changes forced upon it, and as a result its future and that of similar buildings seem more secure than hitherto.

Shropshire

Shropshire at the time of Domesday was very much in a state of flux. Much had been laid waste, and much was still uncultivated. Nonetheless, there were eighty-seven mills in Domesday.

A combination of factors accounts for the present paucity of mills in the county. First, parts of Shropshire became heavily industrialized in the eighteenth and nineteenth centuries and many local mills disappeared. Where small watermills did survive, mainly in the north and west, the universal difficulties experienced by mills in the last hundred years led to closure and loss, since most were not deemed fit for conversion. Chadwell remains, Claybury is a very exciting project nearing completion, Henley is just being restored, and the recently renovated Daniel's is a quite remarkable mill which fits no pattern.

All Stretton: Dudgeley Mill, near Church Stretton – Ground flour until 1917 and animal feed until late 1960s; sixteen-foot diameter wheel remains; now guesthouse – pit wheel feature of sitting-room; OPEN ONLY TO GUESTS.

Chadwell Mill, near Newport – below.

Cleobury Mortimer: Claybury Mill (TCG) – p.135.

Eardington: Daniel's Mill, near Bridgnorth – Four-storey, cream-washed building, more Suffolk than Shropshire; remarkable thirty-eight-foot-diameter, forty tonne combined pitch-back and breastshot suspension wheel; built 1854; recently restored and producing flour; the biggest working corn-mill in Britain, in village claiming to have had mill since Saxon times.

Henley: Henley Mill, near Ludlow – Large, brick-built mill on attractive Domesday site currently (1988) being restored.

Chadwell Mill, near Newport

Visitors to Chadwell may be greeted by some remarkably fierce farmyard geese, and by friendly ducks, chickens and cats. It is an early Victorian, three-storey red-brick mill under a tiled roof, part of a complex which includes a millhouse and three converted farm buildings now used as self-catering holiday cottages. Very much a functional vernacular building, I find Chadwell pleasing, although its owner, Mrs Partridge, thinks it not particularly attractive.

An interesting working mill, Chadwell possesses one unusual, possibly unique feature. The two-acre millpond running almost parallel to the Shropshire/Staffordshire boundary is fed by a natural spring known as St Chad's Well. Local tradition claims that the saint used the spring for baptisms as he travelled the newly established See of Lichfield in the eighth century. Today the spring has two functions, for, after providing power for the mill, it supplies drinking-water to the area.

The site has been home to a mill for many centuries; there is evidence to suggest that there was an iron forge here. The use of a stream limits the positioning of a mill building, but the use of a millpond makes it easier for water to be drawn off at different points. Perhaps for this reason the site of Chadwell Mill has varied – the present building is a little way from that of its predecessor.

As in so many instances, the mill ran into trouble at the end of the nineteenth century but it was rescued and restored between 1919 and 1922. It then continued to operate, though latterly with increasing difficulty, until the early 1950s. When the present owners took over the mill, they first repaired the water-wheel and then returned the mill to commercial operation, producing stone-ground flour for sale. The enclosed twenty-three-foot-diameter wheel is iron-rimmed; oak spokes and seventy-two oak buckets supply the drive for two pairs of French Burr stones.

Other features of considerable interest at Chadwell are the auxiliary shafting and double pulleys still visible within the mill. Power for use with agricultural machinery was transmitted over 400 yards to the neighbouring farm, Chadwell Grange, via a wire-rope drive – a fascinating demonstration of the imaginative uses to which adaptations of mill machinery can be put.

Cleobury Mortimer: Claybury Mill

Claybury stands in a lovely setting in the valley of the River Rea (one of the many unsung rivers of Britain) just south of Cleobury Mortimer. It may well be on the site of a Domesday mill, though neither Jim Bartlett, who now owns it, nor I would be prepared to swear an affidavit to that.

A corn-mill which may have been used for producing animal feed for the farm opposite, Claybury was last operated commercially in 1933. An attempt was made early in the Second World War to use the mill but the collapse of the weir frustrated the effort. However, the attempt saved the internal workings from the scrap-merchants.

Claybury, a seventeenth- or early eighteenth-century mill, was derelict when Mr Bartlett acquired it in 1981/2, and he has been engaged in repairing it for the last six years. When he recently took on the tenancy of Newnham Mill, near Tenbury Wells (p.105), he established Rea Valley Mills, and has begun producing flour in commercially viable quantities. Once Claybury is operating again, it will be used primarily as 'back-up' for Newnham.

There are three pairs of French Burr stones in the mill which were originally powered by a sixteen-foot-diameter, seven-foot-wide cast-iron and wooden breastshot wheel. The wheel was made by the local company, Turton's, in 1876 and is of historical interest, for it is believed to be the final wheel they produced before they went out of business. When the wheel, currently still in poor condition, is repaired, it will not be used to power the stones as the leat is no longer viable – the result of a local dispute over ownership of the river bed. Power will be provided by a post-war Lister compression-engine producing 16 hp – equivalent, Mr Bartlett thinks, to the wheel's output.

Rea Valley Mills were involved in the setting-up of the Traditional Cornmillers' Guild in March 1987. Like one or two other members of the Guild, Jim Bartlett came to milling from a very different background (in his case, teaching), but he has become totally absorbed in the challenge it presents. I believe that the future of the craft, and therefore of mills, lies with this new breed of determinedly 'professional' small-scale millers.

Somerset

At the time of Domesday, Somerset was a large county which already possessed a considerable agricultural acreage. Unlike the other counties in the Exon Domesday (Devon and Cornwall), it had many mills, and the majority of the sites remain, even if the mills have disappeared or their purpose has been greatly changed.

Not all the mills listed below are on Domesday sites but most are on sites of some antiquity. Although I have dealt in detail with the county, I am conscious that many more mills exist in Somerset than I have been able to indicate. It is one of the most rewarding counties for the budding industrial archaeologist to investigate.

Because of the popularity of Somerset as a holiday centre, several of the mills in the list are heavily visited, and it must be said that there is a proponderance of 'touristy' places among them. But Hornsbury, Dunster, Orchard, Wookey Hole and the 'newcomer' Cutterne Mill have all avoided the worst pitfalls; the enthusiast may be surprised at the care taken in the presentation of these mills. The Mill on the Brue is a marvellous background to a holiday for children, and the fibreglass wheel at Wootton Courtenay may be the forerunner of many more. Piles and Clapton represent the more traditional mill – I would love to see Piles producing even small quantities of flour, but it would probably disappear entirely under the weight of visitors!

Clapton Mill (TCG), near Crewkerne – Three-storey stone mill worked continuously since built in 1864; on earlier site – possibly even thirteenth-century; twenty-one-foot-diameter wheel is powered by two sources – Clapton Beck and River Axe; water from beck flows along iron conduit and turns wheel by overshot means; water from Axe converts wheel to breastshot function; same ownership for five generations.

Holford: Combe House Hotel – Twenty-six-foot iron overshot wheel, dating from 1893; performed variety of functions, primarily powering tannery pump; building used as storage shed for hotel; wheel can be inspected – explanatory note in building.
Somerton: Mill House – Enclosed twelve-foot cast-iron pitch-back wheel; restored and regularly worked, although open only by prior appointment; nineteenth-century wooden gearing.

Wookey Hole Paper-Mill, near Wells – Produces handmade paper using electrically powered equipment, originally water-powered then steam; modern overshot water-wheel; owned by Madame Tussaud's – entry charge includes caves and museum displays.

Allerford: Piles Mill (NT)

As often happens, the exact age of Piles Mill is difficult to determine, and the situation is not helped by a degree of confusion as to the meaning of the name. The word 'Pylle' or 'Pill' is said to describe a tidal creek and implies that the River Aller was once tidal or navigable to this height. Whether it was or not, I think it likely that this was Pyle's mill – the name Pyle appears in parish records during the sixteenth and seventeenth centuries.

Piles is an immensely charming mill, within feet of the often horrendously busy A39, yet well protected by a curtain of bushes and trees and, like Allerford across the road, somehow managing to retain its dignity in the presence of hordes of visitors. 'A remarkable picturesque object – rural in the highest degree' is how the Reverend John Strete saw it in 1796, and there has been little change since, although a certain amount of rebuilding took place in the last century.

The external appearance of the mill is rather functional, its woodwork painted an austere black, as is the ten-foot-diameter overshot wheel with its thirty wooden buckets. Against that impression is the setting of the mill, nestling into the side of a steep hill, its tailrace (a misnomer this – it frequently dries up) trickling under a pretty, if tiny bridge past clumps of iris. Inside the mill are some internal machinery (not original) and a small collection of agricultural implements rather grandly titled a 'museum of local interest'.

For much of its working life, which lasted until the 1930s, Piles was a corn-mill, but it then spent some years in cider-making. Appropriately, the major items on the ground floor are an apple-crusher, used on the site, and a large cider-barrel. On the first floor there are two pairs of millstones, French Burr and millstone conglomerate. A third pair of stones was transferred to Dunster Mill (p.140) a few years ago. The water-wheel was operated simply by raising a flap on the iron pentrough, and this could be done from inside the mill. The stones were driven through the iron-spur pit-wheel. Among the implements on the first floor are a sack-hoist, beam scale, wagon-jack, ploughshare and drag shoe, used in braking wagons descending a hill – vital equipment in countryside as hilly as this!

Bruton: Gants Mill (Mill on the Brue)

There is some uncertainty as to whether Gants Mill, on its present site beside the Brue, is one of the six mills recorded in Domesday for Bruton. The first records for a mill on the present site do not appear until the late thirteenth century, after Sir Hugh Lovel of Castle Cary granted land to John Le Gaunt.

Le Gaunt appears to have been a prosperous man, his wealth coming almost certainly from wool, an industry undergoing a period of considerable prosperity at the time (p.42). In around 1293 he is known to have held the lease of a fulling-mill at Coombe, to the north of Bruton, and about ten years later he gave 'a certain watermill and another fulling-mill', built on the land granted him by Lovel, to his brother Walter and his wife. The family retained possession of the lands and mills for perhaps thirty years, after which they passed through several changes of ownership and various tenancies. The major owners during the succeeding centuries were the Weston family, who acquired 'the two fulling mills called Gauntysmylles' in 1429 and held them for 200 years.

For most of this period Gants Mill remained a fulling-mill, but as the woollen industry began to concentrate in the Cotswolds and, from the early eighteenth century, Yorkshire, it seems probable that the mill was converted to use as a corn-mill at some time during the late seventeenth or eighteenth century.

In around 1800 the mill underwent a further change when a silk-throwster, Theophilus Perceval, acquired it, investing £10,000 in its conversion to a silk-mill. Gants Mill is an important mill historically because of its involvement in three major industries but the period it spent under the ownership of Perceval is of further interest for, to a degree, he appears to have reversed the general trend in the silk industry at that time. It was a period of retrenchment following years of difficulties, yet Perceval was able to employ up to 250 people in the mill which was extended to accommodate the long floors where silk was thrown. Conversely, just as the silk industry was beginning to recover following the adoption of free trade policies in the 1820s, Perceval seems to have become less successful, and in 1830 the mill was put up for sale.

After the next conversion of Gants Mill (to a flour- and grist-mill), it was leased to the Lockyer family, who operated it successfully for the best part of a century. They were faced, as earlier generations had been, with water-supply problems, particularly in summer. The problems were solved by installing first a steam-engine and later a semi-diesel. A major refit was undertaken in 1888, when much of the present internal machinery was installed together with a twenty-inch British Empire turbine supplied by Armfields of Ringwood.

The mill still operates, producing animal feed and, occasionally, wholewheat flour. As a working mill, it is not opened regularly to the public, although the Shingler family, who bought it from the Lockyers in 1949, are prepared to show it to interested visitors. But Gants Mill has already entered into another phase in its remarkably varied history, for Brian Shingler, his wife and two friends now use the fields and woods of the eighty-acre site as an activity holiday centre for children between the ages of eight and fourteen. There are several mills in this book with claims to being unique – this is definitely one of them!

Chard: Hornsbury Mill

At first glance Hornsbury appears to be the sort of mill from which the enthusiast will run screaming. It has everything for the casual visitor – a museum, craft shop, restaurant, function suite, bar, *en suite* accommodation and goodness knows what else. Its own literature calls it 'the cream tea centre of the West'. The beautifully manicured gardens with the River Isle rippling through them will probably be overflowing with visitors, young and old. It is undeniably commercial, but the present owners have ensured that the mill student is well looked after, providing an informative leaflet.

Hornsbury Mill was first recorded in 1327, and the present flintstone mill is of early nineteenth-century construction – accurate dating is hindered by the degree of modernization that has taken place over the years. Between 1902 and 1942 the mill worked commercially in the hands of George Chaffey, but it fell victim to changing fashion hastened by the war. It then lay idle for twenty-five years before being restored and tea-rooms and a craft shop introduced. As a further attraction, the collection of bygones amassed by Mr Austin Wookey was added at this time. The present owners bought the mill in 1984.

The overshot wheel by Bodley Bros of Exeter was installed by a local millwright in 1870. It's an eighteen-foot-diameter, six-foot-wide wheel, carrying forty-eight elmwood buckets, supplied by water from a leat which leaves the Isle at the top of the south bank. Each bucket holds up to twenty gallons of water. Beside the glass inspection panel there is a miller's privy – an early example of *en suite* plumbing. The auxiliary machinery, including the control wheels, is contained behind glass in the restaurant lounge. There are three pairs of millstones near the crown wheel on the first floor, with one pair opened up to show the 'harps'.

Beyond the mill is the Yesteryear Museum. This rather cosy title encompasses the wide range of nineteenth- and twentieth-century artefacts acquired by Mr Wookey. Again, I think the mill's own literature provides a neat summary when it says: 'The collection is ... too varied to even summarise easily.' Certainly there's no discernible 'rhyme or reason' to it, but the museum contains many fascinating pieces and is worth visiting for the pleasure of recognizing some forgotten item of domestic life – a reminder of how rapid has been the pace of change in recent years.

Dunster Mill (NT)

At the time of the Domesday survey, William de Mohun had large holdings in Devon, Dorset, Somerset and Wiltshire, including Dunster, where he later founded a priory. One of de Mohun's two mills in 'Torre' was almost certainly on the present site. Dunster Mill seemed to face few problems apart from the age-old squabbles between miller and farmer as it continued its largely profitable task of grinding corn for the manor over the succeeding centuries. Milling generally proved profitable in the West Country, the growth of the woollen trade in the sixteenth and seventeenth centuries leading to the building of fulling-mills.

Dunster enjoyed a major refit between 1779 and 1782 after the aptly named Mr Mills of Bristol leased it from the Luttrell Estate at a very reasonable rent of £50 a year. Mr Luttrell seems to have been concerned that his view should not be affected by the alterations and that he should not have to pay for the repairs – very practical and sensible considerations. Detailed accounts of the work survive, and some are reproduced in the excellent leaflet on sale at the mill. It's possible that the expense broke Mills, for he left at the end of 1782, just as the repairs were completed. An alternative explanation is that the work took so long that he simply lost heart in the venture. Whatever the reason, Mills left behind a fine, well-fitted corn-mill which prospered for much of the following century.

Inevitably trade declined as competition mounted from the roller-mills at ports where imported grain produced cheaper, if poorer-quality, flour. By the 1930s the mill was producing animal feed, and it reverted briefly to corn grinding only during the Second World War; its two wheels were restored and a bakery was added to supply the castle and village. After the war the mill returned to grist-milling finally closing in 1962. The Luttrell Estate was given to the National Trust in 1976, and in 1978 the mill, by now in very poor condition, was leased to Mr and Mrs Arthur Capps.

The Capps have specialized in the repair of old buildings and were fortunate to have another specialist, Reg Sutton, last miller of Williton (p.142), to advise on the repair of the machinery and dressing the stones. From the outset, the aim was to restore Dunster to its Victorian form, and this the family set about accomplishing early in 1979. Remarkably, the first phase of the work was completed within a year, and the mill was even able to grind a little flour. Improvements have been made throughout the 1980s, and the standard of the mill and its machinery is now higher than at any time since the 1782 refitting.

The mill has some distinctive features, chief among them the twin twelve-foot overshot water-wheels of wood and iron which can be worked separately or in tandem. An observation platform has been built over the wheels and mill-leat, itself almost a mile long and drawing its water from the River Avill. Three pairs of French Burr stones, one from Piles Mill (p.137), are turned by conventional gearing.

Dunster Mill is a remarkable, even heady mixture of old and new. An old craft, revived using a combination of traditional methods and modern practice (including the sensible application of grants), is housed in a building of wonderfully mixed ancestry, the whole overlaid with the dust of flour-production. Sadly, Mr Capps was in poor health in the 1980s and, for a time, the future of the mill was somewhat clouded. The position was resolved in late 1987 when the young and enthusiastic Paul Marriott, previously in computers, acquired the lease. History and continuity count for much in milling – Mr Marriott has acknowledged this by retaining the plaque commemorating the achievements of his predecessors.

Evercreech: Cutterne Mill

When travelling in Britain, I take great satisfaction in observing how often patterns are repeated – a reminder that much of what we call change is simply cyclical. A good example occurred in August 1987 when eighty-six-year-old Charlie Joyce restarted the large water-wheel at Cutterne Mill – fifty-five years after he had stopped it and closed the mill for what must have seemed certain to be the last time.

Cutterne is a good, solid mill beside the River Alham, built without frills in 1628 to serve a small rural community. For the last part of its working life it was a grist-mill. It is probably on the site of one which existed at Domesday, paying rent of just 7s. 6d. to the bishop of Wells or one of his three under-tenants. As the owner, Mike Ralph, points out on one of his sensible, clearly labelled descriptive panels, the expense of digging the millrace and tail meant that mills were invariably rebuilt on the same site. I suspect he writes with feeling, having personally restored the race to its present fast-flowing condition.

The entrance to the mill leads into the stone floor with its two pairs of stones. The high breastshot water-wheel was installed by Maggs & Hindley of Bourton in 1862 – only the buckets have had to be replaced. The other wheels are also of metal, the gearing and auxiliary machinery of standard design.

Cutterne Mill has been restored, with the aid of grants from the Mendip District Council, by Mr and Mrs Ralph, who have already established a small craft shop and folk museum with displays on corn-milling. The upper floor is occupied by bats and is out of bounds to visitors but there are seven acres of natural meadows around the mill where visitors are invited to stroll and to picnic.

Williton: Orchard Mill

Orchard Mill was built in 1616 by Sir John Wyndham, whose family was one of the largest landowners in the area at that time. The history of the mill follows a classic pattern. With a virtual monopoly, it was at first successful, but its fortunes fluctuated over the centuries, with a definite downturn in the late 1800s during which time (almost certainly due to the effect of roller-milling, as we've seen in many other instances) it probably ceased work entirely for a short period. Milling continued during this century, but less and less corn-grinding was taking place at this type of mill, and Orchard Mill was reduced to grinding alabaster at one time in the 1930s. Like Dunster (p.140), the mill revived in the Second World War but, unlike its neighbour, Orchard did grind some corn in addition to the inevitable animal feed after the war.

By this time Reg Sutton was the tenant. An accepted expert in his craft, he was later, at the age of eighty, to be closely involved in the repair of Dunster Mill. Partly due to his ill health, Orchard Mill slowly did less work, and it was effectively no longer working by the time of its 350th anniversary in 1966. The Suttons left the mill in 1977, and it was reopened as a museum in 1979 by Michael and Alison Rawlings. The next tenants also carried out restorations, and more major work has been completed by the present tenants, Robert and Wendy Millar.

The mill is becoming established both as a museum of agricultural implements and Victoriana, and as a craft centre. The Millars are also offering meals at the millhouse. The overshot wheel is once again turning, and perhaps one day corn will again be ground here. The Millars have a young family and have taken care to produce a very good questionnaire about the mill, aimed at children. The little guidebook written by Robert Millar is excellent, and I make no bones about acknowledging my debt to it.

Orchard Mill stands on the edge of Williton, in flat meadowland by a marshy stream, the Swilly. The millhouse retains its seventeenth-century elegance, although there have been additions to it, while the inside of the mill is satisfyingly dusty. The museum exhibits are set out on all three floors of the mill. A problem with many of the 'museums' springing up around the country is that they look like, and are, indiscriminate collections of unrelated items which *might* interest the 'punters'. At Orchard Mill all the items in the museum are what they claim to be, and very interesting some are as a reminder of the recent past – and of how far domestic and agricultural machinery has progressed in the last hundred years or so.

The large external overshot water wheel (eighteen feet in diameter, four feet wide with fifty buckets) is a reconstruction of the wheel installed in 1871. Not all the internal machinery is original but only a purist could possibly complain about that; for the rest of us it is well displayed, and Robert Millar is justifiably proud of its smooth running.

Wootton Courtenay: Mill Pottery

The Mill Pottery is included not just for Michael Gaitskell's imaginative use of an old mill for his work or even for the use of a wheel to provide power and generate electricity (the ceramic-mill is water-powered) but primarily because the rust-coloured overshot wheel is made of fibreglass and possibly unique – Haxted Mill (p.157) has fibreglass buckets but not a wheel.

Mr Gaitskell, who was a university lecturer until deciding to concentrate on his passion for pottery, found that the old wheel was beyond repair and approached the naval dockyard at Plymouth for help. He was allowed to spend some time rummaging in the dockyard's scrapyard, finding several useful items, including a gearbox for which he paid the 'exorbitant' sum of £50. He also obtained advice from the Navy on the making and installation of the new wheel.

The site is old: 'Otone' was held by William de Falaise in 1086, and it already possessed a mill. The present mill and associated buildings form an agreeably unspoilt complex on the edge of a village which has suffered from some less than agreeable new building in recent years. Milling in this lovely, narrow valley cannot always have been easy if recent experience is anything to go by, for in the wet summer of 1987 lack of water was an unexpected problem; over the hill on the north-facing slopes there was a surfeit. Perhaps partly for this reason, milling stopped here in 1860, some thirty years before the general decline of small mills.

Staffordshire

The Domesday survey of Staffordshire has fewer entries than all but two of the surveyed counties, and they – Middlesex and Rutland – were considerably smaller. The reason undoubtedly lay in the 'wasting' of Staffordshire by King William's army following the uprising of Mercia in 1069.

Not surprisingly, in view of its industrial connections, Staffordshire has many more industrial mill sites than agricultural, a fact not exactly reflected in the short list below. A great number of mills remain in the towns, by rivers and canals. Though many were not necessarily water-powered and have been abandoned in recent years, they provide a fascinating insight into the industrial history of this part of the West Midlands. Visitors to Leek, for example, have a veritable plethora of mills to seek out when they have exhausted Brindley's Mill.

Cheddleton Flint-Grinding Mills, near Leek – p.145.

Great Bridgeford: Worston Mill – Large red-brick complex, built about 1814, now a pub; undershot wheel and other ancillary machinery; mixture of styles (including American) in not entirely successful internal conversion.

Leek: Brindley Mill – p.146.

Shugborough Park Farm, near Stafford – A working corn-mill forms part of a range of red brick farm buildings built in 1805.

Stone: The Mill – p.147.

Tutbury: The Old Mill – p.147.

Cheddleton Flint-Grinding Mills, near Leek

The two working watermills in Staffordshire are very different in character. Brindley is firmly enmeshed in an urban environment, while Cheddleton, only a mile or two to the south, lies a little off the road and gives the impression of being part of a rural community.

At the time of writing, Cheddleton appears to be short of funds and a little run-down but it has a definite charm – even when visited while closed. The approach is off the main A520 south of Leek along a rough and narrow but, happily, very short section of the Caldon Canal towpath.

The Cheddleton site is believed to date from the thirteenth century and contains two mills: North, built in the mid eighteenth century to grind flint for use in the pottery industry, and South, which was strengthened and converted from corn-milling as the pottery industry expanded in the latter years of the century. Water from the River Churnet supplies the twin water-wheels, one twenty-two feet in diameter, the other 20½ feet, which are separated by only a few feet of water. The level of the Churnet was lowered in 1980, and water now flows under the wheels, converting them to undershot from the original low breastshot. Neither is currently in good shape.

Cheddleton officially opens only on Saturday and Sunday afternoons, but the Cheddleton Flint-Mill Preservation Trust, which owns and runs the site, has sensibly provided clear information plaques on the walls of all the buildings. Each plate is numbered and contains a diagram and arrow pointing to the next, providing a self-guided tour of the site. It's a simple idea and could easily be adopted in a variety of situations.

The process of grinding flint or stone is described on the plaque on the North Mill. Hoisted to the first floor, flint was tipped into a grinding-pan for milling to a fine powder. Grinding was achieved by the action of a chert runner stone passing over a harder bedstone positioned under water. The result was a creamy paste known as slop. This was allowed to settle, the water was drawn off and the remaining substance, slip, was kiln-dried and formed into blocks. It was then shipped to the potteries, where the ground flint was used to improve the texture of earthenware. Demonstrations relating to the pottery industry are occasionally held in the South Mill.

Cheddleton has on display a slip-drying-kiln, an edge-runner mill, a centre-feed mill and an important Robey horizontal engine fitted with patented drop-valve gear and used by Minton of Stoke-on-Trent to power their mill from 1928 until the late sixties. Moored on the canal side is a horse-drawn narrow-boat, the *Vienna*. The tight-knit little complex is completed by a small, attractive mill cottage and a few ruined outbuildings.

Leek: Brindley Mill

On the north-west side of Leek, beside the A523, Brindley Mill nestles between the tall buildings of a textile company. When first viewed from the bridge over the River Churnet beside the factory entrance, this small mill is made to appear even smaller by its setting.

The present mill is built in a rather uninteresting local brick, enlivened by some decorative windows. It has been working since the mid-eighteenth century, with a break between 1940, when it was abandoned, and its reopening by the Brindley Mill Preservation Trust in 1974. In addition to the mill workings, the building houses the Brindley Museum, illustrating both the history of milling and the life and work of the civil engineer James Brindley, who started life as a millwright but is best known as 'the father of English canals'.

The mill has long been popularly linked with Brindley, and the evidence, though circumstantial, is convincing. The arches and keystones of the windows and doors are of a design associated with Brindley, and the building bears, on the first floor, the inscription 'TI 1752 JB', suggesting a possible connection between him and a local landowner, Thomas Jolliffe.

The Brindley Mill received an award from the Royal Institute of Chartered Surveyors in 1978, and it is not difficult to see why. Inside, superbly restored, well-lit and maintained machinery greets the visitor and, more important, there is a pleasant welcome from the volunteer stewards. The mill is fully operational, with frequent short demonstrations of the working machinery.

Visitors are invited to start a tour of the mill by watching the sixteen-foot-diameter water-wheel with its forty elm boards turning slowly in the flow from the Churnet. Inside the building, on the ground or meal floor, is the sluice gear which raises a gate to allow the flow of water under the wheel. The mill has three sets of tentering gear to adjust the gaps between the grindstones on the floor above. The great spur-wheel at Brindley is overdriven – that is to say, it is positioned above the millstones which here are made of pieces of French Burr stone bound together by metal bands. The stones are four feet in diameter and both weigh about twelve hundredweight. The hopper, used during demonstrations of corn-grinding on this floor, is a replacement and only a quarter of the size of the original.

The second or garner floor contains the museum exhibits, among them a surveyor's level and a notebook which belonged to Brindley. In the centre of the room is a tableau showing a miller bending over sacks ready for tipping into the hoppers. Clearly illustrated panels around the walls have excellent notes on a variety of associated themes including the millwright's and sawyer's trades and, hardly surprisingly, several more on Brindley himself.

Stone: The Mill

The mill at Stone doesn't appear in the Domesday survey of Staffordshire, although milling took place here for at least 400 years until the 1960s; corn was ground for the monks of the priory until the Dissolution. The late-eighteenth-century mill, now an hotel, is reached along the narrow and industrialized Mill Lane and is a pleasant and civilized oasis at the end of the lane.

The mill-leat is carried through a small rock garden into the building at first-floor level and originally turned a twenty-five-foot overshot wheel. In 1890 this was replaced by a turbine operating three pairs of stones. Inside the mill, water falls into the original wheel-pit, while upstairs in the restaurant the thirteen-foot spur-wheel and a large hopper are central attractions – the 'wheel' of Stilton also looked pretty good on my visit.

If the mill is of interest both for its history and for its conversion, the millhouse is almost more important. It was the birthplace of Richard 'Stoney' Smith who was to develop Smith's Patent Germ Flour. This uninspiring name was replaced by the much pithier and more saleable 'Hovis' on the suggestion of an Oxford schoolmaster, Herbert Grimes, who brilliantly adapted the Latin tag '*hominis vis*' – 'the strength of man'.

Tutbury: The Old Mill

Driving south on the A50 into Tutbury, there is a picnic area donated by British Gypsum in 1985, with a symbolic millstone, a rather sad thing, half buried in the ground. The five-storey Tutbury Mill stood here until demolished in 1972. Built for cotton-spinning shortly before orders for cotton began to fall off in the 1880s, it was leased by Staton's (now part of British Gypsum) in 1890 and converted to the production of plaster. The ceiling of the Tower Ballroom in Blackpool is just one example of plaster supplied by Tutbury Mill.

Just outside the town is the Old Mill (there is now some dispute over the right to the title), a corn-mill claimed to have been on the site since pre-Domesday times, although the present three-storeyed mill is of eighteenth-century construction. It ceased work as a corn-mill in 1914, when the Chapman family of Nottingham adapted it for use as a tannery, which survived, though latterly in different ownership, until 1986.

The sheepskin shop and tea-room run by the Chapmans remain, and there are two enclosed low-breast undershot wheels, twelve feet in diameter, under which water still passes, though they no longer turn and are currently rather dilapidated. One of the wheels, which is illuminated, can be viewed from a little window in the tea-room, where good tea and cakes are served.

Suffolk

No county as rich in waterways as Suffolk could fail to possess a great number of mills, many of them in situations of considerable beauty. Equally, as with all the other counties now considered to be within 'easy reach' of London, these mills have attracted the attention of wealthy buyers. Many, perhaps the majority, have been turned into expensively renovated homes where *hoi polloi* are definitely not welcome.

These mills are now sheltered behind new, well-manicured high hedges, no longer visible and certainly not working. We have cause to be grateful for those, such as the Allens at Letheringham and the Thorolds at Glemham, who are anxious to share their pleasure in these historic places. Nor must we forget the groups who, by dedication and determination, have rescued such important mills as Pakenham and Woodbridge. Flatford is at least preserved, and Alton is an adornment to 'its' museum. Sudbury may no longer be a working mill but this fine building in its lovely edge of town setting has been very sensibly adapted – perhaps as well as any.

Baylham Mill, near Needham Market

I do not see my function in this book as being to indulge in too much special pleading (although it might be said the whole book is a special plea), but in the case of Baylham Mill I shall make an exception.

A mill of outstanding architectural and historic merit, Baylham was still in good condition when photographed by Leslie Syson for *The Watermills of Britain* (published in 1980). A beautifully proportioned, three-storey weather-boarded mill with a distinctive two-storey lucam, it represents the best in mill design. Sadly, the exterior is now looking very seedy, and there is a run-down feeling to the whole complex.

There were two mills at Baylham in 1086, and close to the present mill there is a sixteenth-century moated farmhouse. This is an area full of interest and history on a river, the Gipping, which for centuries was one of the great providers of power for mills. What a pity it would be if this mill, perhaps its finest adornment, were allowed to fall further into decay.

East Bergholt: Flatford Mill (NT)

It is regrettable that the mill at Flatford continues to be leased by the National Trust to the Field Studies Council and is not open to the general public. This is in no way a criticism of the Council, an admirable body which provides so many with both education and pleasure. Nor is my regret logical, for the mill contains no machinery and is therefore of limited value to the mill buff. Furthermore, the Trust leases many other properties, though none, I think, of greater importance in an historical sense.

Flatford Mill is inextricably linked with the name of John Constable, and it is ingenuous of 'experts' to point out that he neither was born there nor worked there for more than but a fraction of his life. His magnificent talent was developed in and around '... all that lies on the banks of the Stour. Those scenes made me a painter ...' – surely it would be fitting if, one day, a major exhibition of his works could be mounted permanently at Flatford Mill.

Golding Constable, John's father, inherited the lease of the mill in 1765 but moved to a larger house he had built in East Bergholt two years before John was born in 1776. Golding originally intended his son to become a clergyman but was disappointed in this and in his second choice for the boy, milling. The younger Constable had early indicated his preference for painting and, although opposed by his father, he persevered, encouraged by his mother. After his brother Abram had taken on the running of the business in 1799, John was allowed to live and train in London, although throughout his life he continued to return for inspiration to his beloved Stour valley.

The most accessible and popular view of the mill buildings nowadays is from the path across the millpool. It presents a pleasing picture of jumbled styles, with the millhouse predominating. From this angle the mill itself is hardly visible, squeezed between the house and the granary. Built in about 1733, its two – and later four – pairs of millstones were originally operated by two small wheels within the mill. Later an undershot water-wheel fourteen feet wide and twelve feet in diameter was installed in a larger version of the brick building still visible immediately over the millrace.

From the front the mill is seen as an elegant building on two floors, with the miller's house adjoining it. This was a timber-framed building when put up in the early seventeenth century, but it, with two adjoining cottages, was later given a brick façade. Both *The Mill Stream* and *The Haywain* which include Willie Lott's cottage, were painted from a standpoint beside the mill. By contrast, *Flatford Mill* was painted beside the footbridge on the west bank of the river, just past the timber-framed Bridge Cottage in which the National Trust now has a small exhibition on the artist – which brings me back to my starting-point.

Letheringham Mill, near Easton

At the time Little Domesday was compiled, the mill at Letheringham belonged to Geoffrey de Mandeville (Magnaville) and formed part of the manor of Letheringham, itself one of three divisions within the parish. The estate survived for over 800 years and was not finally broken up until the Duke of Hamilton sold it in 1921.

For many years Letheringham was a useful place to have tea, after a visit to nearby Easton Farm Park. With the death of its previous owner, there seemed a possibility that public access would be lost – a great pity, for Letheringham looks just as most of us expect mills to look. A charming mixture of pink paint and weather-boarding under a roof at least part peg-tiled, the mill stands in a beautiful garden bordered by the Deben at its most seductively attractive. There is a woodland walk beside the river which, like the garden, is best experienced in the spring but is never less than delightful. The mill is early eighteenth-century, while the millhouse (not open) is, in part, Tudor.

Happily the new owners, Rod and Hilary Allen, intend to reopen the mill for teas sometime in 1988. When Letheringham Mill closed, the bulk of the auxiliary machinery was taken across the county to Kelsale Windmill, but the Allens hope eventually to show the fourteen-foot undershot wheel which once operated two pairs of stones. The wheel is not, at present, in good nick; indeed, its condition is remarkably similar to that at Little Glemham (below) – not entirely surprising as they are both a mixture of metal and elm, and both ceased working in the 1920s. However, with an enthusiast like Dennis Thorold already tackling the problem at Glemham, just a few miles away, (see below) the Allens won't lack for help and encouragement!

Little Glemham Mill, near Wickham Market

Little Glemham Mill is reached by a narrow track from the by-road between Little Glemham and Blaxhall. Originally Beaverham (Beversham) Mill, it is said to be on a Domesday site, although the present mill is early nineteenth-century. It is a small weather-boarded building under a simple mansard roof of corrugated iron. The material may not be attractive (it adds little to the beauty of the adjoining millhouse) but it almost certainly saved the machinery inside the mill from destruction (cf. Woodbridge, p.154). The millhouse is in a pleasantly weathered brick with a pegged tile roof; I assume that the mill's mansard was also once tiled. Much of the house is late Tudor but there have been other, well-integrated, additions.

Little Glemham last milled flour in the early 1890s and ceased work entirely in 1923, when the production of animal feed became uneconomic. In 1887, in an attempt to increase its efficiency, it was converted to use both steam- and water-power, and by the end of its life it was working with a Blackstone oil-engine.

After it was abandoned, the mill fell into gradual decline. The present tenant, Dennis Thorold, discovered it almost by chance and, after pressing for a preservation order on it, talked himself into moving in and setting about the task of restoration! He both makes and restores clocks, models and automata, with work on display in (among others) the Science Museum in London and the Smithsonian Institute in Washington. For good measure he restores furniture and carries out work for such organizations as the Historic Churches Trust. The repair of Little Glemham Mill should present him with few difficulties.

The internal water-wheel is undershot, wooden with iron shaft and paddles. There are three pairs of stones. The wheel is remarkably similar in design, size and even condition to the wheel in Letheringham Mill (p.150) but here repair work has already begun. When repairs are complete, Little Glemham will be both an excellent example of what small country corn-mills looked like for centuries, and an adornment to the chain of well-preserved mills in this part of Suffolk.

Pakenham Watermill

'Pachenham' had two mills and eight beehives in 1086, according to Little Domesday. Both the mills were watermills, and one stood on this site. Today the parish of Pakenham is unique in Britain in that it has two working mills, one of which is a windmill. It is about to lose its claim to exclusivity, for Llynon Windmill on Anglesey should be grinding by the time this book is published, and that gem among watermills, Howell Mill (p.196), is in the same parish and has been working since 1352 – almost as long as Pakenham. So Pakenham will, in future, be 'unique in England' but no less worthy of a visit for that.

Pakenham is one of those mills, by no means unusual in Suffolk, which continued to work long after similar mills had ceased to function elsewhere in the country. It finally closed in 1974, ending a period of unbroken corn-grinding extending over 900 years. As is often the case, the structure of the mill then deteriorated rapidly, and when the Suffolk Preservation Society purchased it, it was suffering from dry rot and the attentions of the deathwatch beetle. The mill was restored by the Society between 1978 and 1981, much of the work carried out by 'volunteer apprentices and young people from Eastern Electricity' and gaining for the Society a Europa Nostra Diploma in 1985.

Following restoration, three millers now use the mill for grinding flour which is sold commercially. Three pairs of stones are powered by an overshot metal wheel built and installed by Peck of Bury St Edmunds in about 1900 and supplemented by a turbine engine. On the stone floor the Society maintains a good range of machinery accompanied by well-written notes.

The mill is a particularly fine three-storeyed eighteenth-century pantiled building of considerable architectural merit. Added interest is given by the result of recent excavations which have revealed that it is based on the foundations of a Tudor building. This may help to explain some of the structural problems – the newer south end is some nine inches lower than the rest.

Stowmarket: Alton Mill, Museum of East Anglian Life

I have deliberately restricted the number of mills transferred to museums to a minimum in this book, preferring those on original sites. But it is necessary to include some examples to complete the pattern of uses to which mills are being put, and Alton has an interesting history, retaining all its old machinery. In addition, its outbuildings include a two-seater privy, believed to be unique because of its individual culvert.

The mill stands on a site, the Museum of East Anglian Life, which complements it well. The museum is a fascinating blend of the charmingly amateurish (in which I include some of its exhibitions of aspects of domestic life) and the utterly professional, typified by the Boby building with its outstanding examples of industrial machinery, all clearly labelled and explained.

The mill belonged to Alton Hall in the Tattingstone area, and it, or its predecessors, is believed to date back to at least the 1060s. It stopped milling only in the 1960s and could easily have faded into the sort of oblivion that has been the fate of vast numbers of mills in the past century. A proposal to create a reservoir in the Tattingstone valley appeared at first to represent a death sentence for the mill. However, at a public enquiry the Suffolk Preservation Society suggested that the mill should be moved to Abbot's Hall, Stowmarket (now the Museum of East Anglian Life).

A series of grants allied to a generous public response enabled the project to be completed between 1973 and 1975. As so often, this bare statement conceals a great number of difficulties. The positioning of the mill was a major problem. Since overshot wheels require water to be fed from a pool on a higher level, the only feasible area at Abbot's Hall was in the far corner of the museum site. The walk is not long, no more than 400 yards, but a virtue has been made from a necessity, and horse-drawn transport is often available for afternoon visitors – those of us who go in the mornings are presumably hardier!

Removal and reassembly were not difficult in the case of the mill and the cart-lodge; their basically timber-framed construction lent itself to the process of numbering each timber in relation to a master plan. The millhouse was dismantled and reassembled brick by brick, an arduous but rewarding task which led to a series of fascinating discoveries about the age and 'make-up' of the house. Briefly (for the booklet *The Alton Watermill* available on the site contains full details), parts of the millhouse are almost certainly older than first supposed, and the mill and outbuildings probably so; I suspect that this is often true of vernacular buildings.

The recent history of the mill, and of its owners and tenants, is remarkably well documented, largely because one family, the Southgates, owned it from 1879 until its removal to Stowmarket. Again, the booklet has a great deal of detail, much of it based on interviews with surviving members of the Southgate family and their tenants.

Sudbury: Mill Hotel

As is its custom, the Little Domesday Book, covering Essex and Norfolk in addition to Suffolk, records details of livestock not given in the main volumes of Domesday. The census shows two horses, twenty-four pigs and 120 sheep in Sudbury – which is more detail than it affords the mill. Faced with no evidence other than tradition, we can only assume that the mill site has not changed over the centuries. The present mill is a remarkably large and handsome beast, very well renovated in the 1970s, when it was turned into a hotel.

A century or so after Domesday, records began to be better kept, and in 1260 Richard de Clare gave the meadows around the mill to the town. His granddaughter confirmed the grant some seventy years later, retaining the right to dig earth in the meadows for the repair of the millpool. In 1608 William Gladwyn, the miller, was held responsible for the repair of the causeway leading from Sudbury to Brundon in Essex. A deed of title to the mill, dated 1640, is among several displayed in the foyer of the hotel.

The mill stands beside the Stour, on the edge of the town, with attractive views from its public rooms over the millpool and meadows. The sixteen-foot cast-iron undershot wheel, used to power four pairs of millstones and other machinery, was among the items restored during the renovations. The work was carried out, using traditional techniques wherever possible, during the 200th anniversary year of the founding of the makers, the famous local (Wickham Market) firm of Whatmore & Binyon. Their name and the date of its manufacture, 1889, are still visible on the spokes of the wheel behind its plate-glass cage situated in the main bar.

Woodbridge Tidemill

Perhaps because I take great joy in estuaries – their solitude, wild life, even their configuration, I approach tidemills with a special excitement. Eling (p.101), Carew (p.189) and Woodbridge have a particular fascination for me, and I remember feeling cheated when I failed to find the remains of St Issay in Cornwall.

Part of the romance of Woodbridge lies in its 'nick-of-time' rescue and renovation. Some think the result of the restoration is a museum, lacking atmosphere but, though it *is* a museum, it is a model of its kind, and surely there is a place for the educational mill. As it happens, I have heard a similar complaint levelled at the restoration of Eling, and on the evidence available I doubt that the purists will be any happier with Carew, when it is finished.

The bulk of the ground-floor machinery at Woodbridge is enclosed and none too visible, but the short guide incorporates sensible black-and-white photographs which identify all the main features throughout the mill. Not much of the oak water-wheel can be seen, which is a pity, for it has impressive statistics – it is eighteen feet in diameter with fifty-six elm floats. Equally impressive is the axle, eighteen inches in diameter and weighing 1½ tons. The wheel and axle were installed in 1976.

It was the breaking of the old axle shaft in 1957 which spelled both an end and a beginning in the history of Woodbridge Mill. It was clear that after 800 years the mill would never again work commercially. Perversely, the 'rotten hulk on the Deben' now began to attract what might be termed inspired amateur attention. Nonetheless it was a further eleven years before a gesture of great generosity supplied the essential spur to translating good will into positive action. In 1968 Mrs R.T. Gardner bought the mill and presented it to the Woodbridge Tide Mill Trust. The Trust, with additional support after 1972 from the Friends of Woodbridge Tide Mill, began the task of raising £50,000 (a staggering increase on the first estimates, in 1950, of £400) for the repair of the mill.

The foundations needed immediate attention, and the mill now stands on new 'feet'. The corrugated iron sheeting which had disfigured but also protected (cf. Little Glemham p.150) the mill for fifty years was replaced by weather-boarding. Structural repairs continued, but it was not until 1977 that Mrs Gardner was able ceremoniously to hand over the key of the mill. Five years later a new millpond was completed – the bulk of the old one had been converted to a marina basin – and the tide was once more used to drive the machinery, if only for demonstration purposes.

The stone floor of the mill houses an exhibition tracing the work of restoration. There are well-preserved examples of auxiliary machinery on both this and the second floor. The upper beams in the roof are supported by six very fine oak 'knee joints' – five are original and there are three more in the mansard roof (not open). The views of the river from the second-floor windows are always good and in certain lights breathtaking.

One of the charms of Woodbridge is its visibility. It can be studied from the official path beside the boat-building yards, from the marina or from the opposite bank at either Sutton Hoo or Kyson Hill. From all these vantage-points the old mill still draws the eye, effortlessly dominating the riverside frontage of Woodbridge.

Surrey

At Domesday Surrey was hardly the developed county it is now – indeed, compared with Kent and Sussex it was a very uncivilized place. Not surprisingly, it had many fewer mills than either of its neighbours.

In later centuries watermills flourished, particularly along certain rivers. Given their relatively short lengths, the Tillingbourne and the Wandle are prime examples of exceptionally hard-working rivers. The Tillingbourne possessed eight mills manufacturing a variety of products in its ten-mile length. The Wandle has an even more fascinating industrial history, for there were already thirteen mills on it at Domesday, and by the middle of the seventeenth century there were claimed to be thirty-eight mills operating along its mere nine miles. Even during the 1920s more than half a dozen survived.

In the following list I have included two very different Tillingbourne mills and the historically important Snuff-Mill on the Wandle at Morden Hall Park. The Snuff and Liberty's Mills are also the nearest surviving mills to my home on this remarkable river, an almost unique blend of bustling industry and rural backwaters. The three closely grouped Dorking mills all have great appeal, and they give hope that these old town mills need not be lost to future generations – even if access to them happens to be facilitated by the presence of public footpaths.

Cobham Mill – At present showing signs of being restored after a long period of decline; formerly two buildings with undershot wheels between them, joined by covered footbridge; one small brick and tile building remains between River Mole and A245; cast-iron wheel lying in waterlogged pit; some other machinery remains in mill; sluices still operative; charming place – let us hope optimism is not misdirected.

Dorking: Castle Mill – Early nineteenth-century, four-storey wood and brick building on River Mole; slated mansard roof; some recent restoration work is not in character; remains of breastshot iron wheel containing mixture of iron and wooden paddles; once drove three pairs of stones; lies behind and below Watermill pub on A25 east of town; reached by a public footpath. NOT OPEN.

Dorking: Pippbrook Mill – Much-restored (in 1980s) long, pleasing, brick building; slate roof; wheelpit – axle but no machinery visible; said to be part seventeenth-century; fine eight-pointed tie-irons incorporated as decoration on wall; Pippbrook stream, though short, once supplied power to six mills; footpath crossing stream and linking roads passes front; used by several small businesses including advertising agency. NOT OPEN.

Dorking: Pixham Mill – Tall and elegant three-storey white-painted brick-built mill; weather-boarded gable, also white-painted; said to be early nineteenth-century – has similarities to nearby Castle Mill; well restored and beautiful mill cottage next door is older; very satisfying grouping; public footpath along side of drive and around mill beside river. NOT OPEN.

Elstead Mill – Elegant five-storey eighteenth-century brick-built building, on River Wey; steeply raked mansard roof with cupola; in design and construction one of finest surviving brick-built mills; maintained in superb condition; has had variety of uses, including fulling, paper-making and malting; very pleasant, well-kept grounds; part restaurant, part private house; internal wheel visible behind glass on ground floor of restaurant. HOUSE NOT OPEN.

Gomshall Mill and Gallery, near Guildford – Once one of many corn-mills along the beautiful and historically important River Tillingbourne; ceased operating in 1950s; well restored, with original water-wheel and some internal machinery; contains restaurant, picture gallery, craft shop and antique showroom; beside busy

A25 and very popular.

Guildford: Town Mill, Millbrook – said to be site of fulling-mill in Tudor times; eighteenth-century three-storey red-brick building with very noticeable late nineteenth-century extension; hipped tiled roof and tile-hung gable ends; now workshops and storage for Yvonne Arnaud Theatre.

Haxted Mill Museum, near Edenbridge – below.

Hurst Green: Coltsford Mill – Eighteenth-century brick and weather-boarded mill, now restaurant; steep slated mansard roof; iron overshot wheel, sixteen feet in diameter, four feet wide; once drove four pairs of stones; ancillary machinery; mill machinery in working order behind glass partition; for sale May 1988, future therefore uncertain.

Merton Park; Liberty's Silk-Mill – p.150.

Morden: Snuff-Mills, Morden Hall Park (NT) – p.159.

Ockham Mill, near Ripley – Fine four-storey brick building, brick decoration on walls and around windows and doors; two-storey wooden lucam; mill and adjacent millhouse dated 1862; no wheel or machinery left; private house, part of large and mostly attractive complex including Georgian farmhouse; can be seen from public footpath crossing River Wey; mill has recently changed hands; new owners are proposing to continue restoration work begun by previous owners.

Shalford Mill, near Guildford (NT) – p.160.

Haxted Mill Museum, near Edenbridge

Haxted has a long tradition of corn-milling but does not now grind corn, the result of a decision by the owners to concentrate on providing a history of watermills through a small museum in the mill. Extensively restored by both past and present owners, Haxted retains its 150-year-old overshot water-wheel combined with machinery gathered from other mills. Historically, the most important item is the great spur-wheel of the mill, believed to be the original oak wheel of 1580.

The collapse of the old iron buckets in 1972 left the water-wheel in superficially poor condition, but the ironwork, including a cast-iron axle, was still serviceable, and Haxted became one of the first mills to acquire buckets made from fibreglass – to my knowledge Wootton Courtenay (p.143) has the only wheel constructed entirely in this material.

Haxted is a double-fronted white-painted weather-boarded mill of great charm, well maintained and an excellent example of the mill architecture of this area. The western half of the mill is oak and is believed to date from about 1580. The eastern part is late eighteenth-century and of pitch-pine. Haxted Mill stands on the Kent/Surrey border. The River Eden, which supplies its power, is an equally good example of the use to which many seemingly unpromising streams were put. All six mills on the Eden were corn-mills but the river has a tributary, the Eden Brook, which, because it touched upon the Sussex Iron Belt, was used to power the forges and furnaces of the iron-mills.

The mill is assumed to be one of the 'two watermills and 4 acres of meadow in Edenbridge' owned by William de Sardenne in 1347. The earliest specific mention of the mill is in the will of Sir Reginald de Cobham, the first Lord Cobham. In 1361 he left Haxted to his wife Joan, together with a second mill, 'Christemesse' (now 'Christmas') Mill at Cobhambury, just to the east. The older part of the present mill stands on the foundations of the fourteenth-century mill. The mill was in continuous use as a corn-mill until 1919 and produced animal feed until the end of the Second World War.

A unique hydraulic water-level control installed in Christmas Mill in 1910 was rebuilt in 1980 and presented to the museum. Among other machinery in the mill is a typical small Cornish overshot water-wheel used to drive surface working machinery in the tin-mines. A farm mill, several wheels and a number of machines used in the milling process can be seen; all are used in illustrating the history of milling.

Merton Park: Liberty's Silk-Mill

Little more than a mile from the Snuff-Mills (below) on the Wandle stand the remains of 'the Liberty Site'. On it various forms of textile-printing were carried out over a period of about 250 years. The site is part of an area in Merton which is currently undergoing (dread word) 'redevelopment' and may not survive for long – hopefully some at least of this historic area may be preserved.

Among the buildings on the site is the 'colour-house', an eighteenth-century printshop used in the thriving days of the calico-printing industry. There have been suggestions that this building, with its flint in-fill taken from the remains of Merton Priory, was the priory chapel – I doubt it. The colour-house is a listed building, as is the wheelhouse, with an external undershot wheel. Cast-iron and dating from the 1840s, it is twelve feet in diameter, and powered the rinsing spools on which the cloth was placed for washing out excess dyes after printing.

As the calico industry declined, so the silk industry entered a period of prosperity, and Edmund Littler established his silk-printing business at Merton Abbey in the 1820s. At first, specialists such as Liberty's imported Indian cloth, but quality suffered as demand rose, and Arthur Liberty turned increasingly to the home market. In 1877 a partnership began between Liberty's and Littlers which ended only when Liberty's acquired the silkworks, by then a substantial site, in 1904.

Liberty's continued to operate on the site until 1977, moving from hand-block printing to fully automated high-speed machines as technology developed. Printing on the site finally came to an end in 1981.

Morden: Snuff-Mills, Morden Hall Park (NT)

The taking of snuff reached a peak in the eighteenth and nineteenth centuries, and even the growth in tobacco-smoking during the nineteenth century had little effect on the production of snuff. It was not until women began smoking cigarettes after the First World War that the snuff-taking habit suffered a dramatic and lasting loss of popularity. Mitcham had a number of companies engaged in snuff-making, the majority based along the Wandle.

Originally snuff was ground by hand, using the whole of the tobacco leaf, but with the development of taxes on imports the manufacturers turned to using only the poorer, hard parts of the leaf. This was more easily ground by mechanical means and, in any event, demand was increasing. The introduction of mills began in the late seventeenth century, and they soon replaced all but the most specialized hand-grinding operations.

The snuff-mills in Morden Hall Park stand on either side of the Wandle. They were originally linked by their low-breast iron wheels, with wooden paddles, between which there was a sluice to allow water to pass when the mills were not working. The smaller of the two mills is white-weather-boarded and appears, on external evidence, to be quite old – possibly even seventeenth-century. Beside it is Morden Cottage, a larger building, part weather-boarded; at one time it was lived in by the mill-owners. This has been let on a long lease to Merton Council, who use it to provide a romantic setting for the local Registry Office.

The second mill is brick-built and of little architectural interest; the National Trust uses it as a base for its travelling theatre company for young people – the second mill in the county to be used for this purpose (Town Mill at Guildford is the other). Next to this mill is the clapperboard Mill Cottage, once the home of the mill foreman. The wheel of the 'new' mill was removed with its remaining machinery some years ago, leaving only the wheel of the older mill *in situ*.

Even though much of the complex has been very run down in recent years, it still conveys a remarkably rural impression – heightened by a rather interesting small Victorian wooden dairy building just downstream of the mills. With the whole area once more under their control, the National Trust is now proposing to carry out repair work. Long-term plans are to make a feature of the mill, hopefully with the wheel turning again. The mills are not open but can be viewed by visitors to the park.

Shalford Mill, near Guildford (NT)

The present mill at Shalford is early eighteenth-century. It is an impressive three-storey building, with interesting external walls. The first floor is brick but the upper storeys are tile-hung over an oak and chestnut frame. At the front the second floor juts out over the River Tillingbourne, providing protection from the weather (cf. Moor Mill for a smaller example, p.107). At the back of the mill a trio of elegant brick arches (a pleasing and relatively common feature in mills in west Surrey) channel water to the low breastshot wheel.

The iron wheel, twelve feet in diameter and eight feet wide, has wooden paddles which supplied power to three pairs of stones via a vertical shaft fashioned from a single pine trunk. Most of the machinery is original, and there is some ancillary machinery, including a couple of wire-brushing machines and an oat-crusher.

The mill worked until the outbreak of the First World War and, after renovation, was presented to the National Trust in 1932 by a group of anonymous benefactors calling themselves Ferguson's Gang. The members of this group employed pseudonyms such as 'Sister Agatha', 'Bill Stickers' and 'The Bloody Bishop'. Dedicated to preservation, they were responsible for raising a great deal of money for the Trust between the 1930s and fifties, while successfully concealing their true identities, even from senior members of the Trust's staff.

Sussex (East)

At Domesday Sussex was still in the process of being fortified by William the Conqueror's most trusted barons, to whom he had given the five Rapes – that unique subdivision of a county. It was also a county whose settlements were largely grouped along the strip of land between the sea and the Downs. Nevertheless, considering the number of settlements, it had relatively few mills, and many of them were near the sea.

Sussex had an industry, the iron industry, in the centuries that followed the Survey, but it had faded away by the end of the eighteenth century. What is a little surprising is the paucity of corn-mills in the east of the county. There are more examples than I show here, but most are private dwellings, some are stores and some

Surrey – Pippbrook Mill, Dorking. The short Pippbrook stream once supplied power to six mills; this considerably restored but pleasing mill is now used by several small businesses.

Surrey – Haxted Mill Museum, near Edenbridge. The archetypal white weatherboarded mill, here adapted as a museum of mill history.

Surrey – Elstead Mill. A remarkably beautiful group of mill buildings on the River Wey, marred only by the modern windows in the mansard roof.

Surrey/London – Liberty's Silk-Mill, Merton Park. Liberty's famous mill, currently in a rather poor state, now being restored as part of a new development scheme for the site.

East Sussex – Bartley Mill, Bells Yew Green, near Frant. The thirteenth-century mill on this site belonged to nearby Bayham Abbey. Flour continued to be ground until the early 1900s and the mill has recently reopened.

East Sussex – Park Mill, Bateman's, Burwash. Volunteers have restored this attractive brick-and-timber mill, originally built by a Wealdon ironmaster in 1634.

East Sussex – Michelham Priory Mill, Upper Dicker. Medieval foundations still underpin this typically Wealden mill largely rebuilt in the last two centuries.

West Sussex – Woods Mill, Henfield. An attractive four-storey weatherboarded building, very typical of many Sussex mills; headquarters of the Sussex Trust for Nature Conservation.

West Sussex – Burton Mill, near Petworth. Following extensive repairs the mill began grinding corn again in 1980 – exactly two centuries after it was first recorded, close to a Domesday site.

West Sussex – Warnham Mill, Horsham. This lovely mill with a fine roof of local stone and very well-repaired Victorian internal machinery now houses an antiques business.

West Sussex – Lurgashall Mill, Weald and Downland Open Air Museum, Singleton. This charming small mill comes from a village a few miles north of Singleton and is one of over thirty buildings of vernacular interest re-erected at the museum.

Warwickshire – Arrow Mill Hotel, Alcester. Several large mills remain on the Rivers Arne and Arrow and have been converted to other uses in recent years. This solid, red-brick building is now a hotel.

West Midlands – Sarehole Mill, Hall Green, near Birmingham. Sole survivor of over fifty watermills operating around Birmingham earlier this century this agreeable complex is now municipally owned.

Wiltshire – West Harnham Mill, Salisbury. Architecturally one of the most remarkable mills in existence, Harnham still retains much of its vigorous Tudor charm.

Wiltshire – Lower Mill, Bishopstone, near Salisbury. A thatched mill attached to an attractive mill house in the valley of the short but fascinating, and unspoilt, River Ebble.

North Yorkshire – Crakehall Mill. The present charming little mill, on a Domesday site, is mostly seventeenth century. It stands beside the Crakehall Beck in a lovely, well-maintained village.

North Yorkshire – Gayle Mill, near Hawes. Familiar to walkers along the Pennine Way, this solid mill was built for the cotton industry in 1784 but has also been a woollen-mill and a saw-mill.

North Yorkshire – Darley Mill Centre. In an interesting mixture of buildings of different sizes and periods, the centre houses several showrooms and an excellent display on mills and milling.

North Yorkshire – Raindale Watermill, Castle Museum, York. This tiny mill from the moors above Pickering now stands on the banks of the Foss in York, dwarfed by the castle walls.

South Yorkshire – Worsbrough Mill Museum, Barnsley. The entrance to this exceptionally well-run mill museum – one of several in the county providing first-class information on various forms of milling.

South Yorkshire – Abbeydale Industrial Hamlet, Sheffield. Two of the wheels – the 18-foot high breast, and 14½-foot overshot – which provided power for this remarkable complex. Water for both came from the large pentrough.

South Yorkshire – Shepherd Wheel, Sheffield. A cutlery-grinding plant on an old mill site in a deep, narrow valley. An unbelievably rural setting less than two miles from the city centre.

are in a poor condition. As a result, I have concentrated on West Sussex, with its greater variety of mills.

Bells Yew Green: Bartley Mill, near Frant – below.
Burwash; Park Mill, Bateman's (NT) – p.162.
Upper Dicker: Michelham Priory Mill – p.162.

Bells Yew Green: Bartley Mill, near Frant

Bartley Mill has certainly been in existence since the thirteenth century, and the abbot of Bayham Abbey, which owned the mill until the Reformation, was evicting tenants as early as 1311. There was more trouble in 1556, when a jury from Frant decided that the appropriately named miller, Thomas Baker, 'several times has taken excessive money', and he was fined 4s.

The Barham family purchased the mill shortly after this and held it until 1723. The Ashby family were the next major holders of the mill, occupying it until 1859, although only on a lease after 1801, Thomas Ashby having sold the property to the owner of Bayham Estate, the Marquess of Camden. The Estate continued to lease Bartley, which ground corn until shortly before the First World War, when it briefly became an engineering workshop. Given the history of the area (Frant was a great iron-working parish), this seems very appropriate, but the mill reverted to agricultural purposes after the war.

The family firm of H.S. Pledge, who have a long tradition of milling in the Ashford area of Kent, bought Bartley Mill in 1985 and began the task of renovating it. Almost at once they discovered that the fall of water was insufficient for the necessary supply of power. A fresh source has now been provided, drawn in part from an old hammer-pond used during the period when the iron industry flourished in the Weald and establishing, albeit indirectly, another link with the history of the area.

Inside the mill the twelve-foot-diameter cast-iron wheel, installed in 1969, is enclosed behind glass; upstairs there is some auxiliary machinery, and a well-mounted display, including old photographs, on the history of the mill. There is a restaurant, with a few 'crafty' things for sale, and the mill produces flour for sale using organically grown wheat from its own farm. Some craft shops have been set up in nearby outbuildings.

Delightfully untechnical, this newly reopened mill is exceptionally well lit and laid out. If at present it lacks a degree of authenticity, a few years working will add a patina of dust and cobwebs. As seems to be universally the case with watermill staff, everyone at Bartley Mill is welcoming and helpful. When we arrived five minutes before their nominal closing time one particularly wet and cold evening in the middle of the 'summer' of 1987, both the owner, Piers Garnham, and his millwright stayed to answer a series of questions when they would have been justified in showing us the door!

Burwash: Park Mill, Bateman's (NT)

Park Mill is a very attractive three-storey brick and timber building standing beside the River Dudwell at the far end of the garden of Rudyard Kipling's home, Bateman's. It was built by a local ironmaster in 1634. The view of the upper storey and roof of the mill from the millpond is particularly pleasing in autumn, when the leaves of the trees which ring the pond are turning.

Beside the mill is one of the oldest working water-driven turbines in the world, installed by Kipling in 1903 to generate electricity for the house. The restoration of the mill, which had become very dilapidated, was carried out by volunteer labour for the National Trust. The turbine and generator, unused since the 1920s, were repaired and a replacement was built for the overshot wheel removed by Kipling when he installed the turbine. The new wheel is only half the size of the original, since it has to share the wheel-pit with the turbine and its penstock. Flour is produced for sale.

Upper Dicker: Michelham Priory Mill

Like Park Mill, Michelham stands in a most attractive setting – the grounds of Michelham Priory, founded in 1229. There has been a mill on this site since the fourteenth century, and parts of the original foundations survive. The effect is of a very pretty, almost medieval building, but in truth Michelham has undergone a great deal of restoration, and much of the classic Wealden structure of brick and wood has been rebuilt over the centuries. The bulk of the mill is no earlier than the eighteenth century.

When the mill closed in 1925, all the machinery was removed, and it has now been replaced with carefully crafted modern machinery made in a medieval style. The only exception is the iron pit-wheel which is eighteenth-century. In 1971 restoration work began on this historic mill, and after five years work the mill was ready to operate again.

Sussex (West)

The mills included here have much greater variety than those of East Sussex – indeed, the purist will argue that Coultershaw Beam Pump, like Claverton Pump-House in Avon, has no place in a book on mills. But both use water-power and have their place in the history of the water-wheel. Of the watermills listed here, Burton and Warnham have long, well-documented histories and strong connections with the iron industry which flourished in Kent and Sussex until the end of the seventeenth century. Their recent history is markedly different – proof of the variety of uses to which mills can be put.

Burton Mill, near Petworth – below.
Coultershaw Beam Pump, near Petworth – p.164.
Henfield: Woods Mill – p.165.
Horsham: Warnham Mill – p.166.
Ifield Mill, near Crawley – Nineteenth-century, four-storey brick weather-boarded mill on edge of new town estate; large sixteenth-century millpond; milled corn from seventeenth to twentieth century; external iron overshot wheel; pentrough and other machinery replaced using equipment from other mills; restoration work in hand since 1974 – currently appears to be in abeyance.
Singleton: Lurgashall Mill, Weald and Downland Open Air Museum – p.168.

Burton Mill, near Petworth

Several of the mills described in this book are situated close to each other – convenient when planning visits, but not the reason for their inclusion. One good example of a 'species' often seems to inspire the development of another (pubs are a case in point). Certainly the presence of enthusiasts is an advantage, and Mrs Ann Mills, the present tenant and restorer of Burton Mill, had the help of volunteers from the Sussex Industrial Archaeology Society. The SIAS were also responsible for the restoration of Coultershaw Beam Pump (p.164), just 1½ miles away.

The present mill at Burton is good and solid, if not outstandingly attractive, but is included for its historic connections with the Wealden iron industry and for its setting. By the early seventeenth century Sussex had replaced Kent, where the great Wealden forests had been almost destroyed, as the centre of the industry. The 'drift' from east to west is quite distinct, and in 1635 Burton was being used as an iron forge with water-powered trip-hammers producing wrought-iron for weapons and tools. A piece of forge cinder thought to be of this period and bearing the imprint of the bellows was found in the tailrace in 1979 and can be seen in the mill. Cast-iron would have come from the furnaces at Petworth or Pallingham Lock.

The forge at Burton was still in existence in 1664 but there are no later records and, although some forges survived into the eighteenth century, this one had probably gone within ten years as the iron industry made its final move north to take advantage of cheap coal and developing technology.

First noted in the Land Tax return of 1780, the present mill remained tenanted but in the hands of Burton Park Estate until 1894, when the estate was broken up – the mill and millhouse were sold as one lot. Flour-grinding ceased around the turn of the century, and thereafter the mill appears to have functioned rather as an estate mill. A water turbine replaced the east wheel early in this century, driving a dynamo to produce electricity for Burton Park House. In the 1930s the west wheel gave way to a Gilkes turbine which powered a circular saw and cattlecake-crusher.

Burton Mill stands in surprisingly unspoilt country; the thirty-acre hammer-pond feeding it is surrounded by mature deciduous trees and, at weekends, by anglers. At Domesday the mill and fishery paid annual dues of 260 eels and, even if the Domesday mill was almost certainly *not* on the present site, it's pleasing to note that a combination of milling and fishing continues at 'Botechitone'.

It was the threatened collapse of the road between the pond and the half-hidden mill which led to West Sussex County Council's acquiring the mill in the 1960s. In 1978 they let it to Mrs Mills on a repairing lease. At this time the mill was in poor condition, needing a lot of strengthening to the internal structure before replacements could be sought for the machinery – the turbine at the west end remained and had been repaired. When the repairs were complete, a pair of French Burr stones, with gearing and iron hurst frame, were brought from a derelict mill in Wales, rebuilt and dressed in readiness for flour-production, which began again in 1980.

Coultershaw Beam Pump, near Petworth

Coultershaw is included as an example of the uses to which the water-wheel can be put rather than as a 'mill', although there was a very fine mill of classic proportions on the site until 1923. Coultershaw Mill was recorded in Domesday and again in 1240, when it was given to Schulebrede Priory by William de Percy. Destroyed by fire in 1923, the mill was replaced by a functional concrete and steel box-like structure that I, along with many others, still remember with a shudder. After the death of the last tenant it was, thankfully, pulled down.

In this area of West Sussex many of the developments over the centuries can be shown to have been connected with, or initiated by, one or other of the large estates at Cowdray, Goodwood or Petworth. Expansion of the local transport system began in 1787, when the River Arun was improved to allow navigation as far as Billingshurst. Then in 1794 the 3rd Earl of Egremont personally paid for the widening of its tributary, the Rother, permitting waterborne traffic to travel as far as Midhurst. At Coultershaw Bridge a wharf was built, from which it was possible to transport supplies easily and cheaply to Petworth House and to the town.

A water-pump was installed in 1784 to supplement the water-supply to the house and town, which had previously relied upon local springs. The original wheel was wooden and undershot but it was replaced in the mid nineteenth century by a more efficient breastshot iron wheel, eleven feet in diameter and 4½ feet wide; the oak paddles are modern. There is direct coupling to the three-throw crankshaft of the pump through timber beams (cf. Claverton Pump-House, p.53). Water was originally taken from the culvert supplying the wheel and pumped at 65 psi along a three-inch pipe the 1½ miles to Petworth – operations ceased in about 1960. The alignment of water-wheel and crankshaft was poor, resulting in a great amount of noise, to the considerable discomfiture of the millers working next door.

It is claimed that Coultershaw Pump was capable of delivering up to 20,000 gallons a day to Petworth but it now performs a much more limited task. Water is pumped the short distance to a fountain beside the shed in which the pump is housed, and the pressure is used to operate the fountain. The pump shed is itself of considerable interest. It comes from nearby Goodwood and is a clay-tiled wagon shed rebuilt here by the volunteer workers of the Sussex Industrial Archaeology Society. They have been lovingly restoring and maintaining the site since 1976 and are, as the visitor quickly realizes, still immensely enthusiastic about the project.

Henfield: Woods Mill

Woods Mill is owned and used by the Sussex Trust for Nature Conservation as its headquarters. Set in fifteen acres of nature reserve, it concentrates, not unnaturally, on wildlife, but it's something of a pity that the Trust currently has little information available in leaflet form about the mill. This lack of information is pointed up by the existence of several excellent leaflets on other aspects of the reserve. In fairness, there is a good series of display panels on the lower floor, outlining the history of the mill.

The pleasant four-storey white weather-boarded mill dates from the early eighteenth century but the site almost certainly has a long history. It is quite possible that a mill at Streatham Manor, mentioned in Domesday, may have been Woods Mill. The earliest reference to Woods Mill by name is contained in a survey of the manor made in 1647, following its confiscation by Parliamentary forces during the Civil War. For much of the nineteenth century, until its closure in 1927, the lease of the mill was in the hands of two families. The Botting family occupied it from 1819 to 1858 (the name is still well-known in the area), and from 1883 to 1927 the Coote family leased the mill. The entomologist Dr J.N.D. Smith purchased the mill in 1950, bequeathing it to the STNC in 1966.

Well lit and laid out on three floors, Woods Mill contains the natural history exhibition set up by the Trust. There is a reception area and bookshop on the first floor, the level at which the mill is entered. Extending over three floors is a large and authentic-looking model showing in graphic form the natural history of an oak tree. The upper floor features display panels on the nature reserve, and the species visitors may observe as they walk its nature trail. Freshwater fish swim in a large tank, and a small vivarium houses harvest mice (only one when I was there). In a separate wooden building beside the millpond, plant and insect specimens collected on the reserve are displayed. Dr Smith would surely be delighted with the enthusiastic Trust wardens who catch moths in an ingenious trap on summer nights, identifying them for visitors before releasing them the following morning.

The well-produced panels outlining the history of the mill share the ground floor with the wheel machinery – none of it original. The large external overshot water-wheel dating from 1854 can be studied from the doorway on this floor.

It would be wrong to suggest that Woods Mill should be an automatic choice for the committed mill 'freak' – too much has been changed for that, but it is exceptionally well maintained by the Sussex Trust for Nature Conservation, and its history justifies a visit. It is ideal for children (there is an audio-visual room for use by schools and other organizations), and the welcome from the volunteer staff is unfailingly friendly. I greatly enjoy its atmosphere – and so, apparently do the contented harvest mice.

Horsham: Warnham Mill

Towards the end of the thirteenth century there was a mill at Caldecote, just north of the present millpond, but it was not until about 1580 that Warnham Furnace was built by Sir John Caryll. The east to west 'drift' by the Wealden iron industry has been mentioned when dealing with Burton Mill (p.163), and the furnace at Warnham predates that at Burton by some years. Ironstone for smelting was obtained by digging locally with the spoil used to build up the pond head-dam. The layout is similar to other furnace plants, with the mill standing close to, but below the level of, the completed millpond. Two water-wheels were installed to drive the bellows for the double furnace.

It appears that, for some forty-five summers, the lake was regularly drained and the ironstone seam beneath it worked. Obviously, this had a secondary advantage in that the capacity of the pond was enlarged until it was about half a mile long. I know of no other example of such a scheme.

Warnham was a Royalist mill, producing cannon during the Civil War, and it was one of those destroyed by Colonel Hawker's raid into Sussex in 1645. The mill would not have been rebuilt as a forge after the war because the industry was then in gradual decline as the great oak forests of Kent and Sussex were exhausted. Nonetheless, the site clearly had considerable value as a mill site, and by the turn of the century a corn-mill with a single overshot wheel was standing on the remains of the old furnace mill. On 1 December 1700 the mill was bought by a man named Robert Charman for £250. Twenty days later he resold it for £300 – a useful Christmas present to himself, and proof that speculators are no new phenomenon!

As evidence of another seeming immutable, the rise in the price of property, the cost of the mill (admittedly with 125 acres of farmland) had risen to £17,000 by 1875. It was then bought by Charles Thomas Lucas and is still owned by the Lucas family. Mr Lucas carried out many improvements, including the installation of a steam-pump to drive the wheel when the water-supply was low. At first glance this seems unnecessary, because a pond of some thirty-five acres should have been sufficient to supply water for one wheel driving, at most, three pairs of stones. The answer is that water from the millpond was by now being drawn off to supply a reservoir and lakes in Warnham Court. The mill continued to grind corn and animal feed until 1928.

Warnham Mill is a most attractive building, with a particularly fine roof of local Horsham stone. The interior of the mill, containing the beginnings of a small museum and the contents of the antiques business of the tenants, Mr and Mrs Dickins, is a charming jumble. It is also a very welcoming place, with a strong 'feel' of history – somehow even the heavy traffic constantly passing by fails to affect it. Restoration of the mill was carried out between 1982 and 1984, using local craftsmen and materials (often from mills in the Horsham area), which, I think, contributes greatly to the sense of continuity.

As an example of the care taken, Mr C.J. Lucas, the present owner, employed local millwrights to rebuild the eighteen-foot Victorian cast-iron water-wheel. Peter and Anne Dickins hope to use the wheel by harnessing it to a generator to provide heating for the mill.

Singleton: Lurgashall Mill, Weald and Downland Open Air Museum

The Weald and Downland Open Air Museum was fortunate in that its foundation, in 1967, coincided with the upsurge in interest in vernacular architecture. Barley's standard work *The English Farmhouse and Cottage* had appeared in 1961. On a broader canvas, television was soon to discover the advantages, and relative cheapness, of having an expert explore facets of rural or urban England – among others, the irreplaceable Alec Clifton-Taylor would impart his infectious joy in good buildings, and scorn of bad, to millions of viewers.

The Weald and Downland Museum has always argued that buildings should be preserved *in situ* wherever possible, but when this is not so, it considers the buildings for re-erection at Singleton. Over thirty buildings have been saved in this way, and a similar number are waiting to be rebuilt on the site. A comparatively recent development has been the acquisition of artefacts representing country crafts, building-trades and agriculture. Many of these will furnish buildings, while others will form a valuable additional collection.

The museum is planning to develop a number of themes on the site. Lurgashall Mill will form, with a windpump and treadmill, the major part of one of these themes – in this case, the importance of water-, wind- and animal-power. The mill ceased working in the 1930s and was presented to the museum by the Leconfield Estate in 1973. There is a close parallel here with Alton Mill at Stowmarket (p.152), for Singleton is not ideal for a mill, with an overshot water-wheel requiring a drop of twelve feet from upper to lower millpond. Excavation work on a new millpond was carried out while the mill was being dismantled and rebuilt. The mill was in position by 1977, but work on the interior and the machinery took another three years. Another problem which had to be overcome at Singleton was the lack of a natural water-supply. Bearing in mind that it was always intended to make Lurgashall a working mill, producing flour for sale, a continual supply of water was needed to 'fuel' the millpond, and the solution adopted was to install a recirculation pump.

Lurgashall probably dates from the seventeenth century, but it was modified and partly rebuilt at least once in the next century. This amount of change is by no means unusual, but a possible explanation for the degree of rebuilding is the evidence, visible on the wall, of a second wheel. Assuming this was not part of the original mill, the structure might have had to be altered to accommodate it, and the additional stresses may have weakened the mill. The twelve-foot diameter cast-iron water-wheel is from Costers Mill at West Lavington and replaces the original wooden wheel.

The gearing and machinery have no unusual features – but then Lurgashall Mill is important precisely because it so perfectly typifies the great majority of mills which served their communities across the centuries. In what are still, relatively speaking, their early years, the aim at museums like Singleton and St Fagans must surely be to seek out the *representative* building rather than the unusual.

Gerallt Nash at St Fagans once gently pointed out to my wife that the Weald and Downland Open Air Museum was established long *after* the Welsh Folk Museum (p.201), but for anyone even remotely interested in the vernacular buildings of either country both are essential visiting. And how fortunate we are to witness the growth of so many exciting modern museums.

Tyne & Wear

One of the most romantic settings I know is at Jesmond Dene, where the mill has deteriorated alarmingly in recent years. It is now a ruin – but admittedly attractive. What adds to the sadness is that the Council maintains Jesmond Dene Park in fine condition, employing MSC workers to assist in the task – why cannot the work be extended to cover restoration of the mill? Perhaps one day the broken wheel will be repaired and will turn again for the delight of strollers in the park.

Newcastle upon Tyne: Jesmond Dene – Remains of wheel in ruined mill; attractive parkland setting beside River Ouseburn; public access to park – mill unsafe and fenced.

Warwickshire

In 1086 Warwickshire consisted of two distinct areas – the south and east widely cultivated, the north and west still largely uncolonized. Interestingly, this divide was repeated when industrialization came to the county in the form of the eastern coalfield. Division of a different type came about with the administrative changes of the 1970s.

Warwickshire mills seem to have suffered more than most from conversion in recent years; sadly not all of it has been very good – Arrow Mill, though not perfect, is an exception. The rather disturbed recent history of Great Alne has just taken a new twist, while the authenticity of claims regarding Guy's Cliffe has always caused conflict. The jewel in the Warwickshire crown is undoubtedly Charlecote – a lovely mill being used for its correct purpose.

Alcester: Arrow Mill Hotel – below.

Great Alne Mill, near Alcester – Large mill; after period housing museum of the history of flying, now again grinding corn; turbine driven for much of this century; one of several on River Alne of historic interest; part of site has recently been acquired and is being developed into five luxury dwellings; milling continues in mill which is now NOT OPEN.

Guy's Cliffe Mill, near Warwick – Claimed to have Saxon origins; present 'Saxon' mill built in 1822; millhouse is older – seventeenth-century; timber-framed and stone; much altered and together form a restaurant; small working wheel in restaurant millrace visible under glass panel.

Hampton Lucy: Charlecote Mill (TCG) – p.171.

Little Lawford Mill, near Rugby – Handsome corn-mill and millhouse; no wheel but remains of sack-hoist.

Shipston on Stour Mill – Very visible, large complex by bridge on R. Stour; Shipston Mill sells animal feed; millhouse has been heavily converted to an hotel; no sign of machinery. NOT OPEN.

Stratford-upon-Avon: Lucy's Mill – Large mill on Avon; better than average conversion to flats.

Studley: Old Washford Mill near Redditch – Large black-and-white mill converted to pub; one of first mills adapted to needle-making (cf. Forge Mill, p.106); wheel enclosed by glass; waterside gardens; to my mind a strident conversion of a historically interesting mill.

Warwick: Castle Mill – Remarkable Georgian Gothic mill in castle grounds; not worked in over a century; retains external wheel.

Alcester: Arrow Mill Hotel

Arrow Mill is a good-quality three-storey, red-brick building, standing in fifty-five acres of land about a mile south of Alcester, a town with a pronounced milling history, situated on the junction of two rivers, the Alne and the Arrow. Other mills in the area include Forge Mill (p.106), Old Washford Mill (see above) and Great Alne Mill (above). The first two were among the first to be converted to needle-making when that industry became centred around Studley. Like Arrow, Great Alne was always a corn-mill.

The history of the mill is said to go back to Domesday, although it is really only in the last 150 years that much detail is recorded. The Sisam family owned the mill for almost a hundred years, from 1828 until 1921, when the grinding of corn stopped and the stones were replaced by rollers. Animal feed was ground until 1962, after which the mill was closed and converted into a restaurant.

The size of the mill and its setting, with the mill-stream flowing under it, a fine millpond and the river winding past, made Arrow Mill a 'natural' for development, and it now has fifteen bedrooms. I confess to approaching all these conversions – particularly when large breweries (Bass in this instance) are involved – with trepidation, but helpful staff are an asset, and I was allowed to look round at leisure. One or two well-worn mill-stones are in evidence but, mercifully, there is little 'olde worlde mylle' about the place. The iron-framed undershot water-wheel, with wooden paddles, fairly whizzes round in its glass cage!

Hampton Lucy: Charlecote Mill

There were several mills in this area at the time of the Domesday Book – Charlecote had two and Hampton Lucy one, valued at only 6s. 8d. I don't know how much the BBC paid for the repair of the west water-wheel in 1978, when they used the mill for filming *The Mill on the Floss* – considerably more than the original value of the entire mill!

The handsome mill and house were built by the Lucy family, owners of Charlecote Park, in the eighteenth century. It has certain interesting features, not least the use of differing materials on either side of the roof – tiles for the south, and slates on the north, a result of raising the roof and decreasing the pitch during a later addition. The mill also possesses some fine studded doors, a feature found in several Warwickshire watermills.

By the 1950s, when it ceased operating, the mill was relying almost entirely on engine-power. On taking up the lease in 1978, the present tenant, John Bedington, began the process of restoring the mill to working order. Charlecote Mill now produces wholemeal flour and some animal feed. The wheel used for milling is undershot; the machinery is largely conventional but, as an example of how millers have always been prepared to incorporate 'modern' technology, grain is now stored in bins lined with galvanized steel as a protection against rats and mice.

Scattered around the mill are various milling artefacts, but the great pleasure of Charlecote has to be the building itself – architecturally in the very first rank of surviving working mills. Now open only by appointment.

West Midlands

No doubt administratively effective, 'West Midlands' covers an area in which mills are almost bound to be thin on the ground, due to centuries of urbanization. Sarehole proves the point – the only survivor of fifty or more in the Birmingham area. A few other mill buildings remain, often converted beyond recognition or deserted, and can be sought by the enthusiast along rivers and canals. Some of these 'mills' would not come in the scope of this book, as they were never water-powered.

Hall Green: Sarehole Mill, near Birmingham – below.

Hall Green: Sarehole Mill, near Birmingham

It is possible that there was a mill on this site during Norman times but there is no mention of it under Yardley ('Gerlei') in Domesday. There were certainly mills in the area – the number of streams and rivers would have ensured that, but the first specific reference to a mill here occurs in 1542, when permission was given to a local man to build a corn-mill. He employed John Bedell as builder, and a hundred years later the mill was still known as 'Biddle's Mill'. It was bought by the Eaves family in 1727, and among their tenants was Matthew Boulton, later to establish the Soho Manufactory at Handsworth – generally accepted as the first factory where labour was organized and therefore the precursor of the industrial town of the nineteenth century. Some time after Boulton left, Richard Eaves rebuilt the mill, improving the water-supply to the millpond by cutting a half-mile headrace from the River Cole. The work, involving various loans and mortgages, overstretched Eaves, and in 1775 the mill was sold following his bankruptcy.

Among Richard Eaves' improvements were a granary and a blade-grinding workshop. For about thirty years, the mill ground both corn and edge tools but with the growth of specialization in the manufacturing industries (cf. Forge Mill, p.106) it reverted to corn-grinding – successfully, for in 1851 a second wheel was installed and the blade-grinding shop was converted into a house for the miller. A steam-engine was installed to provide additional power, and the typical pattern was established – rapid expansion of milling in the early years of Victoria's reign followed by a dramatic downturn with the arrival of roller-milling in the 1890s. Milling ceased in 1919 but the mill was tenanted until 1959. Restoration work began in 1964, and the mill became the responsibility of the Birmingham City Museums and Art Gallery six years later.

Sarehole qualifies for the description 'unique' because it is the sole survivor of the fifty or so watermills operating in and around Birmingham until the beginning of the century. A factor in this dramatic loss was the growth of Birmingham as an urban area – although more flour was needed, there was even greater pressure for land for development.

Of different periods, the buildings in the tight-knit little complex form a pleasant grouping. The single-storey south wheel-house was the original blade-grinding shop and now houses a reconstruction of the shop showing that here the grinder sat upright (cf. Abbeydale and Finch's, pp.181 and 88). The cast-iron overshot wheel added in 1851 is housed next door. Adjoining it is the three-storey mill 'proper', with its rather elegant lucam. The well-maintained ancillary machinery for both wheels is on the ground floor here next to a high-breast, cast-iron wheel with wooden buckets. On the stone floor two pairs of millstones are set up for operation, with a further pair exposed to show the dressed faces.

The granary is used for exhibitions, part permanent, part temporary. Local children visit the mill and relive a day in its working life – their essays are displayed upstairs, alongside a good range of farm implements. Downstairs there is a fine collection of carts, including a magnificent Gloucester Bow, a horse-drawn blacksmith's bellows and a mobile corn-grinder with stones which would have been powered by a traction-engine.

Wiltshire

As a centre for the woollen industry (Defoe thought it the principal industry of the county), Wiltshire should be full of working mills, but it isn't. More correctly the old mills have undergone a variety of changes and, almost more than anywhere else in Britain, now fulfil a range of functions far removed from their early purpose. I am talking here primarily of the larger mills; the smaller ones have almost all become private houses.

We must be grateful that the loss of so much vernacular building 'stock' in Wiltshire is not a universal problem. Let us hope that it will act as a warning of what can happen, not through wickedness but rather by default. With very few examples to choose from, particularly in the more industrialized north of the county, I have deliberately listed a number within easy reach of Salisbury. They are in pleasant surroundings and, more important, are representative of the range of mills to be found in the county – from decrepit to over-restored, with some gems in between!

Bishopstone: Lower Mill, near Salisbury – Two-storey timber mill on brick base; thatched roof; leat passes under mill – no machinery visible; externally in excellent repair; attached, at right-angles to two-storey brick (white-painted) millhouse; various waterways used as feature of charming garden; one of several mills remaining on River Ebble (see below);. NOT OPEN. Croucheston Mill (well signed at west of village) is large, unattractive commercial mill producing agricultural fertilizers etc.

Blackland: Mill Farm (TCG), near Calne – Corn-mill on site of monastic mill dating to 1215; present building late eighteenth- or early nineteenth-century; eighteen-foot breastshot wheel – three pairs French Burr stones.

Coombe Bisset Mill, near Salisbury – Dark weather-boarded mill on River Ebble; brick base, tile roof; iron external wheel – broad, undershot; one of few run-down buildings in pleasing village with impressive three-arch packhorse bridge. NOT OPEN.

Great Cheverell Mill – Two-storey red-brick corn-mill; no external machinery. NOT OPEN.

South Newton Mill, near Salisbury – Red-brick two-storey mill on River Wylye south of village; exposed position by A36 points up rather 'raw' look following restoration; timber barn very obviously renovated. NOT OPEN.

West Harnham Old Mill, near Salisbury – below.

Winterbourne Gunner Mill – Small, rather dilapidated, complex on River Bourne; including three-storey red-brick mill under slate roof; millhouse with weather-boarded and thatched outbuildings. NOT OPEN.

Wylye Mill – Fine nineteenth-century mill in lovely village now, thankfully, bypassed by both A36 and A303; three-storey, brick with a little stone; good brick arch; beautiful garden on River Wylye. NOT OPEN.

West Harnham Old Mill, near Salisbury

Harnham Old Mill is largely Tudor on an early medieval site. It has a very decorative external appearance, the ground floor of alternate flint and stone areas creating a squared pattern. The first floor is brick under a lovely uneven tiled roof. The mill stands on a causeway, with the River Nadder flowing under it through a brick water-course.

The quality of the mill has led to suggestions that it may have been intended for an alternative use. The closest comparison is Bourne Mill (p.94), generally believed to have been a fishing lodge first and a mill second. I have reservations about that theory, but it cannot be denied that no other surviving mills are so remarkably well built and decorated as these two. Equally, it must be noted that there are very few of comparable date, built during a period of wealth – often based on wool – and generally reflected in vigorous, confident and essentially happy buildings. Cutterne Mill (p.142), some thirty years younger, lacks the *brio* of the earlier mills, but then it was intended to be a functional building in a relatively remote rural setting.

Whatever its origins, Harnham has enjoyed a varied history as a mill. In its time it has been a fulling-mill, a corn-mill and even a paper-mill. It is now a craft shop and café; no machinery remains, although it seems safe to assume that the wheel(s) would have been undershot. Attached to the mill is a much later four-storey red-brick building of Georgian appearance. Converted to a hotel, it entirely lacks the quality of the mill and may once have housed auxiliary machinery for it.

Yorkshire, North

Much of North Yorkshire was waste when Domesday was compiled, and though it is possible that some mills escaped the attention of the Commissioners, the probability has to be that they had been destroyed during the time of King William's attacks in 1069-70. Most of the mills listed below are of later date – only Crakehall is certainly a Domesday site. Yore Mill is very popular with visitors, as is Darley – both reflect the growing tourist industry in this area.

One mill not on this list, and not open, is Easby Abbey Mill, near Richmond; I mention it because it is currently a boarding-kennel for dogs – another use for an old mill.

Aysgarth: Yore Mill – p.176.
Bainbridge: Low Mill – Small mill on River Bain; last worked early 1900s; eighteenth-century breastshot wheel; two pairs of stones; recently restored.
Crakehall Mill – p.176.
Darley Mill – p.177.
Gayle Mill, near Hawes – Historic mill, on side of Gayle Beck; tall cottages beside beck were combing-houses for mill; operated first as cotton- and then as woollen-mill; later a saw-mill, now a joiner's shop; turbine is probably oldest still working; sturdy three-storey building with six bays, remarkably little altered; visible from Pennine Way, which passes close behind it; recent attempt by Yorkshire Dales National Park to buy mill has failed and future is in some doubt. NOT OPEN.
Pateley Bridge: Foster Beck Mill – Very large (thirty-foot-diameter) external pitch-back wheel; was a hemp-mill until 1960s; has experienced a chequered career in recent years; currently being restored as inn (for second time!)
Skipton: George Leatt Industrial and Folk Museum, High Corn-Mills – For long part of Skipton Castle Estate (stands in shadow of castle); now an industrial and folk museum; two water-wheels, one (twenty-eight feet in diameter) drives machinery.
Sleninford Mill, near Ripon – p.177.

Stamford Bridge: Corn-Mill – Six-storey, brick-built eighteenth-century mill; now a restaurant; metal undershot wheel remains and turns.

York: Raindale Watermill, Castle Museum – p.179.

Aysgarth: Yore Mill

Yore Mill has crammed a remarkably full 'life' into its 200-odd years of existence! Built in 1784, at the same time as Gayle Mill (p.175) and Hawes Mill, which later housed the first Wensleydale cheese factory, Yore was operated as a corn-mill but failed and was in poor condition by 1822, when it was repaired. It was then used for the production of worsted cloth before burning down in the early 1850s.

It was rebuilt on the same site and considerably enlarged, becoming an impressively solid Victorian mill. It now looked like, and for a time was, a cotton-mill and is said to have produced shirts for Garibaldi's army of Redshirts. Between 1912 and 1956 it ground corn, and after that, was used for the distribution of animal feed.

The Yore Mill's latest and (judging by the number of tourists it attracts) most successful manifestation is as home to a Coach and Carriage Museum – it also houses a tea room and craft centre. Anyone parking in the large car-park at Aysgarth and heading for the village has to pass the mill, seemingly rising sheer from the River Ure.

Crakehall Mill

A mill with a long, well-documented history beginning in 1086 with the Domesday Survey and including a period in the ownership of the Neville family of Middleham Castle. Crakehall was forfeited in the fifteenth century, becoming Crown property until sold by James I in 1624. The milling family of Hobson worked the mill from the late nineteenth century until closing it in the 1930s. Colonel Whitaker Holmes bought it in 1977, after it had lain in a derelict condition for close on fifty years. He repaired sluices, re-excavated the millpond, restored the original mill machinery to working order and replaced the wooden buckets of the fifteen-foot-diameter, nineteenth-century low breastshot wheel. In 1980 the two remaining pairs of stones began once again to grind corn.

Crakehall is a most charming mill, much of it dating from the seventeenth-century, although the top storey is probably around 1800. Small and compact, it has the Crakehall Beck flowing beside it, creating a very satisfactory image of what a village mill should look like. It is a fitting memorial to the man who restored it and who sadly died in 1986.

Darley Mill

Darley Mill represents the split personality of the mill/craft-centre concept taken to the limit. The ground floor is given over to an excellent milling display – well laid out, with instructive panels containing a good mixture of general and valuable local information on mills. For probably the majority of the visitors to the mill, its stone floor and grain store devoted to showrooms for bed linens and crafts and gifts respectively are of most interest. The attached old barn has a range of household linen items; a restaurant and tea shop complete the complex.

Even after a modernization programme principally designed to show it off to good commercial advantage, the mill is an attractive place, with a miller's cottage standing at an angle to the main mill. The buildings are of different periods and sizes; the three-storey mill (comprising the middle section) is flanked by the two-storey millhouse, with a Georgian frontage added in 1767, and the cow byre. A detail worth studying is the waggon porch, which was designed so that grain could be unloaded under cover direct to the drying-tank or grain store. When finished, the meal or flour was returned to the roadside, where it immediately became the responsibility of the grain-supplier, regardless of weather conditions.

Darley Mill has six pairs of stones set in a circle round the main shaft. In dry periods the Darley Beck could not provide enough water to turn the large, twenty-seven-foot-diameter, pitch-back wheel, so an auxiliary steam-engine was installed in the 1850s. The wheel is a hybrid of a type which became increasingly popular in the nineteenth century – cast-iron rim and centre axle; spokes and panels of elm. It is at the back of the mill and is an instant attraction to children as they leave the car-park.

The millrace consists of a reservoir and conduit, and the view from the millrace footpath is of a classic farming landscape. Small fields, bounded by mortarless dry-stone walls, are today used for sheep and cattle-grazing. For centuries these fields produced cereals and peas; with limited transport facilities, it was essential to have access to a local mill to convert them to foodstuffs for people and animals. Darley Mill is a good example of the once successful community mill of the area and, because of its layout, can be studied independently of the craft centre.

Sleninford Mill, near Ripon

Sleninford (so spelt by owners – generally Sleningford, but not at Domesday!) Mill stands beside the beautiful, hurrying waters of the River Ure, close to the handsome bridge at West Tanfield. It is in the grounds of a small caravan and touring park; the mill is used as the information centre with one room devoted to leaflets extolling the virtues of a wide range of Yorkshire attractions. Sadly, it is not operating, although the bulk of the machinery is still on the site. As part of a large estate clearly intending to capitalize on its assets, I would have thought a working mill would have attracted additional revenue.

The Manor of Ripon belonged to the see of York from a very early time, possibly that of St Wilfrid in the seventh century. There almost certainly were mills in the area but, though they were relatively major parts of the estate, there is no specific mention of a mill at either 'Scleneforde' or neighbouring 'Nordestanlai'. The first record of a mill at Sleninford occurs in 1328, when the land passed into the ownership of Fountains Abbey. The present millhouse was probably finished about 1773 – there is an inscription of that date over the front door – but the mill buildings are possibly a little earlier.

The cast-iron Poncelet wheel (fifteen feet in diameter by five feet wide) was installed in the 1800s and continued in use until about 1950. Sleninford is a good example of an estate mill, for, in addition to powering the auxiliary milling machinery, it drove a saw bench and grindstone and pumped river-water to the estuary. To complete the picture, wire-rope gear drove a turnip-cutter and straw-chopper in the barn across the yard!

How could such a labour-and-energy-intensive set-up have failed? The usual answer is changing farm practice, speeded by the shortage of labour during the Second World War, allied to the introduction of electric-power. In this instance there is a simpler explanation: the land around Sleninford Mill was quarried in the 1950s and sixties, with the extraction of two million tons of aggregate, and access to the mill became almost impossible.

The part of the mill containing the machinery is not open to inspection, and the upper floors appear unsafe, but, at a cursory glance, the machinery does not seem to be in bad condition. The iron mill-shaft, bevel-geared pit-wheel, wallower and cast-iron cog are all visible, while on the stone floor there are said to be three pairs of grinding-stones (French Burr, composition and millstone grit).

With car-parking space and good facilities, including provision for disabled people, I can only repeat that it seems that an opportunity is being lost when a mill set in such beautiful surroundings is not functioning at least as a tourist attraction. Perhaps one day the wheel at Sleninford Mill will turn again, attracting those who, in the words of that inscription of 1773, are forced to 'Toyle in fortune's Giddy Spheare' and who, increasingly,

Do not too Rafhlye deeme Amyfse
Of him that bydes Contented here.

York: Raindale Watermill, Castle Museum

Standing on the banks of York's 'other' river, the Foss, in the shadow of the castle walls and close to the site of the medieval Castle Mills, is Raindale Mill. A tiny mill from Raindale valley on the moors north of Pickering, it has an instant appeal, if only because it seems in imminent danger of being engulfed by the castle!

Raindale became a mill only in the early part of the nineteenth century, when an external overshot water-wheel fourteen feet in diameter, powering a single pair of stones and associated machinery, was installed at what had been a small cottage. The mill ground local wheat for bread-making and produced some animal feed. The Boulton family worked the mill from the beginning of this century until, in 1915, the stream supplying water to the leat installed for the mill changed course and the water-supply dried up.

Henry Boulton offered Raindale Mill to Dr John Kirk, the founder of Castle Museum, in 1935, but the advent of the Second World War delayed its transfer, and the mill was not brought to the site until 1953, finally opening in 1966. A lovely place, beautifully maintained – and one of the few remaining examples of the sort of unpretentious mill once found in abundance all over Britain.

Yorkshire, South

A recurring problem when dealing with Yorkshire is the alarming way in which settlements have 'migrated' over the years. The classical North, East and West Ridings of Domesday differ from, say, Pevsner's 1960s interpretation, while the most recent administrative changes, in the early 1970s, have resulted in yet more adjustments.

The present county of South Yorkshire contains few corn-mills, yet in Worsbrough it possesses a mill containing all the elements for a classical study of the history of corn-milling. By contrast the county has a rich concentration of industrial water-powered sites, and there can be few finer industrial museums anywhere in the world than those listed below.

Barnsley: Worsbrough Mill Museum – p.180.
Sheffield: Abbeydale Industrial Hamlet – p.181.
Sheffield: Sharrow Snuff-Mill – Tobacco-powdering mill; overshot wheel; close to Abbeydale.
Sheffield: Shepherd Wheel – p.182.
Wortley: Top Forge – p.183.

Barnsley: Worsbrough Mill Museum

The soke mill at Worsbrough was valued at 2s. in Domesday, among the lowest recorded in the book, but its actual location on the River Dove is not certain. This is a commonplace situation but it applies particularly to Yorkshire, perhaps the worst-recorded of all the counties, due to a combination of size and continuing unrest in the years leading to the preparation of the Survey.

The mill buildings are of various periods. The oldest part of the mill has been dated to 1625; it is a practical two-storey structure of sandstone. Two fireplaces at the north end confirm this was once the miller's home. The three-storey New Mill was added in the 1840s and is a good example of solid Victorian building with a touch of quality – I particularly like the windows. The millhouse is on higher ground and set at a right-angle to the mills overlooking the yard; the total effect is of a very satisfactory grouping.

The comparatively brief history of the New Mill encapsulates the developments of the period. The earlier mill had operated a service to the local farming community which had not changed since medieval times, even to taking the one-sixteenth toll before grinding. The new mill, with its steam-engine, was able to take advantage of greatly improved transport facilities created by the arrival of the Dearne & Dove Canal and the South Yorkshire Railway. This development, echoed in much of the Midlands and North, led to the rapid expansion of industry, ensuring a period of unparalleled prosperity for Worsbrough Mill. By the mid 1840s it had five pairs of stones producing a range of products, but the widespread introduction of roller-mills in the 1890s reversed the trend, and in a matter of years Worsbrough, like many other mills, was reduced to grinding small quantities of corn and producing feed for livestock. The New Mill closed, its engine scrapped, in 1922; the Old Mill continued working into the 1960s, by which time it was in a very poor condition.

The County Council took on the task of repairing the mills in 1972 – the result of their work was a national conservation award. Structurally the mill was unsound but much of the machinery remained, and a rare 1911 Hornsby hot-bulk oil-engine, rescued from a scrapheap, was rebuilt and installed as a replacement for the steam-engine. The overshot iron water-wheel (fourteen feet in diameter), had replaced a wooden wheel in 1864 – it supplies power to three pairs of French Burr stones which grind a small quantity of wholemeal flour for sale. Ancillary machinery, in exemplary condition, includes an oat-roller, kibbler, sack-hoist and separator. A pleasing feature of the mill is the voluntary admission charge and the provision of a good free leaflet.

Water for the millpond originally came from the Dove by a lengthy headrace. The building of a reservoir to act as feeder to the canal affected this supply, and alternative arrangements, rarely satisfactory to either miller or water authority, were implemented. Disputes were frequent, and a final resolution did not come until 1949, when the last miller discovered that the enabling Act for the Canal of 1793 was still on the Statute Book and that it included a £20-a-day penalty clause should the flow of water to the mill suffer. The Docks and Inland Waterways Executive, by then responsible for the reservoir, and probably aware of a dozen similar Acts with potentially ruinous clauses, quickly proposed a sensible compromise.

Sheffield: Abbeydale Industrial Hamlet

South Yorkshire is exceptionally fortunate in its industrial museums – Abbeydale and Worsbrough (p.180) are both outstanding examples bearing comparison with Styal (p.68) across the Pennines. Unlike Worsbrough and Styal, which owe a great debt to the inspiration of individuals, Abbeydale represents that rare thing, a successful committee project, in this case by the City Museums Department.

The River Sheaf, on which Abbeydale stands, is one of many fast-flowing streams which together supported more than 150 mills in the Sheffield area during the seventeenth and eighteenth centuries. The history of the Abbeydale site begins in the thirteenth century, for on or near it the monks of Beauchief Abbey had a smithy. One Hugh Stephenson was a tenant in the seventeenth century, and the records of the site are fairly complete since 1714. Major developments occurred in the late eighteenth century following the enlargement of the dam to four acres, making Abbeydale one of the largest water-powered sites on the river.

The main products were crown scythes (basically heavy-duty), patent riveted scythes (more easily produced and effectively an early form of mass production) and a wide range of agricultural edge-tools. Production continued until 1933 – not always smoothly, for there were several periods in the nineteenth century when unrest among the work-force led to violence (cf. Shepherd Wheel, p.182). Between 1842 and 1912 there were three explosions: two of an accidental nature, killing a total of three men; and one deliberate. During the Second World War Abbeydale returned briefly to life, producing steel for the war effort.

On walking round the site, the impression is that the visitor has arrived while the work-force is temporarily absent, perhaps at lunch. Working-tools lie waiting to be picked up, and only the lack of noise and heat from the furnaces betrays the fact that this is indeed a museum. On some days craftsmen do demonstrate the use of water-powered tilt-hammers, enhancing the fancy that Abbeydale is still a working hamlet. The complete sequence of production from the preparation of clay crucibles in which steel was melted to the protective painting used on the scythes is demonstrated in the various buildings.

Power for the machinery was provided by water-wheels fed from the dam above and behind the site. The tilt-hammers are driven by an eighteen-foot-diameter high-breast wheel developing around 30 hp – necessary because the machinery weighs some twenty-three tonnes when in motion! The grinding-hull, where the scythe blades were sharpened on grindstones weighing up to two tonnes, required a wheel of similar proportions. Slightly smaller in diameter, though much narrower, is the blowing-engine water-wheel. The blowing-engine supplied the draught to heat the hearth of the tilt forge. A small iron wheel powered the boring-machines. These last two wheels are overshot. Three of the wheels are supplied with water through the same pentrough; a separate shuttle, or sluice, over the blowing-engine wheel allows individual control of the flow; only the grinding-hull wheel has its own pentrough.

The visitor is free to stroll round the whole complex, including an audio-visual display, stores, the manager's house and the counting-house – the 'office'. Abbeydale is not the place for a brief visit: leisurely investigation is repaid with a very tangible sense of history.

Sheffield: Shepherd Wheel

Shepherd Wheel is typical of the mills which sprang up wherever suitable fast-flowing rivers were found. There is, however, a noticeable contrast with Abbeydale (p.181), where a number of products were produced and several crafts employed. Here, in the long, narrow, heavily wooded valley of the River Potter, there was a cutlery-grinding plant, its ten sandstone grindstones powered by a large (seventeen feet by six) overshot wheel. The water for the wheel was drawn from an equally long, narrow dam above the small building.

It is possible that this is a site of some antiquity – a plaque on the wall suggests that it may be the 'Potar Whele' mentioned in a will of 1584. The present building takes its name from an eighteenth-century owner, and in this secluded setting it is somehow difficult to imagine Mr Shepherd or his successors experiencing the sort of problems with the work-force that beset John Dyson, owner of Abbeydale in the 1840s, where the grinding-hull building was blown up with gunpowder following Dyson's use of non-union labour. Nowadays the two sites share a common ownership, the Sheffield City Museum.

Shepherd Wheel is not easy to find, although it is on some sort of nature or industrial heritage trail; unhappily, when I visited it, the difficulties were compounded by a lack of signs (probably vandalized). Parking is almost impossible; it reminds me of a similar problem in Jesmond Dene Park, Newcastle (p.169), where the local authority seems to be determined to ignore the existence of the motor-car.

Wortley: Top Forge, near Sheffield

Perhaps I spent too long working in and around gas-works, but I admit that my visit to the industrial site at Top Forge was to be more duty than pleasure. A first view hardly helped – the site is difficult to locate and easily overlooked (literally, since much of it is level with, or below, the road). But the millwright, Duncan Smith, was working on the site, and he stayed for almost two hours, conveying his knowledge of, and sense of excitement in, Top Forge, transforming my visit.

Top Forge was built between 1605 and 1625 and is thought to be the only ironworks of its kind still on its original site. In its time it has produced iron for nail-making, but its prime purpose was the forging of railway axles, a purpose it fulfilled until 1910.

Even to a non-engineer, the scale and completeness of Top Forge are most impressive. A wide range of lovingly tended machine tools remain, bearing a more than passing resemblance to large creatures from pre-history. Yet these are no dinosaurs, more slumbering giants capable of stirring and undertaking the work for which they were fashioned, as they do on several occasions a year. A dramatic demonstration of the meaning of water-power is provided when the sluices at Top Forge open, water begins to flood down from the dam and the large pitch-back wheel gathers speed. One of the two breastshot wheels also works, and machinery on display includes tilt- and forge-hammers, wooden jib-cranes and many small working engines.

For me, Top Forge is a perfect evocation of the type of small industrial site on which Britain's prosperity was built. Far from the popular image of a pretty mill in an idyllic pastoral setting, it still represents a vital stage in the history of the water-wheel.

Yorkshire, West

Like South Yorkshire, West Yorkshire has few sites other than industrial mills. The two below, housed in old mills, are both excellent museums.

Bradford: Bradford Industrial Museum – Very large four-storey mill;

includes examples of prime movers in local industry; breastshot wheel restored and coupled to electric drive; engineering and textile displays.

Leeds: Armley Mills Industrial Museum – Outstanding Georgian mill on River Aire; built 1806 – last worked 1969; carding- fulling- and corn-mill and once world's largest woollen-mill; contains breast- and overshot wheels with much other machinery; working water-wheel, fulling-stocks; various exhibitions.

Wales

Clwyd

Clwyd County Council has made great efforts to preserve its industrial heritage in recent years. Its most important current project is at Pentrefoelas, where the entire village is being redeveloped. In addition, there is an excellent Industrial Trail at Bersham, which included Felin Puleston. Sadly, it and King's (or New) Mill on the Erddig Estate have gone in the last few years, one in a dramatic explosion. This is particularly galling, for both had a long and fascinating history. King's Mill was also quite remarkably fully documented because, almost from the first reference to it in 1315, it was at the centre of centuries of attempts by locals to rid themselves of the archaic 'suit of mills' (more commonly known as soke rights), which they did not finally achieve until 1854.

Loggerheads: Pentre Mill, Loggerheads Country Park, near Mold – Corn-mill believed to have been built prior to 1796; added to at various times; cast-iron and timber overshot wheel driving two pairs of stones – only one now working; operated as combined corn- and saw-mill between 1880s and 1921; well-maintained mill, now part of Information Centre in Clwyd C.C.-owned Country Park.

Pentrefoelas Mill – p.186.

Rossett Mill, near Wrexham – half-timbered corn-mill; building has date 1661 carved on it – possibility that it may be fourteenth-century in origin; large nineteenth-century external breastshot wheel, cast-iron with wooden paddles; part now used by local council – part currently (spring 1988) being converted, apparently to house.

Rossett: BASC Gift Shop – heavily adapted mill, opposite Rossett Mill, being used by BASC as a gift shop; undershot wooden water-wheel turning free; has remains of older wheel in series with it; mill is three-storey white-painted brick with large modern four-bay extension; latter has produced violent reactions – Pevsner is positively apoplectic, I confess I can live with it.

Pentrefoelas Mill

The 'man of the mill' was one of thirty-seven separate vocations noted in Pentrefoelas in 1857. The majority of the activities listed were connected with the essential maintenance of a large manorial estate. With the breaking up of the estates and of their associated rural industries, villages like Pentrefoelas went into what appeared to be terminal decline. Even the advent of the motor-car and of tourism had little effect on this straggling village alongside the A5 – indeed the growing weight of traffic simply increased its problems. This is by no means a unique situation, it applies in many parts of England and Scotland as well as in Wales, but at Pentrefoelas proposals are being introduced which, it is hoped, will restore the community to its past strengths.

The watermill has both a practical and symbolic part to play in the imaginative programme being undertaken by Welsh Heritage. The intention is nothing less than to recreate a living village, which can be seen as a development of the ideas already being implemented at the Welsh Folk Museum at St Fagan's, Cardiff (see p. 201), and on a smaller scale at Erddig, Wrexham.

The present mill was built in 1817 and is a sturdy, attractive building lying right beside the A5. The cast-iron overshot wheel is eighteen feet in diameter and 43½ inches wide; it was cast at Llanrwst Foundry and contains 56 elm buckets. Water is supplied along a slate launder from a smallish mill-pond, fed from the River Nug. Since Clwyd County Council took a twenty-year lease on the mill, they have already begun work on restoring the early nineteenth-century machinery. It powers three pairs of stones, including French Burr and Anglesey millstones. The internal timbers are being sandblasted, and clear perspex sheets will be installed to protect visitors from the moving parts of the machinery.

The hope is that the mill will be open to the public by the middle of 1988. As with all the projects at Pentrefoelas, the mill has to be commercially viable and the intention is that it should soon be selling its own flour in 32 kilo bags. George Heald, the son of the last miller here, has been acting as adviser, and the whole project is under the enthusiastic direction of Berwyn Evans of Welsh Heritage.

I referred above to the symbolism of the part played by the watermill in a community. So often the demise of the village watermill during the last century has been accompanied by a running-down, not just of other skills, but of the population and prosperity of the whole area. With the restoration of mills such as Pentrefoelas perhaps we can begin to see a return to a degree of self-sufficiency among many communities, not just in Wales, but throughout Britain.

Dyfed

One of my 'core' counties, and full of fascinating mills. They range from very basic corn-mills to woollen-mills and include museums and the only tidemill left in Wales.

Carew and Y Felin at Cenarth are mills standing in very different but wonderfully dramatic settings; Black Pool is handsome, Middle Mill and Tregwynt are more practical but interesting mills. Felin Geri and Y Felin at St Dogmaels are maintaining the traditional mill and proving that it can work successfully. Others in the list demonstrate 'new' uses for mills.

If you have the opportunity, do take the (slightly misleadingly named) Factory Trail at Dre-fach Felindre. It really does provide a potted history of what has been, and is, happening to mills – not just in Wales but throughout Britain. But then, on a wider canvas, so does the whole of Dyfed and, as elsewhere in Wales, there is a growing awareness of the importance of these historic places – would that the situation applied in some English counties.

Aberystwyth: Felin Gyffin – Small, two-storey corn-mill dated 1714; overshot cast-iron and timber wheel, installed 1870s; flour-production ceased in 1930s, animal feedstuffs about 1970; millhouse a restaurant.

Canaston Bridge: Black Pool Mill, near Narberth – p.188.

Capel Dewi: Rock Mills, near Llandysul – Small, water-powered woollen-mill – one of few remaining in Wales; founded 1890 – still in same family ownership; original wheel; water provides power for carding and spinning; produces woollen yarn for sale in own shop.

Carew: French Tidemill – p.189.

Cenarth: Y Felin – p.190.

Cwm Cou: Felin Geri, near Newcastle Emlyn – p.191.

Dre-fach Felindre: Museum of the Welsh Woollen Industry, near Newcastle Emlyn – Old water-powered machinery amongst exhibits tracing development of the industry in Wales; adjoining Melin Teifi has seven looms producing woollen cloth for sale – water-wheel is to be installed in original position; a number of water-powered woollen-mills survive in West Wales – museum maintains invaluable list; a 'factory trail' walk passes many of the mills in the area of Dre-fach Felindre; trail represents a fascinating microcosm of present situation in whole of Britain – some working, some derelict, some converted.

Furnace: Dyfi Furnace, near Aberystwyth – Founded in 1750s on seventeenth-century silver-refining site; blast furnace – used local charcoal but iron ore from Cumbria; bellows driven by water-wheel; adapted for use as saw-mill early in twentieth century – thirty-one-foot-diameter water-wheel added at same time; close to picturesque Dyfi Falls; restored by Cadw, Welsh Historic Monuments.

Llandysul: Maesllyn Woollen-Mill Museum – Nineteenth-century mill, one of many based on Yorkshire mill design in Teifi Valley; built 1881, much of original machinery still operating and some driven from restored water-wheels; working mill museum aiming to provide nineteenth-century atmosphere; various displays including audio-visual woollen and craft goods for sale; nature trail.

Llangolman: Pont Hywel Mill, near Clynderwen – Small, delightful eighteenth-century corn-mill in very rural valley on Preseli Hills; no machinery; remains of leat; interesting conversion by Richard and Fran Boultbee to use as slate workshop-showroom; uses local slate in products.

Ponterwyd: Llywernog Silver/Lead-Mine – Small mid-nineteenth-century mineral mine; mining ended 1910 – site abandoned until 1973; now Mid-Wales Mining Museum; among exhibits depicting history of mineral mining in Wales are six water-wheels including fifty-foot-diameter great wheel of mine; four are working.

Porthrhyd: Melin Maesdulais, near Carmarthen – p.192.

St Dogmaels: Y Felin (TCG), near Cardigan – p.193.

St Nicholas: Tregwynt Woollen-Mill, Letterston, near Haverfordwest – Remote site in deeply wooded valley; group of buildings established in fulling-mill site in eighteenth-century; worked continuously for 200 years – owned by same family since 1912; wide internal water-wheel still turns; water-course; visitors can watch weaving in progress; shop.

Solva: The Corn-Mill, near St David's – p.194.

Solva: Middle Mill, near St David's – p.194.

Treffgarne: Nant-y-Coy Watermill, near Haverfordwest – Pleasant, restored mill by busy road (A40); overshot external wheel and some internal machinery; small museum; scenic walk to Treffgarne Rock.

Canaston Bridge: Black Pool Mill, near Narberth

Black Pool Mill presents an imposing picture when seen from the road; the unpainted back is less impressive, although the presence of the Eastern Cleddau immediately behind the mill adds to its visual appeal. The mill was built in 1813 and is a tall, four-storey, white-painted stone building with balancing two-storey extensions at either end. Water flows under the building. The original eleven-foot-nine-inch-wide water-wheel drove four pairs of stones for corn-grinding. At the end of the century the process became uneconomic and the wheel was replaced by a turbine powering seven pairs of stones. The mill continued to operate until the 1950s.

Black Pool Mill was restored in 1968, with the turbine and other machinery driven by electric motor. Recent work on the sluices has resulted in an increase of water-flow along the leat, and in 1987 the turbine and wheels were able once more to turn on water-power.

The mill features a museum of nineteenth-century model steam-engines and a well-equipped wheelwright's shop. There are walks along the river bank and a forest walk. A display of replicas of the extinct animals of Wales, including bears, reindeer and wild boar, not to mention the Welsh Dragon, does not seem entirely appropriate, if only because the last is not extinct – it is the creature I watch devouring fifteen white-clad sacrifices at Twickenham or the National Stadium each year!

Carew: French Tidemill

One of three surviving tidemills in Britain, and the only example left in Wales. The setting is even more romantic – and certainly more remote – than that at Woodbridge (p.154). The mill straddles the mudflats of the Carew River, just a couple of hundred yards below the dramatic ruins of Carew Castle.

There is evidence to suggest that there was a fresh-water-powered mill close to the castle but among the earliest records of the mill is a lease of 1558. At the time the mill belonged to the Crown, but after what appears to have been a period of neglect by tenants it reverted to the ownership of the Carew family. The date of construction of the present four-storey building is not known but it must have been built around 1800. One suggestion as to the acquisition of the name is that there is French influence in the design and that mill experts fleeing from the Revolution in France worked on the mill.

Carew was fortunate in that it could attract two types of business – the usual local farming work was supplemented by coastal trade provided by small craft. The mill possessed two wheels and was able to grind barley, corn, animal feed and fertilizers, including bonemeal; the bones were stored in the attached two-storey building. Granted this variety, it is a little surprising that the mill ceased to work as early as 1937, slowly becoming derelict.

The wheels are undershot and are set beneath the mill in the causeway. The causeway was built, damming the river and creating a twenty-three-acre millpond; in order to supplement the limited tidal flow. The danger of flooding led to the body of the mill being raised above the high-water level, a common precaution. Both wheels are of iron with wooden paddles and are sixteen feet in diameter; the unrestored north wheel is the wider. The arrangement of mill and machinery follows a conventional pattern, the ground floor containing the bulk of the machinery and the spur-wheel – driven via a vertical pitch-pine shaft. There are six pairs of stones on the stone floor. On this and the second floor are a variety of machines including an oat-roller and a cattlecake-crusher. The garner floor retains the sack-hoist mechanism.

Initial work on renovating the mill began in the 1960s and was completed in 1972, winning two major conservation awards. In 1984 the lease of the mill passed into the hands of the Pembrokeshire Coast National Park. The Authority has continued restoration work and has installed an audio-visual unit as part of a policy of developing the educational value of the mill. It is hoped that the south wheel will soon be turning some of the auxiliary machinery again. I've written elsewhere about the (alleged) emphasis in all three surviving tidemills on a museum-like atmosphere (Eling, p.101, does produce a little flour). Some may regret this; I am only happy that they remain for our enjoyment.

Cenarth: Y Felin

No book celebrating mills could possibly omit the mill at Cenarth. It vies with Thrum Mill in Northumberland – now a private house (see p.129) – for the prize as the most dramatic and picturesquely sited mill in Britain. Happily, after a period of neglect, it is now being restored and visitors are welcome. The rapidly moving waters of the Teifi tumble over the shallow waterfalls of Cenarth in front of the small mill perched in what seems a most precarious position on the edge of the bank.

The present three-storey mill probably dates from the eighteenth century; it has two pairs of stones powered by an undershot wheel of wood and cast-iron construction. The stones were used for the grinding of oats and barley. There is a small kiln for drying oats on the ground floor, a common feature in areas of high rainfall. The layout of the mill and machinery is conventional.

Cenarth village has a long, well-documented, history. Giraldus Cambrensis (Gerald of Wales) visited it in 1188 during his travels through Wales, writing of the church of St Llawddogs, the mill and bridge and an orchard and garden beside the river. After crushing the Welsh in the war of 1282-3, Edward I became lord of the manor in 1284, passing his lands in Wales to his son in 1301 when creating him the first Prince of Wales.

In the early part of the fifteenth century many mills in the area were destroyed by the supporters of Owain Glyndwyr as part of a campaign to remove the hated Norman influence – a campaign which, in a sense, ended only when Raglan and other Marcher castles were slighted by English and Welsh alike in 1646-7. Cenarth may have survived; it certainly remained a Crown possession until it was sold by James I in 1613.

In the next few years the mill went through several changes of ownership but after that brief, unsettled phase was bought by the Vaughan family, passing to the Cawdor family early in the nineteenth century. At that time the earls of Cawdor were the largest landowners in Wales, and the mill must have been a valuable asset, functioning as a community mill until after the Second World War before falling into the all-too-familiar pattern of decay during the 1960s and 1970s.

Y Felin remained in the hands of the Cawdor family until the 1970s, when all their estates in West Wales were broken up to pay death duties. In 1983 Martin Fowler and his wife bought the mill and began the slow process of restoring it to working order. While doing so, they are involved in another aspect of the life of the village, running the post office.

Cwm Cou: Felin Geri, near Newcastle Emlyn

Felin Geri is one of the remarkably few mills which really do fit the image of a typical small mill. It stands in the remote and lovely wooded valley of the River Ceri near its junction with the even lovelier Teifi. The farm buildings, including the mill, are somehow all of a piece and satisfying even to someone who may never have heard of vernacular architecture. A bakery sells produce made from flour ground on the site. Friendly and familiar farm animals are everywhere and, for good measure, the staff are charming and helpful. Not that all this has occurred by chance. The whole project has been carefully planned, and the restoration work earned the mill a European Architectural Heritage Award in 1975.

Felin Geri has done well to obtain grants from various sources – the Capps at Dunster (p.140) are others who have succeeded in this respect. There sometimes seems to be a degree of prejudice against those who use ‘the system’ to support their restoration but, for my part, I reject the implied criticism. The preservation of our heritage, industrial or natural, takes precedence over some imagined superior moral standpoint involving unsupported amateur action and ‘by the sweat of my brow’ restoration (not that receiving grants removes the necessity for hard physical effort). Such large conservation bodies as the National Trust and the RSPB do not hesitate to use grants – nor does the farming community in general, and we rightly applaud them for their professionalism.

Apart from the mill's 'looking good', its history follows a classic pattern. The details are contained in an excellent leaflet which could almost serve as a primer on mill history. The first record of the mill, as so often, is in a legal transfer of the seventeenth century, when the keeping of records became more organized. In this case it is a marriage settlement of 1610, although the mill is thought to date from the 1580s. As part of the Cilgwyn Estate, the mill had an important role in the local community, and it is frequently mentioned in succeeding transactions.

Felin Geri was enlarged early in the nineteenth century, with the addition of a third storey. There was a widespread move in the mid nineteenth century to replace wooden wheels with iron, and Felin Geri followed the pattern. In 1872 a wheel cast at the Cardigan Iron Foundry was installed, although, as elsewhere, wooden cog teeth were retained to ensure quiet running. In the early 1880s more 'labour-intensive' methods were installed at many estate mills, and Felin Geri added a saw-mill powered by a second wheel. Standing side by side in the mill-stream, the wheels are overshot but turn in opposite directions, as the earlier wheel is pitch-back, providing the additional power required for corn-grinding. The introduction of roller-milling proved a body-blow to most old-style corn-mills, and the saw-mill became the main source of income during the early years of this century. The Second World War delayed closure of many mills, and Felin Geri struggled on into the 1950s, operating as a saw-mill.

Duncan and Sarah Fitzwilliams bought the derelict mill in 1972 – an appropriate purchase as his family had owned Felin Geri for much of the nineteenth century and had deposited the historically valuable papers of the estate in the National Library of Wales. Mr Fitzwilliams formed a partnership with Michael Heycock and began the process of restoring the mill, not just to working order but to economic viability. During the next few years they expanded production and, importantly, their markets. A judicious use of extra attractions has helped to make Felin Geri one of the most successful of the new breed of working mills, but I have to say that, sadly, the addition of a 'Wild West' fort in 1987 has not added to the charm of the complex.

Porthrhyd: Melin Maesdulais, near Carmarthen

For most of the eighteenth and nineteenth centuries Melin Maesdulais, a three-storey, late-eighteenth-century corn-mill, ground oats and barley for local farmers. In common with many other small mills, it was converted to a woollen-mill in the 1890s, and its name

Clwyd – BASC Gift Shop, Rossett, near Wrexham. An attractive three-storey brick mill now used as a gift shop. An extension, on the left, has been the subject of some controversy.

Dyfed – French Tidemill, Carew. This fine tidemill lies across the Carew River, just below the romantic, ruined Carew Castle. It has been extensively repaired in recent years.

Dyfed – Felin Geri Mill, Cwm Cou, near Newcastle Emlyn. This tiny mill has two wheels which turn in opposite directions. It stands in a beautiful position in the deeply wooded valley of the River Ceri.

Dyfed – Y Felin, St Dogmaels, near Cardigan. First recorded in the 1640s, but almost certainly the mill of St Dogmaels Abbey just across the road. The wheel is from a disused mill at St David's.

Dyfed – Y Felin, Cenarth. Set in most picturesque fashion above the Cenarth Falls, this lovely little mill has recently reopened to the public.

Gwynedd – Felin Faesog, Tai'n Lon, Clynnogfawr. One of two lovely old mills in Gwynedd, this seventeenth-century mill is not working but contains a small museum showing Welsh country life.

Gwynedd – Felin Isaf, Llansantffraio, near Colwyn Bay. A typical mill setting – Felin Isaf on the banks of Y Nant-y-Garreg Ddu. The smaller Clover Mill dates from the 1680s, the main mill from 1749.

Gwynedd – Howell Mill, Llanddeusant, Anglesey. A lovely, timeless place in a remote part of Anglesey. A genuine working mill which has served its community unceasingly for over 600 years.

Powys – Bacheldre Mill, Church Stoke. Work on restoring the mill, strongly built of good local stone, only began in 1985 but the machinery was in such good condition that the mill is already producing flour.

South Glamorgan – Melin Bompren Corn-Mill, St Fagans. Reconstruction of this fine example of a corn-mill from Dyfed on its new site at the Welsh Folk Museum took seven years to complete.

South Glamorgan – Esgair Moel Water-Powered Woollen-Mill, St Fagans. One of many beautifully preserved buildings at St Fagans, this woollen-mill is from Llanwrtyd Wells.

Central – Clock Mill, Tillicoultry. The well-preserved lade used to provide water to power the wheel of the Clock spinning mill.

Highland – Mill of Tore, Balnain. This good example of a well-preserved community mill stands deep in lovely countryside in Glen Urquhart.

Lothian – Preston Mill, East Linton. A very attractive estate mill, built in 1660. The kiln (behind) is possibly two centuries older.

Highland – Clack Mill, Highland Folk Museum, Kingussie. A rare survival of the once common clack mill. This well-restored example is from Back on the Isle of Lewis.

Strathclyde – New Lanark Mills. The lengthy process of renovating this remarkable complex of cotton-mills built by David Dale and Robert Owen along the River Clyde is nearing completion.

Tayside – Mill of Blair Atholl, Pitlochry. Parts of this popular tourist attraction on the A9 probably date to about 1613. Closed in 1929, it was renovated in the 1970s.

was changed to Maesdulais Factory. It continued in production until 1925, after which it fell into disuse and considerable disrepair. When Geoff Brace bought the mill in 1977 the only piece of machinery remaining was the water-wheel – he has installed all the internal machinery. The significance of that remark is that Mr Brace has not hesitated to use modern machinery in the restoration, which was completed in early 1983.

Melin Maesdulais is powered by a belt-driven overshot water-wheel, fifteen feet in diameter, driving the millstones and ancillary machinery. After being separated out using a Barnard's Horizontal Smutter, the grain is 'hoovered' from the first to the second floor for storage before returning to the first floor to be ground. Magnets remove any metallic impurities.

All the internal machinery is also capable of being powered by a modern oil/electric-engine. Mr Brace takes the view – quite properly, I think – that there is no point in ignoring modern technology when it can be harnessed to ease the miller's burden. Naturally, the product must not suffer, and so he, like most millers, continues to use traditional French Burr stones, as the slow-grinding action associated with these millstones results in a flour of a quality unimpaired by overheating, a common fault in flour produced by roller-milling.

St Dogmaels: Y Felin, near Cardigan

A number of the mills listed in this book have connections with religious establishments. Few are physically closer – divided by a road – than Y Felin is to the twelfth-century St Dogmaels Abbey. Yet, logical though it may be to presume a relationship between the two, no firm evidence exists to link them. Industrial archaeologists have frequently faced this problem in the relatively short time the discipline has existed, and it appears not to be near resolution. Is the purpose of industrial archaeology to record facts or can it offer an interpretation – perhaps after the study of associated evidence? This is not the place to step into a (sometimes bitter) dispute between factions, but St Dogmaels provides a nice, if minor, example of the dilemma. The absence of proof will weigh heavily with what might be termed the scientific school, while the interpreters will conclude that the mill was the abbey mill.

The records of the mill date from the 1640s, a period when the formal recording of legal transfers and sales began to be treated seriously. It was obviously a typical community mill and a valuable asset. For that reason, perhaps, it has had relatively few owners. The Pembrokeshire landowning family of Webley Parry owned the mill during the late eighteenth and early nineteenth century, adding the third storey and renewing the machinery of the mill. Later the

Gwynne family acquired and worked the mill until the 1920s, after which it struggled to survive. The Second World War brought a brief reprieve, but by the 1950s the redevelopment of the abbey, by the Department of the Environment (predecessors of Cadw), seemed paradoxically to spell the end of the mill.

It was not until 1977, when Mike and Jane Hall bought Y Felin, that the situation improved, and within ten years they had achieved the near miracle of restoring the mill to working order, creating a commercial enterprise. From the start of the restoration, the Halls were determined to employ the same or similar materials used in the original mill. When replacement was necessary – in the case of the overshot wheel – a wheel was taken from a disused mill at St David's and combined with the axle and hub of the original wheel. Oak and beech were used in the wooden parts of the mechanism, and unseasoned elm for the new paddles. The surprisingly small millpond, which had been filled in during the 1950s, was cleared and reflooded in 1981.

Y Felin is a three-storey mill with an oat-drying kiln attached – a common feature of the west coast of Britain. The original tiles have gone, to be replaced by a steel sheet over an open fire. At one time the kiln would have been fired by a fore-runner of modern smokeless fuel called culm, a briquette formed of local clay and coaldust. Interestingly, in Cardiganshire this was usually provided by the farmer whose oats were to be dried.

The fourteen-foot wheel provides power to three sets of stones – one French Burr, two Derbyshire, and the mill now grinds speciality flours in addition to wholemeal, which is sold to local bakeries. On the way to achieving their aims, the Halls have found time to help several newcomers to milling. Their enthusiasm seems unabated, for when we arrived unannounced, on a cold winter Sunday afternoon, they were out, but on their return Mr Hall promptly opened up the mill for four of us to walk round.

Solva: The Corn-Mill and Middle Mill, near St David's

The two mills on this old site lie along a narrow road, about one mile inland and above the once thriving coal- and lime-trade port of Solva. The corn-mill belonged originally to the bishops of St David. The present mill is of eighteenth-century origin, though considerably restored and strengthened in recent years. It last worked in 1950 but all the machinery, both external and internal, remains. The leat, which originally supplied water to both mills, has been excavated, and the new owners of the Corn-Mill (the Palmers) are considering the possibility of restarting the overshot wheel for display purposes.

The mill is open as a tea-room and craft shop and for the sale of 'kitchenalia'.

Middle Mill was a water-powered woollen-mill transferred here on 31 January 1907 from St David's by the Griffiths family, who already owned the corn-mill. The external cast-iron wheel with wooden paddles is still in position; it originally powered the carding-machines using water drawn from the leat of the corn-mill. The mill was converted to oil in the late 1940s – shortly before electricity arrived in the area. The present owner, Mr Grime, hopes to reach an arrangement with the Palmers to draw water from the newly restored leat to drive the wheel. Of the internal machinery only the drive-wheel remains, together with one old fulling-machine.

Gwent

Gwent has suffered from a loss of mills in recent years, but Skenfrith remains and is a traditional working mill with a very long history. Sadly, it is not open to the public.

Skenfrith Mill (TCG) – Working mill beside Norman castle; first recorded 1300; parts of present mill date to 1500s with additions in 1650 and 1867; two pairs of French composition stones; produces range of flours and animal feed; NOT OPEN but undershot wheel can be seen turning from public right of way.

Gwynedd

In Gwynedd there are two mills of quite remarkable quality. I venture to suggest that you will come no nearer the heart of the mystery of mills and their recurring fascination than at Howell Mill (Melin Selar) and Felin Faesog. But don't disregard Felin Isaf, a mill with a long history containing a high percentage of its original fabric.

Golan: Brynkir Woollen-Mill, Garn Dolbenmaen, near Porthmadog – References to cornmill on site since fourteenth century; converted from seventeenth-century fulling-mill on River Henwy in 1830; continuous working since in ownership of same family; looms etc now powered by turbine and mains electricity; original overshot wheel still turns; present buildings can only be termed functional; all woollen products on sale in shop made on premises; same owner (W.H. Evans) is considering restoring Bryncir Corn-Mill, Melin Llecheiddior, to working order.

Llanberis: Welsh Slate Museum – Museum of slate-quarrying industry on site of Dinorwic Slate Quarry Workshops – closed 1969; fifty-foot-diameter, five-foot-wide pitch-back wheel with

140 buckets – largest iron wheel and second largest water-wheel in existence (after Laxey, p.111); built Caernarfon 1870 – provided power for workshops for fifty years; will hopefully turn again if water-supply can be restored.

Llanddeusant: Howell Mill (Melin Selar), Anglesey – below.

Llansantffraid: Felin Isaf, near Colwyn Bay, Clwyd – p.197.

Tai'n Lon: Felin Faesog, Clynnogfawr – p.198.

Tanygrisiau: Melin Moelwyn, near Blaenau Festiniog – Small fulling-mill in area not associated with fulling; evidence suggests established in eighteenth century or earlier; present mill 1880s, ceased to operate in 1964; external overshot water-wheel; original machinery including 'Kilburn' fulling-stocks; restored and run by Gwynedd C.C.

Llanddeusant: Howell Mill, Anglesey

With Felin Faesog (see below) at the other end of the county, Howell Mill or Melin Hywel or Melin Selar makes an almost perfect introduction to the pleasures of old mills. Both are typical examples of the small country mill which has existed throughout England and Wales since Saxon times, serving tiny communities. Both give an effective impression of being entirely genuine, and the 'rightness' of their atmosphere has to be experienced – it is almost tangible. Both are run by remarkable people, yet there the similarity between them ends, for Howell is still working after being in existence on this site for 600 years, and Mr I.W. Owen, who runs the mill for his aunt, Mrs Williams, speaks English as a courtesy to his visitors from that country. By contrast, Faesog has not worked for years and houses a museum, albeit depicting Welsh country life, developed and run by a relative newcomer, Kathleen Smith.

Howell Mill was built beside the Afon Alaw over 600 years ago. It was extended in the 1850s, and probably on other, earlier occasions, but is basically the mill which, Mr Owen proudly stresses, has never stopped working and serving its community since 1352. It operates as a corn-mill but also sells bought-in animal feed. The family have owned it since at least 1817, and for much of that time payment was probably mainly in kind or by toll. The latter was usually a bushel of oats – eight quarts; a bushel of wheat or barley – six quarts.

The large, external wheel is overshot, fed by a leat which passes the farmhouse in which Mrs Williams lives. There is a pond with ducks, a dog who 'borrows' sandwiches from Mr Owen, and a number of peacocks. Inside, the mill machinery and gearing are conventional, with beechwood teeth on the cogs. Note that the three working pairs of French Burr stones are set in a straight line.

Among the problems facing all old working structures are

deterioration (a particular problem facing mills, with their continual stress) and subsequent, often botched restoration. Howell Mill was partly rebuilt in the 1970s, and in 1978 the architect sensibly entered the result in a conservation competition organized by Times Newspapers and the Royal Institute of Chartered Surveyors. Today the plaque confirming its first place in the competition is borne proudly on the wall of the mill. Those of us who occasionally meet architects socially and can confirm that they are often urbane, civilized fellows who know which way to pass the port, sometimes fall to wondering why the sight of a drawing-board seems to turn the balance of their collective minds. In the circumstances, I think it only right to acknowledge this rare success!

Please note that Howell is a working mill and is shown only as a courtesy to visitors. If you arrive at an inconvenient time, when business is being transacted, or at lunch, you must expect to wait. In this most lovely and peaceful of valleys, one of the most pleasant spots I know inland on Anglesey, that will be no hardship. Alternatively, you could take yourself off to look at the local landmark – Llynon Windmill, a stone tower-mill, three storeys high and well restored by the local Ynyf-Mon Borough Council. Once Llynon is grinding corn again, poor Pakenham (p.151) will lose its claim to be the only parish in Britain with working wind- and watermills.

Llansantffraid: Felin Isaf, near Colwyn Bay, Clwyd

Felin Isaf is an almost unique survival – much of the stone fabric and roof structure are original, and the mill dates, in part, from the 1680s. The mill stands in a beautiful, heavily wooded valley just below the A470, and the stone used was quarried from the cliff opposite. The first records are dated 1699, and later records confirm that the mill was being leased and was enlarged in 1749, when a second mill was added. In 1809 the original mill was converted to a clover-mill.

Most of the mill machinery was installed in 1730, although the mill houses some more modern machinery including parts rescued from a windmill and installed in 1891. In 1855 an oat-drying house was built at Felin Isaf. As I've noted elsewhere, the kiln is a common occurrence in the wetter areas of Britain – what makes this one unusual are the curved walls.

Although operations were drastically reduced during this century, the mill didn't finally close until 1942. Happily, the machinery survived and was restored in 1978, with the rest of the mill, under a job-creation scheme. The aim was to re-create nineteenth-century conditions, and for a time the mill ground corn regularly. Educational visits were, and are under the new owners, a speciality of the mill, although, sadly, it is not grinding at present. Modern buildings house the craft and tea shop and, for my taste, detract from the mill – a pity, because it is maintained in really fine condition with excellent signing and display panels.

Tai'n Lon: Felin Faesog, Clynnogfawr

A totally delightful little mill set in a small, remote valley – a survivor of an age which has irrevocably passed away. The communities this sort of mill served were always small, close-knit and self-sufficient until the 'modern' world arrived in the mid-twentieth century with council houses and electricity. How very appropriate that in such an area, where memories remain strong, there should be a small but near perfect museum dedicated to old Welsh country life. Each item in the collection has been selected in a manner which enhances one of several themes, and each is beautifully presented and maintained. For example, the stove is blacked and shiny-clean in a way entirely reminiscent of that in the house in Berkshire where I grew up.

This should not be read as nostalgia for the 'good old days', tempered as it is by memories of learning to read by oil-lamps, of the nightmarish quality of winter mornings washing faces in ice-spiked water (from the sort of pretty, rose-printed wash-basins so sought-after today) and of outside privies beyond the chicken shed! And do not wonder why local people in villages all round Britain flocked to enter the previously undreamed-of comfort of the council house. But memories do fade and fashions change, and now we like to be reminded – in comfort – of those days.

At Felin Faesog, Kathleen Smith has succeeded remarkably well, yet without sentiment, in evoking memories of what is still close in time but already distant in history. Perhaps, granted that this is a remarkable woman, we should not be too surprised. Once Deputy Governor of Holloway Prison, she is a prolific writer, with several television and radio plays to her credit and a book, *Help for the Bereaved*, which has given comfort to millions in both Britain and the USA.

Felin Faesog stands by the Afon Desach and is a mill of some antiquity, dating from the seventeenth century. Most of the machinery remains, including an iron pit-wheel linked to the external overshot wooden water-wheel by a wooden axle. Ms Smith has a list of the mere dozen or so millers who operated the mill from 1682 to its closure in 1938. Much of the restoration work carried out in the period prior to its reopening in 1981 was accomplished with the help of an MSC team.

It is a matter of historic record that the roots of millions of us lie (pre-Industrial Revolution) in communities served by mills like Felin Faesog. And we enjoy visiting them, learning about them, because ultimately, whatever drawbacks they had, the 'folk memory' is good. Kathleen Smith, explains in one of her books why country people were happy: 'They had a good foundation for happiness.' Do not bypass tiny Felin Faesog.

Mid Glamorgan

There is only one mill in the Mid Glamorgan area which currently qualifies for inclusion.

Hengoed: Ystrad Mill, Ystrad Mynych – Earliest recorded date 1721, thought to be older; pitch-back wheel; pleasant site on edge of commercial area.

Powys

Powys has suffered from a loss of mills in recent years – particularly woollen-mills at once-important sites like Newton. Bacheldre is well worth a visit, although it is distinctly on its own in the beautiful but still undiscovered country beyond Bishop's Castle.

Felin Crewi is just one of the many pleasures which lie near to that marvellous cross-country road, the A470, and the Centre for Alternative Technology is only a few miles away for those wishing to compare old and new ideas.

Church Stoke: Bacheldre Mill, near Montgomery – below.
Machynlleth: Centre for Alternative Technology – Modern ten-foot overshot water-wheel included in demonstrations of independent energy systems.
Penegoes: Felin Crewi, near Machynlleth – p.200.

Church Stoke: Bacheldre Mill, near Montgomery

This is one of those odd areas where Powys takes a bite out of Shropshire, and as a result Bacheldre Mill must be a leading contender for the 'first mill in Wales' tag. To reach it, the road passes over the Caebitra Stream, which here forms the boundary between the countries. Bacheldre is a good example of a small community mill which struggled on in classical fashion until the 1960s, when even the production of animal feed could no longer maintain its viability. There is nothing fancy or unusual about it – just a sturdy, well-built three-storey mill of local grey stone with a slate roof. The quality of the 200-year-old building (listed as of historical interest) is reflected in the surprisingly good condition of the internal gear when Trevor Ripley purchased the otherwise run-down mill site in 1985. Remarkably, only the teeth of the crown wheel had to be replaced and the hopper repaired. As a sort of bonus, Mr Ripley found a set of stone-dressing tools and wedges in the mill.

If the story of many mills traces a familiar pattern over several centuries, so does that of their new owners or tenants over the last few years. The seventies and, even more, the eighties have been a period when many people decided to make the sort of break earlier generations were unable or reluctant to do – and, of course, the break has often been dictated by circumstances, such as redundancy.

If not directly to the land, the return frequently involved work which has its roots in the nation's rural past. Men and women have discovered skills and applied them – first to crafts, then to running small country 'guest houses' and finally to less obvious pursuits, such as renovating mills and even producing flour. The Ripleys fit into this pattern, leaving secure work for the 'Min. of Ag.' and turning to a skill in which they had no expertise. They, like others, have been fortunate in finding that millers are generous with both time and advice, and they are, I think, a little surprised to be grinding their own flour on a commercial basis so soon after entering the business. They have sensibly taken out some insurance in the shape of a tea shop, four holiday lets and a caravan site.

Bacheldre Mill has an external overshot metal wheel, powered by a small pond. Ducks swim on the pond, sheep graze around it, chicken feed busily and farm cats stare unmoving into long grass – a scene which cannot have changed much in 200 years. The pond is fed by a stream which is adequate for present needs but may need supplementing at some time in the future. The half-mile-long mill-leat has for long been blocked, and it is possible that an engine could be installed to ensure a reliable supply of power. Alternatively, water could be re-circulated by pump. Experience gained in the next few months will almost certainly help provide a solution – it's the sort of situation millers have resolved over the centuries, and it's pleasing that so many eager owners are facing, and enjoying, this challenge.

Penegoes: Felin Crewi, near Machynlleth

Felin Crewi was originally a fulling-mill, built in the seventeenth century. It was later converted to a corn-mill, and the beautiful specimen of a king-post which it now possesses places the date of conversion between 1700 and 1750. The three-storey stone building is part of a complex which includes a white painted miller's house with outbuildings and a modern single-storey extension overlooking the mill pond.

The present fifteen-and-a-half-foot cast-iron pitch-back wheel was brought here from nearby Melin Ffridd. It replaces an old wheel which was twelve and a half foot in diameter, and it is possible to see, both inside and outside the mill, some of the adjustments that were necessary to accommodate the larger size wheel. Leaning against a wall of the mill there is a fine example of a clasp-arm wheel; the original spur wheel, it was 'retired' in the 1940s. Inside the mill the layout of the conventional machinery is particularly impressive – for example the working of the damsel can be very easily studied. Information about the mill and its history (the latter missing from the brief guide) is clearly presented on sensible information boards. The mill produces small quantities of stone-ground flour from its original stones, and there is a nice patina of dust on the machinery.

Outside, a short nature trail along a lovely river walk through a miniature gorge leads to the weir some hundred yards upstream from the mill. Water is carried via an underground millrace to the millpond and onto the wheel by a traditional slate flume. There is a café, and a licensed restaurant (open only during evenings in high season).

Mr and Mrs Partridge, who own Felin Crewi, are still developing the site, for which they have already won several commendations, including a Prince of Wales Award. They have made a particular effort to cater for disabled visitors, and the mill, café and nature trail are all accessible to wheelchair users. The excellent lavatory block, which includes facilities for nursing mothers, was opened by Bob Donaldson, a doughty fighter for disabled people in Wales. It was paid for in part by money raised through a sponsored entrant in the London Marathon.

South Glamorgan

The two working and two static mills listed below are all at the Welsh Folk Museum, St Fagans, near Cardiff. The earliest major centre for the study of preserved vernacular buildings – and still the best, the museum already houses around twenty buildings and regularly adds more.

The Welsh Mills Group is based at St Fagans, and its secretary, Gerallt Nash, is one of the museum's staff. In its short existence the Group has already achieved a great deal in publicizing the wind- and watermills of Wales. It encourages working millers (even English-born ones!) and offers authoritative advice on restoration. The Group's annual publication, *Melin*, is informative while avoiding pedantry, and the long-term future for the surviving Welsh mills has been markedly more assured since its founding, in 1984.

St Fagans: Deheufryn Gorse-Mill – Dates from about 1850 – transferred from near Colwyn; used for crushing and tearing gorse shoots for cattle fodder; direct drive from axle of wooden overshot wheel to arrangement of spiked rollers; static display – perhaps fortunately, granted vicious appearance of spikes.
St Fagans: Esgair Moel Water-Powered Woollen-Mill – below.
St Fagans: Melin Bompren Corn-Mill – p.203.
St Fagans: Rhayader Tannery Complex – Stone and timber buildings from Rhayader, Powys; displays complete tannery process including overshot wheel used to power bark-crusher; bark was added to tanning-pits in which hides were immersed; static display.

St Fagans: Esgair Moel Water-Powered Woollen-Mill

In the last years of the eighteenth and early years of the nineteenth century, the woollen industry in Wales began an unprecedented period of expansion. Within a few years it developed from a small-scale 'cottage' industry to one of the major employers in the country. This was especially true of parts of Powys (Newtown was known as 'the Leeds of Wales'), where many of the larger mills were patterned on those of Lancashire and Yorkshire. Not all were, and typical of the smaller woollen-mill built in the period, to what might be termed an old-fashioned design, is Esgair Moel, established in about 1780 at Llanwrtyd Wells.

Esgair Moel is a long, low, white-painted, two-storey building built of local stone. Where it differed from many smaller mills was that it was equipped to carry out a whole range of processes, extending from dyeing through teasing to carding, spinning, twisting, weaving, fulling and finishing. The machinery for these processes is powered by an eight-foot internal wood and cast-iron wheel, supplied with water pumped from a pool. Attached on either side of the wheel are a tappet-wheel, to raise the fulling-hammers, and an iron cog powering the belt-drum which operates the remaining machinery – simple but efficient.

The mill is still working, and visitors can watch the various phases being demonstrated by craftsmen. All is just as it has been over the centuries – except for the site, for Esgair Moel was removed from its original site in 1953 and reconstructed at the Welsh Folk Museum, St Fagans.

St Fagans: Melin Bompren Corn-Mill

Melin Bompren is a three-storeyed, hip-roofed stone building from Cross Inn, New Quay, Dyfed. Attached to it is a two-storey corn-drying kiln. The mill was built around 1852 and stopped working in 1957. During its working life it had only four, or possibly five, millers. After the retirement of the last miller, Mrs Hettie Jones, the mill deteriorated in condition, but happily it was donated to the Welsh Folk Museum and was transferred to St Fagans in 1970. After years of patient reconstruction it was opened to the public in 1977.

Melin Bompren is a beautifully set-up mill, typical of the care taken at St Fagans. Stepping inside is like entering a nineteenth-century mill for it has not been prettified and cleverly gives the impression of being a genuine working mill – indeed, it does produce about four tons of flour yearly. The cast-iron overshot wheel (thought not to be the original) is now powered by a modern pumping arrangement. The wheel and an American smutting-machine are the only additions to the equipment of a mill otherwise unaltered in 130 years. The machinery, not all on view, consists of wooden cogged wheels operating conventional gearing. There are two pairs of stones; the French Burr stones would have ground the small amount of corn grown in the area, while a pair of composition stones from Gloucester would have been the day-to-day working stones, used for both barley and oats. Payment to the miller was in kind or by toll.

Melin Bompren's drying-kiln uses thick iron mesh for the upper floor (the one on which the grain is spread), as does the kiln at Cenarth (p.190). In Cardiganshire it was the custom for the farm to supply the culm (clay and coaldust mix – see also St Dogmaels, p.193) along with the oats or barley to be dried. It's worth noting that in this part of Cardiganshire the main crop was barley until well into the twentieth century.

The miller now in charge at Melin Bompren is Marvin Morgan, who is a great walking-stick-maker and enthusiast – examples of his work are for sale and are displayed on the upper floor of the mill.

West Glamorgan

Aberdulais Falls is a frankly speculative entry here. Managed by Rick Poole, who is working hard to find a suitable wheel, it is already a most exciting place for industrial archaeologists and lovers of waterfalls alike – the future could be positively mouth-watering.

Aberdulais Falls (NT), Vale of Neath – Currently ruins only of several industrial mills; exceptionally historic site dating from

1584 to late nineteenth century; involved in development of three metal industries – copper-smelting, ironworking and tinplate-manufacture; corn-milling during eighteenth century in flour- and grist-mills; spectacular waterfall; NT actively investigating possible replacement wheels – they succeeded at Styal (see p. 68).

Parkmill: Corn-Mill – Seventeenth-century working corn-mill by ford; also contains water-powered saw-mill (cf. Felin Geri, p.191); remarkably rural group within eight miles of centre of Swansea; second mill in village is behind post office – converted to private house. NOT OPEN.

Scotland

The watermill in Scotland has, in some respects, undergone an even more dramatic loss in recent years than has its counterpart in England – and certainly Wales. I say 'counterpart' for many of the mill sites, particularly in the Highlands, which do remain and are listed in the publications of several dedicated archaeological societies never possessed vertical mills but were variations of the Greek or horizontal mill, invariably called a 'click mill' in Scotland.

There are still mills of considerable historic interest (New Lanark is the obvious example), mills which are 'traditional' in the English sense (Blair Atholl is one) and others which reflect the use of water-powered mills in industry. But many are now just sites where the industrial archaeologist may exercise powers of detection and deduction. Others, particularly in the Lowlands and Central Region, have been converted to private houses and do not welcome visitors. For the enthusiast with limited time, I suggest that the Grampian Region has most to offer at present.

This change seems to have happened quite rapidly. Leslie Syson, writing only in 1980, mentioned large numbers of sites which simply do not now exist. I made a particular study of some areas in the Borders, Highland and Lothian Regions where Ordnance Survey maps suggested mills and mill sites were to be found – and the bulk had gone or would be of interest only to specialists.

I am conscious that pressure on time limited my exploration of Scotland but I believe that the mills listed in the following pages provide an indication of the variety of mills still to be found in each region.

Borders

As I have indicated in the introduction, the bulk of the sites given in the Ordnance Survey maps of the Border region have ceased to exist and require the detective work of an industrial archaeologist to uncover their secrets. Mills that remain have been converted and do not welcome visitors. The two mills below are, in effect, 'cheats' –

Blyth Bridge was converted to a hotel fifty years ago, and Nether Mill is powered by a turbine!

Blyth Bridge: Old Mill Inn – Deep in remote part of lovely Pentland Hills; pleasant 1930s conversion of old corn-mill (originally to a tea-room) by Sir Walter Darling MP, who bought mill for £150; large metal wheel on outside wall, but mill-lade and internal machinery removed fifty years ago.

Galashiels: Nether Mill – The Peter Anderson Woollen-Mill houses well-lit and presented display of machinery; beautifully restored wheel powered by Liffel water-turbine turns small loom during demonstrations; regular conducted tours; excellent small museum, showing development of town with emphasis on 'social' developments – health and education etc; shop.

Central

The towns and villages grouped at the foot of the Ochil Hills, collectively known as 'the Hillfoots villages', have a long tradition of textile-making. The earliest records of woollen-manufacture in the area are for Tillicoultry during the mid sixteenth century. Initially the work was carried out on hand-looms; indeed, it wasn't until the end of the eighteenth century that the power of the Tillicoultry Burn was first harnessed. By the 1870s the traditional cottage industry had, as elsewhere, been entirely replaced by power-looms – the bulk, though not all, water-powered.

Alva: Strude Mill – below.
Tillicoultry: Clock Mill – p.207.

Alva: Strude Mill

Although it no longer functions, I cannot overlook Strude Mill – indeed, it would be difficult to do so, for it occupies a dominant position above the town, with the Ochil Hills close behind forming a most impressive backdrop. Recent building of houses up to the outer wall of the mill, itself now scheduled for conversion into dwellings, has lessened the impact, but this listed building is still a fine memorial to the age in which it was built, bearing comparison with Stanley Mills (p.221).

A handsome six-storey mill with a bellcote and pediment, Strude Mill was built in about 1827 as part of a larger complex and continued in production until the mid-1960s. Originally housing hand-looms, the mill was later converted, using the Alva Burn, to water-power. Traces of overflow channels and a few pipes are all that remain of what must have been a complex system of waterways.

Tillicoultry: Clock Mill

The Clock Mill consists of three storeys and an attic floor. The clock from which the mill takes its name is on a south-facing gable above the attic window. A water-powered carding- and spinning-mill, it was built in 1824 and continued in use, latterly as a weaving-mill, until the early 1980s. It stands beside the burn, directed here through a deep, well-preserved lade, one of many such channels in the area.

I find the Clock Mill the most attractive of all those in the area, and its present use as both a Tourist Information Centre and a Mill Heritage Centre (complete with audio-visual presentation) should guarantee its future. The centres are both situated on the ground floor, with craft workshops and a display of looms on the first floor. The adaptation has been well planned and laid out, and a replacement wheel, if one could be found, would be a further asset.

To provide water-power for its many mills (ten in 1862), Tillicoultry required a complex system of lades, most leading from a massive wooden dam in Mill Glen (now a public park) above the Clock Mill. For many years it was the duty of the provost to open the dam sluices in the morning. The remains of the dam can still be seen in the park, which seems very popular with young mothers exercising their babies on sunny days.

Clackmannan District Council and the lively and inventive Scottish Tourist Board have together provided funds for a Hillfoots Mill Trail (copies available from the Clock Mill) which highlights several other mills, most still operating commercially, though none is now water-powered.

I've written elsewhere in this book (see Cutterne Mill p.142) about how patterns are often repeated. The following story, taken from notes in the Clock Mill, closely mirrors a story related in the church of Mordiford in Herefordshire, where a couple of buildings (including a cider-mill) were swept away on 27 May 1811!

During the night of 27 August 1877, the River Devon valley was deluged, and at eight o'clock the following morning, when local people had just begun work, '... the rains descended and the floods came.' The burn overflowed, carrying rocks and boulders through the town; at about 8.15 the proprietor of the New Castle Mills was looking at the damage with three millworkers when a bridge that was badly damaged and the embankment on which they stood were swept away. One worker survived, the other three drowned. Their fellow-workers heard the noise and ran out to see what was happening – fortunately for them, as the entire west end of the mill gave way and all the looms and shuttles fell into the torrent. Houses and cottages were wrecked; one resident had just sat down for breakfast when his table was carried away by the flood. History does not relate what happened to him!

Dumfries & Galloway

New Abbey Mill is one of the most important mills remaining in Scotland, and it is good that it is now in the care of the Scottish Development Department. The Bobbin-Mill has been the subject of some ambitious plans in recent years – let us hope that they will now be realized. It is a purely speculative addition to the list. Wanlockhead, though not strictly falling within the remit of this book, is an industrial site where water-power was of considerable importance.

Dumfries: Robert Burns Centre – exhibition is housed in red-sandstone old town mill built 1781 and operating in the poet's lifetime.

Gatehouse: Bobbin-Mill – Currently an ivy-covered ruin; plans for re-development include interpretation centre, craft workshops, museum – all depending on funding.

New Abbey: New Abbey Corn-Mill (SDD) below.

Wanlockhead: Museum of the Scottish Mining Industry – Worth visiting is the unique early nineteenth-century wooden water-bucket beam pumping-engine at Stratisteps; only wheel-pits remain at the museum, where lead-mining continued from the seventeenth to the mid twentieth century.

New Abbey: New Abbey Corn-Mill

The original mill at New Abbey was almost certainly built by the monks of the charmingly named Sweetheart Abbey, a Cistercian foundation begun in 1273. The local name for the mill, Monks Mill, seems to confirm the connection. Further weight is given to this theory by the fact that the village of New Abbey did not develop until the fifteenth and sixteenth centuries, at a time when the monastic tradition was fading but the status of the landowners was increasing.

The first mention of 'the corn-mill of Lochkindeloch' occurs in a deed of 1559, although the present two-storey building is of mid- to late-eighteenth-century construction. It was extended in the nineteenth century and continued to operate until the Second World War. The mill was restored to working order by a descendant of the original eighteenth-century owner and presented to the Secretary of State for Scotland in 1982. It is now in the care of the Scottish Development Department (Ancient Monuments).

New Abbey Mill is a good example of a type of mill which once flourished throughout the Lowlands, grinding oats for human and animal consumption. Viewed from the village square, the white-painted buildings present a pleasingly sturdy vernacular picture, only slightly marred by the presence of what appears to be a modern metal ventilator on the roof of the kiln. The kiln forms the central section of a complex, built, unusually, as a single unit comprising mill, kiln and miller's house.

The cast-iron and wooden pitch-back wheel (fourteen feet six inches), with its launder fed by a half-mile long lade, is situated at the rear of the mill. Pitch-back wheels are not commonly used in small mills, and this wheel has a second unusual feature in that it has nine spokes. It supplies power to turn three pairs of stones – the provender stones for animal feed, the shelling stones for removing the husks from the grain and the finishing stones for producing the finished grain. The bulk of the machinery is conventional and original, although renovated during restoration.

Fife

Fife has no surviving watermills that I could discover, but the enterprising and energetic Levenmouth Environmental Society has produced two 'Walkabout' leaflets containing details of many industrial archaeological sites in Leven and Levenvale.

Several mill buildings are featured in the guides and, though no longer active, might well repay a visit by the enthusiastic molinologist.

Grampian

Grampian is, in some ways, the most exciting region of Scotland, for it has retained several mills of a traditional or semi-traditional nature. Oldmills and Mill of Towie are both making efforts to operate commercially without ruining the 'feel' of the mill. Their methods are different – Towie is working, Oldmills functions for demonstration purposes only – but both are proving successful in the main purpose of attracting visitors.

Mill of Durn is a good modern example of a conversion to a home while Montgarrie is, perhaps, the mill buff's choice. This is a traditional working mill, but one at which visitors are made to feel welcome. The same is certainly true at Newmill Woollen Mill, included here mainly for its architecture and fascinating history, where the always forward-looking owners have produced a useful range of notes to accompany their mill tours.

Drummuir: Mill of Towie – below.

Elgin: Newmill Woollen Mill – group of buildings begun 1798 on site of watermill beside River Lossie; includes a remarkably fine and beautifully balanced front block; was water-powered, later gas and electricity – wheel is said to be buried in factory grounds; a working mill, belonging to Johnstons of Elgin, offering tours; shop has wide range of materials for sale including vicuna – introduced by the company at the Great Exhibition of 1851 in London; company created famous Lovat Check; in ownership of only two families for almost two hundred years.

Elgin: Oldmills p.211.

Kinloss: East Grange Mill – closed for commercial production in 1976; rather decrepit iron and wood wheel still used occasionally for cattle feed; possibility of future MSC involvement in repair project – mill may then reopen.

Montgarrie Mills – p.212.

Portsoy: Mill of Durn – fine quality nineteenth-century meal mill; ceased operating in 1964 and became derelict; recently converted by enthusiastic architect owner to dwelling house; retains many of better features including much internal machinery and central kiln with louvred ventilator; sixteen-foot-diameter wood and iron overshot wheel is in remarkably good condition and may soon be turning again. NOT OPEN.

Drummuir: Mill of Towie

The Mill of Towie is a very pleasing three-storey building of natural stone in a setting, beside the River Isla, which comes close to being idyllic. The present mill dates from the nineteenth century although there has been a mill on the site since at least 1676, grinding oats and barley for the Drummuir Estate.

The mill continued to work until 1978 when the kiln roof collapsed. For the next few years, with no drying facilities, it produced only cattle feed. In 1984 the owners of the mill, Alex and Priscilla Gordon-Duff, decided to repair it, featuring it as the centre of a small commercial complex. They were determined that the restoration should be authentic and were helped in this aim by the willingness of the tenant, Mr Rod Stewart, to undertake the bulk of the repair work. Mr Stewart, who comes from a milling family and first milled oatmeal at the age of fourteen, had been in charge of the mill since 1968.

Much of the good quality internal machinery remained and was renovated by Mr Stewart over the next three years. The interior now looks, and indeed is, remarkably authentic – it shows Victorian mill machinery at its best. The wheel has been re-timbered but the major work involved repairing the kiln roof. The kiln is capable of drying up to thirty cwt of oats at one time and is claimed to be the largest in the area. It is now operational and Mill of Towie is once again able to produce fine quality oatmeal from oats grown on the Drummuir estate.

In addition to repairing the mill the Gordon-Duffs were anxious to provide a good range of other facilities. They have surely succeeded – in addition to a craft shop there is a licensed restaurant (the old grain store), a picnic area beside the river, a nature trail along the five-hundred-yard-long lade, Shetland ponies, farm machinery and facilities for disabled visitors, still a comparative rarity even in commercially-operated mills such as this. The problem with the use of the word 'commercial' is that it tends to raise doubts in the minds of mill-lovers. Here, due in large measure, as I am sure the owners would agree, to the efforts and enthusiasm of Mr Stewart, there is a rare authenticity about the 'feel' of the mill.

The Duff family have owned the estate and the Mill of Towie for three hundred years, and Mr and Mrs Gordon-Duff are particularly pleased that the Historic Buildings Council has given support to their project – believed to be the first time a building of this type has received assistance from the HBC towards the cost of its restoration.

Elgin: Oldmills

There were once seven meal mills along the River Lossie, of which Kingsmills, the original mill on this site, was the oldest. It seems likely that there had been a mill here, in royal ownership, for many years before the first written records appeared in a charter of 1230. The mill and its multures or tolls were granted by Alexander II to the monks of Pluscarden Priory, to the displeasure of the burghers of Elgin. Both the mill and priory lands became the property of the Seatons in 1560, and the mill has changed hands many times since. It was acquired by the Mackay family in 1964, and is now leased to Moray District Council.

The present mill was built at the end of the eighteenth century, following the burning down of the old mill at Hogmanay, 1792. The kiln and storage area were added in the mid-nineteenth century, and the mill continued to work commercially until 1967, latterly for the production of animal feed. With the aid of grants from the Countryside Commission for Scotland, the Mackay Trust restored the mill to working order between 1978 and 1985. Much of the machinery had remained in good order, but the lades had to be rebuilt and the whole site landscaped. Renovation of the machinery was carried out by a millwright from Dingwall, and the remaining work was largely due to the efforts of an MSC team. Progress was hampered by a fire which severely damaged the grain store in the winter of 1983, but this potential disaster was turned to good effect when the store was reconstructed as an exhibition and interpretative centre.

In the summer of 1985, the weirs were reconstructed and a footbridge was built by the Army to allow access to the island created by the division of the River Lossie into three streams. In 1987 a nature trail was opened beside the lade.

Oldmills is an attractive three-storey L-shaped building with its kiln set at one end. It has two breastshot water wheels; the larger, on the east side, is eleven feet in diameter with twenty-four wooden paddles and is responsible for driving the sack-hoist and animal feed mill. The main wheel measures ten foot two inches in diameter, and has thirty steel paddles; it drives all the major flour-milling machinery. Oldmills follows a classic pattern in the use of various woods for the machine parts, and in employing French Burr millstones in addition to a gritstone from Carse Hill.

The mill now produces oatmeal only as a by-product of the continuous process of demonstrating the machinery. The whole concept of the enterprise is to demonstrate to visitors how an old-fashioned mill worked. In addition to the information centre there is a working model of a mill, and a display of farming equipment. The whole site has been laid out in a very effective manner, with good visitor facilities, including a picnic area.

Montgarrie Mills

Montgarrie Mills stand on the outskirts of Alford in surprisingly rugged country for this part of the east coast of Scotland. The mill is a three-storey, five-bay building with a fine tall kiln vent. The building is pleasing, but it is surrounded by a group of corrugated iron additions. It has to be stressed that this is a working mill, and that although there are conducted tours by arrangement on Tuesday and Thursday afternoons it lacks the grooming of an overtly tourist mill, such as Oldmills – readers will not be surprised to learn that I prefer Montgarrie!

Mills have almost certainly existed here for between two and three hundred years. The present building, *c.* 1880, has been owned by the Macdonald family since 1894. It is the fourth to have stood on the site – all three predecessors burnt down. A possible explanation for this is to be found by studying the modified patented temperature gauge on the kiln, which gives a good indication of the working temperature (up to 190°F) required for the drying and toasting of oats. Heat for the kiln is supplied by a furnace fired by anthracite from Wales. The Macdonalds still buy the bulk of their oats direct from local farms or merchants.

Once dried, the oats are automatically conveyed to the first of three sets of millstones. At Montgarrie the husk is removed using a four-and-a-half-foot diameter sandstone coated with emery. The oat dust is removed as the oats pass through a rotary screen. The husks are drawn off as the kernels drop through an aspirator. This process is then repeated, using a second set of stones and machines, after which the kernels are scoured in a set of three rotary brushes. The by-products are used in the production of animal feed.

The cleaned kernels, now groats, are milled in a further pair of stones, in this instance covered with French Burr chippings. As with all forms of milling, the fineness of the grinding is determined by the gap between the two stones. The mill produces six different 'cuts' of oatmeal, achieved by passing the meal over sifters of various sizes.

Montgarrie Mills has always been water-powered, although a little auxiliary power was added in the early years of this century. The present twenty-five foot diameter internal wheel was installed in 1882. It is an overshot wheel powered by water drawn from the River Don. After turning the wheel the water runs underground for over four hundred yards before rejoining the river below Montgarrie bridge.

Highland

There are some quite remarkable mills in the Highland Region, including the two dealt with here in some detail – the Clack Mill from Back on Lewis (in the museum at Kingussie) and Glendale on Skye. The two close together near Braefield are equally fascinating in their own way – Glen Urquhart in particular, though difficult to locate, is, I believe, unique.

Balnain: Mill of Tore – Community mill; overshot wheel fed by longish leat; in remarkably good condition; stands in a field by river and is a joy; we were directed to it by the (English) postman – his wife's auntie used to own it!

Diurinish, Isle of Skye: Glendale Watermill – p.214.

Glen Urquhart, near Braefield – At Inchechart Cottage; remains of tiny mill with water-course and four-foot-diameter wheel; on hillside overlooking superb country.

Kingussie: Clack Mill, Highland Folk Museum – p.214.

Strathpeffer: Old Millnain Mill – Early eighteenth-century two-storey rubble building; external sixteen-foot overshot cast-iron and wood wheel; wooded site beside main road; now a craft workshop, pottery and domestic dwelling.

Diurinish, Isle of Skye: Glendale Watermill

Glendale Watermill is now unique in Scotland, since it is the only remaining thatched Vitruvian or vertical mill. Beside it is another rare survival, a thatched, peat-fired kiln.

The mill, which in architectural terms closely resembles the thatched Greek or Norse mills which once served the Highlands and Islands (see Dounby Click Mill, p.217), stands in a sheltered cove by the shores of Loch Pooltiel. It was built about 200 years ago and ground corn for several local settlements. A single pair of stones, the present pair imported from Rogart Mill in Sutherland, are driven by an overshot metal wheel built by the Edinburgh company of A. & J. Main. Within twelve years of its installation in 1902, the mill had ceased to operate commercially, but this important and remarkable little thatched mill was repaired almost entirely by local labour in 1972 after a lengthy period of near dereliction.

Kingussie: Clack Mill, Highland Folk Museum

The little Highland Folk Museum at Kingussie lacks the sophistication of its larger national cousin at St Fagans in Wales, or even of such English versions as the Weald and Downland Open Air Museum in Sussex (p.68), but it has a very definite charm of its own.

Among the buildings at Kingussie is a clack mill from Back on the Isle of Lewis. It is a Greek or horizontal mill, similar to that at Dounby on Orkney – the name is simply an alliterative variation of the more commonly used 'click mill'.

This mill, which operated until the early 1900s, was collectively owned by five crofters. It was transferred to the museum in the 1940s and reconstructed, using the original vernacular stone material; the shaft is a copy, but the original is in the museum collection. Water to the mill is here supplied by a lade, although the more common practice with horizontal mills was for them to be built over fast-flowing streams.

Isle of Lewis

There are a couple of horizontal or Norse mills on the island which have been restored in recent years. They are at Bragar (restored in 1981 by the West Side Historical Survey) and Shawbost, restored in 1970 by pupils at Shawbost School. This is a typical Norse mill with a thatched roof over a drystone rubble building. A point to note is the lade, whose bottom is lined by flagstones. The tirl has eight paddles.

Lothian

Lothian has the very attractive Preston Mill, perhaps the best-known mill in Scotland, and the increasingly popular Livingstone Mill Farm. In addition to the suspension wheel at the Royal Scottish Museum, there are displays depicting milling methods at the Scottish Agricultural Museum at Ingliston.

East Linton: Preston Mill (NTS) – below.
Edinburgh: Royal Scottish Museum – Has large suspension wheel of 1826 from Grandholm Woollen Mill.
Millfield: Livingston Mill Farm, near Livingston – p.216.

East Linton: Preston Mill (NTS)

The fields of Lower Lothian were always fertile; the whole of Lothian became noted for good agricultural practice during the nineteenth century. Early in that century, Cobbett wrote of the area that it possessed '... such cornfields ... such stackyards as never, surely, were before seen in any country upon earth'. The coastal strip was particularly important for barley- and oat-production, and for centuries the River Tyne supplied water-power for the many mills which lay along its banks. Although it is possible to find traces of several of these mills and one or two conversions to private dwellings, the only survivor is Preston Mill at East Linton, now owned by the National Trust for Scotland.

Preston is a remarkably attractive mill, part of a tight-knit cluster of buildings which includes a circular kiln, probably dating from the fifteenth century. Mill and kiln are joined by a wooden bridge; there is a stable and a cattle shed, now used to house the museum exhibits. The present two-storeyed mill under its charming pantiled roof was built in 1660, operating as the estate mill of the Smeaton family. Powered by a thirteen-foot-diameter low-breast wood and iron wheel cast at the Carron Factory in 1760, it continued to work until 1950, when it was given to the Trust.

Although some maintenance work was carried out, its condition deteriorated, and in the mid 1960s Joseph Rank (now Rank Hovis McDougall) provided funds and expertise for its complete restoration.

A couple of fields away is the Phantassie Doocot, a rare survival of an early dovecot. At first glance it resembles a beehive but the south side has been angled to give a sheltered sloping roof for the birds – common in southern France but unique in Scotland.

Millfield: Livingston Mill Farm, near Livingston

Livingston Mill Farm was originally part of the Rosebery estates and was fortunate in forming part of the designated recreation area bordering the new town of Livingston. The meal-mill, mill-lade and farm buildings were all preserved and have been restored through a Community Project set up by the Livingston Development Council. Voluntary workers have been supplemented by an MSC team and, beginning with the mill-wheel, have largely returned the site to its nineteenth-century appearance.

The present mill was built in about 1770 on an earlier site – possibly sixteenth-century. It stands in a loop of the fast-flowing River Almond, and water for the mill enters the millpond from a long mill-lade, returning to the river just below the mill. There is an early nineteenth-century drying-kiln attached to the mill which continued to operate until the 1940s. Although it suffered from considerable deterioration in the next thirty years, the internal machinery, including the three pairs of stones, remained in place and is currently being renovated.

Livingston Mill Farm has farm animals, a museum of rural life using material collected from local farms, and a conservation area with four water habitats. It has aimed to provide facilities for schools to study the environment and is clearly succeeding. It reminds me, in concept, of Wood's Mill in Sussex (p.165) although the sites are very different. I find it pleasing that Mill Farm has made a special effort to accommodate disabled visitors and claims to provide ninety-five per cent access – a very fine achievement given the problems disabled people face with most mills.

Orkney

Orkney is fortunate in retaining the three mills listed. Although only one, Boardhouse Mill, works, all are important survivals – Dounby is the last example on Orkney of a type of mill once common in the Highlands and Islands.

In addition to these mills there is a disused two-storey nineteenth-century meal-mill at Sabiston.

Birsay: Boardhouse Mill – Fascinating site consisting of three mills – two contain wheel but are not used; largest (New Barony Corn-Mill) still working; hefty nineteenth-century structure incorporating kiln; three pairs of stones driven by fourteen-foot iron and wood overshot wheel; mill is listed; produces both flour and oatmeal.

Dounby: Click Mill (SDD) – below.

Tormiston Watermill, Stenness – Handsome nineteenth-century three-storey mill; fourteen-foot iron overshot wheel and machinery still in place but not working; part of building adapted in 1973 to restaurant and craft shop; furnace and kiln used as store.

Dounby: Click Mill

Greek, Horizontal, Norse or click mills have a long history in both Europe and Asia. They are a mechanized form of hand-quern, believed to date from a century or so BC. Click mills flourished in remote areas where feudalism rarely penetrated. As a result they were often true cooperative mills, working at little or no charge for very small communities and lacking such feudal 'sophistications' as soke rights.

Very few click mills remain in the British Isles, and part of the fascination of Dounby – the last of its kind on Orkney – is that the island is not generally considered suited to Greek mills with their requirement for fast-flowing streams. In most respects, Dounby is a typical Greek mill, built of vernacular materials – in this instance dry flagstones. Other flagstones, laid over wooden rafters and covered with turf, form the roof of the delightfully simple building.

Like most horizontal mills, Dounby has an under-house or basement containing the wheel, supplied with water from a small reservoir above the mill. The wooden wheel or tirl has two sets of blades – a most unusual feature – arranged in tiers at an angle to the wheel's axis. The wheel turns a single pair of stones housed in the upper part of the mill, known as the meal-house (cf. Dunrossness, below).

The 'click' of a Greek mill is caused by a wooden tongue on the tray containing the corn striking a projection on the upper millstone. The vibration so created maintains the flow of corn to the hole in the centre of the upper stone, almost exactly the effect achieved with a clapper on a Vitruvian mill.

Shetland

Shetland has more Norse or horizontal mills than Orkney – the tiny, well-maintained mill at Dunrossness is perhaps the best known.

Dunrossness: Shetland Croft House Museum – Separate from but in ownership of Shetland Museum; well-preserved nineteenth-century croft house furnished in appropriate *c.* 1860s style; among outbuildings is tiny horizontal or Norse mill capable of turning for brief periods, though lacking water-power to operate for any length of time; water is collected by damming stream and releasing down chute onto tirl (wheel); similar history to Dounby Mill on Orkney (p.217) but a more primitive mill.

Strathclyde

I have listed two very different mills, one each from the cotton and wool industry. New Lanark, in size and historical importance, commands inclusion – the demanding programme of restoration begun in the 1970s is finally nearing completion, and the New Lanark Conservation Trust deserve the highest praise for their foresight and perseverence. The cotton industry has, in recent years, been remarkably well served by its enthusiasts; more than any other industry (except the much smaller needle industry), its history has been lovingly recreated at centres like Styal (p.68) and now at New Lanark (p.219).

Bridgend Woollen Mill is included for its rare internal machinery – architecturally it vies with any mill in the book for representing unplanned building at its worst!

Islay: Bridgend Woollen-Mill

Hardly the most attractive grouping on Islay, Bridgend Woollen-Mill consists of a haphazard collection of corrugated iron and asbestos-roofed one- and two-storey buildings of various ages, ranging from the early to late nineteenth century. The oldest, now derelict, was a water-powered carding-mill, and water was used in the main mill, which continued in production until the early 1960s – weaving is still carried out there. The present internal, undershot wheel, twelve feet in diameter, was installed in 1928.

The interest in Bridgend is in the survival of some remarkable machinery, including a piecing-machine by Robert Archibald of Devonvale. Before the continuous 'rope' was introduced, carding-machines produced a web of fibres, and these slivers of wool had to be combined into a workable length of firm thread. The task of piecing was performed originally by children and later by machines adapted from inventions applied in the cotton industry; this is probably the only working survivor of its kind.

New Lanark Mills

Work began on New Lanark in 1785, and it was to become the largest water-powered cotton-mill complex in the world, surviving remarkably unchanged until the late 1960s. The historical importance of New Lanark can hardly be over-stressed. It grew as a result of a preliminary investigation in 1783 by Richard Arkwright and David Dale of the spectacular Falls of Clyde in the narrow, wooded valley below the ancient town of Lanark. Surprisingly for a country of so many rivers, Scotland has relatively few which are suitable for the demands of large water-wheels. Even at New Lanark, the power had to be harnessed through a tunnel 100 yards long, and along a wide mill-lade.

The proposed partnership between Arkwright and Dale was dissolved before work began on the complex. Initial work was speedily completed: the first mill came into operation within the year (and burned down within a further year), and the other three mills followed relatively quickly. The pioneering work in improving conditions for work-forces employed in large complexes tends to have been associated with the name of Robert Owen, Dale's son-in-law, who took control of New Lanark in 1800. Certainly the education programme, which Owen and his London-based Quaker partners implemented in the early 1800s, was remarkably advanced, but the working-conditions, with families housed in small units and apprentices in well-maintained dormitories, were introduced by Dale.

Robert Owen was a man of immense imagination and breadth of interests, who inevitably wished to develop his pioneering ideas in a wider context. Tempted by an offer to take part in the co-operative at Harmony in Indiana, Owen and his son left New Lanark at the end of 1824, closing an era of unparalleled innovation in the advancement of working-conditions for those employed in a large industrial concern. Not that subsequent owners failed to observe the principles laid down by Dale and Owen: it was more that they absorbed the lessons, and New Lanark ceased to be a revolutionary centre.

As has been noted in the section on the cotton industry, it suffered from declining business relatively early in the twentieth century, but there was general surprise when, at the end of 1967, the then owners announced the closure of New Lanark. The next seven or eight years saw this historic site come close to destruction before the creation of the New Lanark Conservation Trust in 1975 meant that an opportunity had been created to produce a new initiative. The reprieve coincided with various developments, including new housing legislation and the setting-up of the Manpower Services

Commission, which presented opportunities for organizations such as the Trust to develop their plans.

In the decade since, an enormous amount of rehabilitation work has been undertaken on the site. Owner-occupied and tenanted properties have been created behind the original façades; the mill buildings – following the first compulsory purchase in Scotland of historically important buildings – are being restored and converted to a museum, with a visitor centre, already partly open to the public. The school house, the most dilapidated of the buildings, has had its roof restored, and the major work on the project should be completed by 1989.

Tayside

Two very different mills represent Tayside. Blair Atholl was an estate mill, and its history reflects that of estate mills everywhere in Britain. Stanley has connections with Richard Arkwright – it demonstrates the spread of the influence of that remarkable man.

Pitlochry: Mill of Blair Atholl – below.
Stanley Mills – p.221.

Pitlochry: Mill of Blair Atholl

Blair Atholl Mill has a long history which could almost be cited as a classic study of the history of the small estate mill in Scotland – and, indeed, in England.

The mill was built as the estate mill for Atholl Castle at some time in the early seventeenth century. The first miller was appointed in 1613, and although there are no records of the building of the mill, it does seem probable that the main three-storey part of the building was erected at this time. The kiln and granary were added in the early 1800s, the kiln replacing an earlier one, parts of which are below the present tea-room. As an estate mill, Blair Atholl operated a toll system which remained in force until the 1860s. Like many other country mills, it began to suffer from the growing popularity of cheap white flour, produced in the large roller-mills which were developed at many major ports by the end of the nineteenth century.

Blair Atholl struggled on until 1929, after which it was used as a store for many years. It was saved by a combination of two factors: 1975 was designated as Architectural Heritage Year, and the local youth groups undertook a project to clean up the mill; at the same time Donald Cameron Ridley was looking for a mill to restore, and he instituted repair and renovation work at the Mill of Blair Atholl in late 1976.

The mill machinery is largely conventional, although some ancillary machinery, including the grain-drier, is electrically operated. There are two pairs of French Burr stones, powered by a fourteen-foot undershot wheel, and the mill is once again producing both flour and some eighty tonnes of oatmeal for sale to the public. The tea-room uses only home-baked flour.

Stanley Mills

The influence on the cotton industry of Richard Arkwright spread far beyond Cromford (p.81), where his ideas were first introduced and prospered. Arkwright had continual problems with patents and, at Cromford, with the water-supply. Stanley was one of the earliest mills established when the patents were quashed (in 1785), and its siting, on the banks of the Tay, disposed of problems with the water-supply.

Stanley is a large, multi-storey group arranged in a U-shape and incorporates one of the most attractive mill buildings in Scotland – the five-storey Bell Mill. The first mill built on the site by Arkwright and his partners, the Bell Mill is unusual for Scotland in that it is of brick construction on a stone base. A bellcote adds to an impression of some elegance, complemented by a pretty mid-nineteenth-century circular gatehouse with ogee roof.

Not all the buildings are of the same standard but Stanley, now producing synthetic yarns on modern machinery, gives an overall impression of space and airiness not often associated with large cotton-mills.

Up the hill is Stanley village, a late-eighteenth- and early-nineteenth-century addition built for the mill-workers. Modernization (including my *bête noire* – the enlarging of windows) in recent years has slightly detracted from the quality of some of the houses, but the village remains very attractive.

III

Glossary

Glossary

The intention in this glossary is to provide explanations of the majority of terms – and their alternatives (referred to as 'also ...') – associated with milling. By no means all the terms listed are used in this book, which is deliberately non-technical, but they may be found in other literature on the subject. I have included brief references to associated matters, such as historical terms (Domesday, soke rights etc), which crop up with some frequency in this book. Allied subjects needing to be dealt with in more depth are covered in separate short chapters. For other, often more specialist sources, see the bibliography (p.237).

Ark – bin for storing grain – usually associated with toll paid to miller.
Arms – spokes of water-wheel; normally eight in number.
Aspirator – device for cleaning grain.
Auger – rotating Archimedean screw inside wooden trough moving grain horizontally; improved by Oliver Evans (see Descender); also creeper and conveyor.
Axle tree – wooden (latterly cast-iron) shaft linking water-wheel and pit-wheel; also axle.

Back-watering – braking effect on overshot wheel created as floats enter water of tailrace.
Balance weights – lead or iron weights inserted into runner stone to achieve balance – comparable with balancing of wheels on motor-car; patented weights supplied with threaded screw.
Barley – most abundant cereal crop in Britain; lacks high gluten content and is not suited for modern bread-making; used as animal feedstock and in brewing; grown mainly in south and east.
Bed stone – lower, fixed millstone of pair; 'standard' diameter four feet; also called a ligger.
Bill – double-ended wedge-shaped steel tool used for dressing millstones; major tool – with pick – employed in craft; mounted in a thrift; particles of metal from bill entered hands of stone-dressers – hence phrase 'showing your metal' used by millers to check how experienced craftsmen were.
Bin – container for storing grain; on top floor of mill, known as bin, garner or granary floor.

Bist – small cushion of bran knelt on by stone-dresser; modern equivalent is beanbag.

Bit – metal tool used in stone-dressing.

Blade – paddles of water-wheel; may be wood (often elm) or wrought-iron.

Bluestone – millstone from Germany *see* Cullin.

Bolter – machine used in dressing or sifting flour; originally a task carried out by hand, using a temse; mechanical means were introduced in sixteenth century; basically flour is shaken through woven fabric fitted over revolving cylinder; fabric was originally wool, then calico, and is nowadays silk; see also Wire-machine.

Brayer – component of tentering-gear; also known as bray.

Breast or breastshot wheel – water-wheel developed to high efficiency in eighteenth and nineteenth centuries, although first mentioned in sixteenth century; water falls into buckets either just above axle (high breast) or just below (low breast).

Bridge tree – part of hursting; adjustable beam supporting thrust bearing at lower end of stone pivot; raised or lowered to regulate gap between stones for grinding.

Bridging-box – mounting for bridge tree.

Brigging – process of ensuring accurate plumbing of vertical stone spindle.

Buckets – enclosed floats used to trap water in breast and overshot wheels.

Burr stone – high-quality quartzite stone quarried near Paris; used for millstones comprised of segments cemented with plaster of Paris and bound with iron; approximately four feet in diameter, twelve inches thick and weighing eighteen hundredweight; produces best results in flour-grinding; always in short supply and expensive; now becoming rarer; when worn too thin for grinding, often used for decorative purposes or in paving; also called Buhr or French Buhr stones.

Centrifugal reel-separator – used in dressing or grading flour.

Clapper – primitive form of damsel, usually associated with Greek mill.

Clasp-arm wheel – timber wheel with spokes which form a square around axle; wedges are inserted to ensure tight fit; generally considered better than compass-arm but were not as strong as cast-iron – increasingly introduced from eighteenth century.

Click mill – gearless mill – known as click mill for noise it makes; also known as horizontal, Greek and Norse mill; see longer entry under Greek mill.

Clow or clough – a sluice

Cogs – removable teeth of gear-wheel; invariably wooden, originally apple.

Cog pit – space in ground floor containing pit-wheel and some gearing; also cock pit or cog hole.

Compass-arm wheel – wheel with radiating spokes mortised to axle; mortices tended to weaken axle and clasp-arm wheel was generally preferred by millwrights.

Composition stone – artificial millstone; contains carborundum or other abrasive material.

Corn – collective term for grain or seed of any cereal crop; see entries for barley, oats, rye and wheat.

Corn Laws – range of regulatory statutes in existence from time of Edward III to control import and export of corn; most commonly bounties paid on exports or duties imposed on imports; combination of factors in early nineteenth century resulted in great economic hardship; abolished in 1846 by Peel, following his conversion to Free Trade.

Cracking – process of cutting fine grooves – up to sixteen per inch – on flat surfaces (lands) of millstone; also known as stitching.

Cradle – wooden support for hopper; also horse.

Crook string – string controlling angle of shoe feeding grain from hopper to stones.

Crown wheel – uppermost wheel on vertical shaft; drives ancillary equipment, including hoisting-gear.

Cullin – Continental millstone – volcanic in origin.

Damsel – iron rod used to agitate shoe and regulate flow of grain to stones; said to be named for similarity of its unceasing chattering to that of women; essential aural 'tool' for millers; sometimes called dandelion.

Derbyshire Peak – millstone grit is the basis of this, the most common stone used for milling in Britain; quarried almost exclusively in Peak District of Derbyshire, it is cheaper than French Burr and second only to it in quality; also Peak stone.

Descender – controls descent of grain through system; one of several labour-saving innovations perfected by American millwright Oliver Evans in eighteenth century.

Domesday survey – survey proposed by William I at meeting of Witan in Gloucester, Christmas 1085; conducted to discover taxable value of each shire, clarify who owned land and confirm what resources the land possessed; aided by administrative system inherited from Anglo-Saxons, the initial stage of the survey was completed by 1086; the majority of the final circuit summaries were incorporated into 'Great' Domesday but the details of Essex, Norfolk and Suffolk are contained in 'Little' Domesday Book; the Exeter (Exon) Domesday is possibly a circuit summary – it covers Cornwall, Somerset, much of Devon and parts of Dorset and Wiltshire, but it contains much fascinating additional detail (such as numbers of animals possessed by tenants) omitted from Domesday Book; there were about 6,000 mills in existence at Domesday, although this figure is open to conjecture – see p.19; for further information see individual County Gazetteer entries.

Dresser – cylindrical, wire or silk-lined sieve enclosing rotating brushes, used to grade flour; also known as wire-machine.

Dressing – process of preparing grinding surfaces of millstones; stone-dressing involves a complex pattern of 'harps', 'furrows', 'lands' and 'cracking' cut or etched into stone.

Drifting – see Furrows.

Driving-stocks – tilt-hammers used in fulling of cloth.

Dutch Blue – Continental millstone.

Edge runner stones – stones which rotate in a vertical plane; edge forms crushing surface; used in industrial processes and in polishing pearl barley.

Edge-tool works – forges used in production of cutting-tools; can be seen at Abbeydale, p.181.

Elevator – endless belt for raising loose grain; introduced by Oliver Evans (see Descender).
Escape gate – sluice for diverting water from water-wheel to overflow (spillway); also flood hatch.
Eye – centre hole in runner stone through which grain passes to be ground.

Face-wheel – gear-wheel with cogs on the side (face) and not along outer edge; used with pinion (smaller gear-wheel).
Facing – method of checking flatness of millstone surface; alternatively flawing or staffing.
Falling-stocks – camshaft-driven hammers used in fulling-process.
False board – upper part of hatch used in controlling water flow to Poncelet type of wheel.
Felloe – rim section of wheel assembled from parts; also felly.
Fer-de-moline – heraldic representation, in shape of *x*, for mill-rynd – metal bridge across eye of runner stone; incorporated in arms of Lincoln's Inn, London.
Flat rods – iron rods used to transmit power from water-wheel to distant machinery; spectacularly illustrated at Laxey, Isle of Man (p.111).
Flawing – see Facing.
Floating mill – pontoon or barge moored under river bridge or in mid-stream and containing one or two undershot water-wheels and pairs of millstones; efficient but a hazard to navigation; for long popular on Continent, not common in Britain – certainly operated under London Bridge in Middle Ages; some remain along River Danube; also known as boat-mill.
Floats – wood or metal blades or paddles of water-wheel.
Flood hatch – see Escape gate.
Flour-Dresser – Sieving-machine used in flour-grading; see also Wire-machine and Bolter.
Flume – see Lade.
Footstep bearing – thrust bearing for upright shaft or spindle; also called footbrass.
French stone – see Burr stone.
Fulling-mill – mill used as part of cloth-manufacturing process – wool is cleaned and given body by being pounded, originally by foot in bath or trough; water-powered hammers falling on cloth produced better, more efficient result; first referred to in twelfth century; probably first alternative use of water-wheel, hitherto used only for corn-grinding; economically important mill in many areas, particularly in Wales, where known as Pandy; also tucking-mill.
Fulling-stocks – water-powered hammers used in cloth-fulling process, reproducing treading or trampling action of human feet.
Furrows – grooves cut in millstone surface; the sharp cutting or grinding edge of furrows on pairs of stones produces scissor-like effect on grain at each revolution; 'furrowing' describes process of cutting grooves – also drifting.

Garner – top floor of mill, used for grain-storage; also known as bin floor and granary floor.

Gimbal – part of support for runner stone – replaced mill-rynd.

Glut box – top bearing of quant, opened to disengage stone nut.

Governor – regulates gap between stones; governors also controlled flow of water onto wheel.

Gradual reduction – multiple grinding to produce fine flour; used in roller-milling but see also High milling.

Granary floor – see Garner.

Great spur-wheel – large gear-wheel on vertical shaft – often wood, but can be cast-iron; transmits power to one or more stones via stone nut(s); also spur-wheel.

Greek mill – gearless mill first mentioned by Antipater about 85 BC; required fast-moving stream of water to turn horizontal 'wheel' – in reality a rotor formed by attaching paddles to lower end of a vertical wooden shaft; shaft ended in iron spindle which drove runner stone; simple basic design, unchanged throughout Europe, consisted of 'under-house', through which stream passed, and 'meal-house', containing hopper; many variations in shape and number of paddles occasioned by local water conditions; building-materials reflected local vernacular tradition; survived in use among isolated communities into twentieth century – often as communal mill, neither taking nor demanding any form of soke rights; also known as click (for noise it makes), horizontal and Norse mill; best-preserved examples in Britain are both in Scotland – at Dounby, Orkney (p.217) and Kingussie, Highland Region (p.214).

Grinding-hull – specialist mill for grinding scythe and other blades; immensely uncomfortable and hazardous task – its use at Abbeydale (p.181) resulted in a death as recently as 1912.

Gripe-driven – see Overdrift.

Grist – originally any material ground in mill; has come to refer to grinding of animal feedstuffs; often used to boost profits and widely employed in twentieth century to maintain economic viability when corn-grinding declined or ceased.

Groats – roasted oats with husk removed by groat machine.

Gudgeon – pivot at end of axle on which wheel turns – from sixteenth century usually of cast-iron.

Hammer-pond – millpond (usually man-made or extended) mainly associated with forges used in Wealdon iron industry; water supplied power for furnaces and tilt-hammers; changed landscape of Kent and Sussex in sixteenth and seventeenth centuries – many still exist in both counties.

Handspikes – lever tool for lifting runner stone for dressing.

Harp – segment (normally one of ten on surface of millstone; contains lands and furrows in set pattern; basically unchanged since developed by Romans.

Hatch – part of sluice gate set in penstock to control water-supply; often raised from inside mill.

Headrace – section of stream above mill, leading to wheel; frequently referred to as leat, particularly when cut and strengthened by miller; can be of considerable length; also millrace.

Heft – see Thrift.

High-breast wheel – variant of breastshot water-wheel; very efficient; water falls into buckets just above axle level; in low breast just below axle.

High milling – process of grinding grain several times using stones set progressively closer; Continental system, originating in sixteenth-century France; economical, producing more usable flour from each sample and in range of qualities, including bran-free white flour; superseded by roller-milling.

Hoop – see Tun.

Hopper – open wooden box container situated above millstones; grain is fed into it from bin floor by gravity and passes to millstones through shoe.

Horizontal mill – gearless mill; also known as click (for noise it makes), Greek and Norse mill; see longer entry under Greek mill.

Horse – wooden frame supporting hopper; so called for its four legs; also cradle.

Hulling-mill – mill used for husking of cereals.

Hunting-cog – additional cog on one of two meshing gear-wheels; simple, highly effective device to counter wear on cogs by ensuring wheels mesh differently on each revolution.

Hurst or hursting – framework, commonly of timber but latterly metal, supporting millstones and enclosing main gearing.

Hurstle – see Tun.

Hutch – corn bin.

Jog-scry – oscillating sieves used to rough-dress flour.

Kibbler – ancillary machinery used for coarse grinding.

Kiln – oven used for drying grain (usually oats); mainly in north and Wales, where preponderance of oats was grown and where rainfall is higher.

Lade – manmade trough or channel conveying headrace waters to wheel; also known as flume, launder or fleume.

Lands – flat surface of millstone.

Lantern pinion – old form of wooden gearing.

Launder – see Lade.

Lay shaft – secondary shaft in mill used to transmit power to auxiliary equipment, e.g. sack-hoist, saw-mill.

Leat – see headrace.

Ligger – see bed stone.

Low-breast wheel – variant of breastshot water-wheel; very efficient; water falls into buckets just below axle level; just above axle in similar high breast.

Low milling – traditional method of producing flour by passing grain once through stones; see also High milling and Roller-milling.

Lucam – projecting dormer cabin, usually wood, occasionally brick and wood, sometimes decorated; on upper floor of mill; contains hoist gear; wide variation of name, including locum, luccam etc.

Macehead – supports and drives gimbal.

Magnetic separator – device introduced in nineteenth century to remove stray metal from grain before grinding; usually in main bins on upper floor; metal can be very dangerous if it falls into stones – risk of sparks and even of runner stone being violently dislodged.

Many-heights – stepped wedge used for raising or lowering millstones.

Meal floor – floor below millstones, most frequently the ground floor to which flour descends for bagging.

Meal spout – wooden chute carrying flour from stones to sacks.

Middlings – middle grade of flour defined by dresser.

Mill – not as obvious as may appear; historically often referred to pair of stones and not mill building; this is so, for example, in some Domesday entries, i.e. 'two mills' refers to two pairs of mill stones under one roof, not two parish mills; pairs of stones were used for different purposes, e.g. flour and grist; has created confusion for many students of local history – valiantly searching for two mill sites where only one existed; still occurs in some areas, notably parts of Wales; see Pair.

Mill-bill – see Bill.

Mill-dresser – see Stone-dresser.

'Miller's thumb' – with experience a miller could gauge, by testing the quality and condition of grain between thumb and forefinger, how much flour would be produced from a given quantity; claims that miller falsified figures to allow him to take more than his agreed toll were commonplace; Chaucer referred to the miller's flattened thumb as his 'thumb of gold', alleging he took three times his due.

Miller's willow – twig used as tensioning spring between shoe and damsel; more often ash or hazel than willow; later of steel.

Millrace – mill-stream above mill, leading to wheel; can be natural or artificial; when artificial is often of considerable length; also headrace and leat.

Mill-rynd – see Rynd.

Millstones – used for grinding-process; French Burr and Peak (or Derbyshire or millstone grit), composition are most common, although some areas have local stones, and some other Continental stones occur in Britain; stones are of different qualities and are used for various functions; French Burr is considered best (and most expensive to buy) – invariably restricted to milling grain; also see under individual headings.

Molinologist – term for a mill buff or enthusiast.

Multure bowl – see Toll dish.

Noria wheel – vertical water-wheel, Middle Eastern in origin, used for irrigation purposes.

Norse mill – gearless mill; also known as click (for noise it makes), horizontal and Greek mill; see longer entry under Greek mill.

Nose helve – tilt-hammer similar to fulling-stocks.

Oats – probably native to Britain; hardy – grow well in poor northern soils with high rainfall and little sun; require some special machinery for processing – mills with kilns are invariably in oat-growing area; used for oatmeal and porridge and, with its good nutritional value, for animal feed.

Overdrift – method of driving millstones from above, by quants; reverse of standard method – underdrift; sometimes called gripe-driven.

Overshot wheel – water-wheel in which water is fed onto top of wheel and is collected in buckets; weight of water carries wheel down, spilling out at bottom; usually fed by pentrough leading from millpond; efficient; like undershot, common from Middle Ages – illustrated in fourteenth-century Luttrell Psalter.

Overtails – impurities large enough to be sieved out of grain.

Paddles – see Floats.

Paint-staff – wooden straight-edge used for testing the flatness of millstone surface; mixture of red-oxide and water (raddle) is applied to paint-staff which is then passed over surface, highlighting raised areas; occasionally mill-staff.

Pair – described capacity of mill in terms of its pairs of stones – two pair mill etc; American usage substitutes 'run' for 'pair'; see Mill.

Pandy – Welsh word for fulling-mill; occurs in Clwyd, Gwent, Gwynedd and Powys and in pub names in England as well as Wales.

Peak stone – see Derbyshire Peak.

Penstock – wood or metal trough carrying water, usually, but not invariably, from millpond to overshot or breast wheel; also pentrough; is sometimes an alternative term for sluice-gate.

Pick – pointed tool; major tool – with bill – used in stone-dressing; mounted in thrift.

Pinion – smaller of pair of gear-wheels.

Pit-wheel – primary gear-wheel; parallel to water-wheel at inner end of axle; so called because it frequently stood in pit dug in floor of mill; lower part often in water; latterly has been made of iron with wooden cogs.

Pitch-back wheel – a variant of the overshot wheel in which water is directed from modified launder into buckets at back (upstream) side of wheel, reversing direction of rotation; often used to good effect on large wheels – see Laxey, Isle of Man (p.111).

Plansifter – ancillary equipment for dressing flour; uses horizontal sieves.

Plim – to use water to swell cogs or wedges.

Poncelet wheel – much-improved nineteenth-century version (introduced 1824 by French general J.V. Poncelet) of undershot wheel; uses curved, usually sheet-metal floats and an adjustable angled hatch; curvature allows water to enter and leave wheel with minimum shock and loss of energy; claimed efficiency of sixty-five per cent; always built of iron; very popular installation when wheels needed replacing in nineteenth century.

Proof-staff – iron straight edge used to check paint-staff; invaluable tool for mill-dresser, invariably kept in wooden box for protection.

Purifier – nineteenth-century device to extract fine dust.

Quant – driving-shaft in overdriven mill.

Quern – hand-mill for corn-grinding believed to have originated in Neolithic times; see longer entries under Rotary quern and Saddle quern.

Race – water-channel – either above (headrace) or below (tailrace) water-wheel.

Raddle – red-oxide and water mix; painted onto paint-staff to assist in detecting projecting areas on face of stone; also called tiver.

Rap – protective hardwood fender on shoe against which damsel knocks.

Recoil block – a block added to rear of tilt-hammer to restrict length of backstroke; sometimes cushioned by sacking, straw or heather.

Reducing – last stage of white flour production in roller-milling.

Reel – silk-covered wooden cylinder of bolter.

Riggers – levers, with forked ends, which engage stone nuts and lift them out of gear, removing power from millstones.

Rim-gearing – toothed rack on inside rim of water-wheel meshing with pinion wheel; pinion is attached to own (not wheel) shaft and transmits power; normally on large wheels, often in nineteenth-century cotton- and woollen-mills; Higher Mill, Helmshore (p.120) had two pairs of rim-gears operating five fulling-stocks.

Roller-milling – principle, first expounded in sixteenth century, involving metal cylinders in place of millstones; developed in Switzerland in nineteenth century; combined form introduced to Britain 1860s; 'stoneless' mill operating Manchester 1878; system first demonstrated London 1881; proved remarkably successful and by end of century was established as means of producing cheap flour of uniform quality for growing mass market; deficiencies in resulting 'white' flour – loss of vitamins etc – were not recognized for some time; success was founded on several factors: maintenance of millstones was a time-consuming and skilled task; hard winter wheats introduced in USA from 1850s proved difficult to mill effectively – precise adjustments possible with roller-mills simplified the gradual reduction of grain to flour; rollers operated well by steam-engine, lessening dependence on water-supply; rapid expansion of transport system allowed grain to be milled in large commercial mills by dockside on arrival, before being despatched around country; advent of roller-mills heralded a dramatic and irreversible decline in traditional country mill.

Rotary quern – hand-mill, forerunner of modern revolving millstone; replaced backward-and-forward action of saddle quern with circular motion of one stone over another; the lower stone was convex to allow flour to fall naturally to edge; grain was poured into central hole in upper stone, which was turned by a vertical handle; usually a task for two women – one fed grain, the other turned handle; mechanized methods of turning stone came much later, as did marking of surface with grooves; forms of hand-quern continued in use for domestic grinding of grain into medieval times – later in parts of northern Britain; frequently outlawed by estate-owners anxious to preserve soke rights, querns were buried by tenants; examples are still ploughed up – have been mistaken for early fonts.

Run – American term for pair of stones – describes capacity of mill in terms of its run of stones – two run mill etc; see Mill.

Rungs – occasional term for floats.

Runner stone – upper, revolving, stone of pair of millstones; 'standard' diameter is four feet; revolves at 125-150 revolutions per minute; made of various materials – see Millstones.

Rye – needs less nutriment, grows in poorer soils than other cereals; once provided high percentage of bread corn grown – declined in popularity from seventeenth century; less profitable than other cereals and subject to attack by ergot (poisonous fungus); now almost exclusively a fodder crop – straw used in thatching.

Rynd – metal bridge across eye of runner stone; later replaced by gimbal but remained a common heraldic symbol – *fer-de-moline*; also mill-rynd or rind.

Sack boy – device used to hold mouth of flour sack open.

Sack-hoist – used to raise grain from cart or other delivery vehicle to upper (garner) floor; usually takes power from lay shaft.

Saddle quern – earliest form of hand-mill, believed to have originated in Neolithic times; employed a backward-and-forward motion of an upper stone across the saddle-shaped lower stone; many illustrations survive from ancient Egypt of women, or slaves, kneeling at saddle querns; later replaced by rotary quern; also saddle stone.

Scratching – cutting fine grooves on millstone surface.

Screener – machine which removes dust from grain.

Separator – machine for removing impurities from grain; used in place of, or with, screener.

Shaft – see Vertical shaft.

Shelling – removal of husks from oats before grinding.

Shoe – small, tapering wooden trough into which grain falls from hopper and is then fed to eye of runner stone.

'Showing your metal' – see Bill.

Shroud – outer casing of water-wheel which encloses floats, creating buckets.

Shuttle – alternative name for sluice.

Sickle-dressing – method of cutting curved, radiating furrows on face of millstone.

Silks – cylinder of silk cloth through which flour is passed in grading-process using bolter.

Skirt – used to describe both outer edge and outer third of millstone surface.

Skirting-board – low wooden frame around bed stone.

Slip cogs – removable cogs permitting a small gear-wheel (pinion) to be disengaged (almost always from millstones).

Sluice – important component in water-control; may occur where leat leaves stream, as control for millpond, in penstock or for diverting water to overflow; usually consists of a gate that can be raised or lowered.

Smutter – ancillary machinery used to remove various diseased particles, including smut, a fungal growth, from wheat before it is processed; still possessed by almost all operating mills.

Soke rights – medieval right (never part of Statute Law) of mill-owner to demand tenants use his mill for grinding their corn, thus ensuring him of income; origin is shrouded in mystery but certainly appears not to have been widespread in Saxon times or at Domesday (where it is never mentioned); like most English Common Law it probably 'just growed'; cause of constant friction between mill-owner and tenants – cases were invariably resolved in favour of owner; many ingenious attempts were made to avoid conforming, including building rival mills and attempting to disrupt working of 'soke' mill (tenants had right to go elsewhere if grain was not ground within specified periods); even in nineteenth century cases were still being fought and soke rights were finally ended in 1871, when Bradford Corporation paid £8,300 for a share in King's Mill, allowing rights to go by default; also suit of mill.

Sole plate – bottom board of bucket on water-wheel; occasionally the lining of a water-wheel.

Spattle – shutter for controlling flow of grain into shoe from hopper.

Spur-wheel – commonly called great spur-wheel; large gear-wheel on main shaft; transfers power to stone spindle via stone nut; invariably wooden.

Staffing – method of checking flatness of millstone surface; alternatively facing or flawing.

Starts – short pieces of wood or metal supporting floats of wheel.

Stitching – see Cracking.

Stone-Dresser – craftsman who prepares working surfaces of millstones; also mill-dresser; see Bill.

Stone nut – small gear-wheel (pinion) connecting spur-wheel to stone spindle, transferring power to drive millstones.

Stone spindle – shaft supporting and driving runner stone; powered via stone nut from spur-wheel.

Strike – straight-edge used to level grain in toll dish or multure bowl; occasionally known as strickle.

Suit of mill – see Soke rights.

Suspension wheel – light iron water-wheel driven by cogged track around rim.

Tail race – section of millrace downstream of mill.

Temse – medieval term for hand-sieve; hence 'setting the temse on fire' for a good worker.

Tentering – method of regulating gap between bed and runner stones to determine fineness of flour produced; bridge tree is raised or lowered; tentering-gear is used to make adjustments.

Thone – term applied to damp or wet grain or stones.

Threshing-mill – mill equipped to drive stationery threshing-machine; most estate mills were so equipped.

Thrift – turned wooden handle to hold bill and pick, major tools in stone-dressing; sometimes heft.

Throughs – sound, good-quality grain that passes through sieve.

'Thumb of gold' – see Miller's thumb.

Tidemill – mill utilizing rise and fall of tide at river mouth or estuary; water retained in millpond; uses undershot wheels; once very common – only three now remain in good order.

Tilt-hammer – forge hammer used in several industrial processes; operated by camshaft or trip-wheel turned by water-wheel; some of largest and best remaining examples are at Wortley (p.183).

Tirl – the horizontal wheel of the Greek mill; design varied considerably from country to country and even district to district, see Dounby (p.217).

Tiver – see Raddle.

Toll – payment due to miller for providing milling service; commonly one-sixteenth of total ground; like soke rights, cause of endless disputes between miller and customer and primarily responsible for miller's reputation for dishonesty; did not always work to advantage of miller, who, through difficulties in translating grain into money, fell into arrears with own rent and lost mill; financial payments in lieu began to be accepted as early as thirteenth century but were not formalized until Act of 1796; payment in kind was also made – see Howell Mill (p.196), where it continued well into this century.

Toll dish – receptacle for miller's toll; toll was emptied into ark; also multure bowl.

Trammel – wooden gauge used for checking positioning of runner stone and spindle.

Tramp iron – American term for metal in grain.

Trieur – device for removing impurities from grain.

Trough – water channel of either wood or metal supplying water to overshot wheel.

Trundle-wheel – primitive gear-wheel, similar to lantern pinion.

Tub-wheel – horizontal wheel encased in wood.

Tucking-mill – see Fulling-mill.

Tun – removable wooden casing around millstones; often seen in mills converted to pubs, craft shops etc as tables or seats; also hoop, hurstle and vat.

Turbine – developed during the nineteenth century and shown to possess greater efficiency than water-wheels; proved suitable for use in both roller- and conventional-milling and, although requiring alterations to the water-flow, were installed in many traditional mills; lacks 'romance' of water-wheels and only a limited number of (historically important) turbine-powered mills are described in this book.

Underdrift – millstones driven by power transmitted from below; standard method employed in milling – reverse of overdrift.

Undershot wheel – earliest and simplest of water-wheels; water passes under wheel, striking blades and setting wheel in motion; efficiency estimated to be only twenty-two per cent, although some refinements are possible; see also Poncelet wheel, a much-improved nineteenth-century version.

Vat – see Tun.

Ventilating-buckets – designed, by Sir William Fairbairn, with vents permitting air to be forced out as water entered, giving fuller buckets and providing maximum weight to turn wheel; worked in reverse as water began to leave bucket with air entering and hastening exit; became feature of improved nineteenth-century breast and overshot wheels – said to increase efficiency by twenty-five per cent.

Vertical mill – common and most successful form of European watermill as opposed to horizontal or Greek mill (qv); all mills in this book are derivations of basic design.

Vertical shaft – vertical pole, almost always wooden, to which power is transmitted from horizontal axle tree via pit-wheel and wallower; capable of driving more than one pair of stones through use of spur-wheel and auxiliary machinery through crown wheel; sometimes shaft.

Vitruvian mill – mill described by Roman engineer Vitruvius in his *De Architectura* written about 15 BC; forerunner of all European vertical mills.

Wallower – bevelled gear-wheel used to transfer power from pit-wheel to main shaft; has similarities to earlier lantern pinion; latterly invariably of iron; wooden cogs of pit-wheel worked well with metal gearing on wallower; also waller.

Weir – dam across stream or river to divert water to mill; frequently a major cause of disputes in medieval period between mill-owners, when the building of a weir often affected all downstream mills; also between mill- and landowners or tenants whose water-supply for irrigation could be affected; the building of weirs across navigable rivers created more tension and was the cause of many legal actions; possibly more contentious even than the miller's toll; remains of weirs often provide prime evidence for industrial archaeologists of previous existence of mills.

Wheat – most widely cultivated cereal of temperate zone; astonishing and ever-changing variety of strains – autumn or spring planting, high-yielding, disease-resistant; hard American wheats considered best for producing modern 'strong' flour used in well-risen white loaves; soft British wheats have better flavour and are used in 'traditional' bread-making by low-milling process; hard wheats better in roller-mills.

Widdershins – method of dressing stone.

Winter mill – regularly mentioned in Domesday; thought to be used when certain streams were swollen by heavy winter rainfall – presumed connection with winterbournes.

Wire-machine – mechanical sieve for grading flour; differed from bolter (qv) in that cylinder was stationary and flour was swept over wire gauze (or silk) lining by brushes; four grades were usually identified in traditional community mills; also flour-dresser.

Wood – traditionally main material in mill machinery construction; most common uses were: oak for wheels and other large parts; apple, beech or hornbeam for cogs; elm for floats.

Bibliography

My debt to the leaflets produced by individual mill-owners – some to a remarkably high standard – is incalculable. The publications of the Tourist Boards are always useful, while the county and regional series of books published by Robert Hale and B.T. Batsford, by authors with personal knowledge of an area, are invaluable for background information. The list which follows is by no means complete but includes the books (with the date of the edition used) to which I made most frequent reference.

Allhusen, Edward, *John Constable* (The Medici Society, 1976)

Aspin, C., *The Cotton Industry* (Shire Publications, 1987)

Aspin, C., *The Woollen Industry* (Shire Publications, 1987)

Bailey, Brian, *Industrial Heritage of Britain* (Ebury Press, 1982)

Balchin, W.G.V. (ed.), *The Living History of Britain* (Country Life Books, 1987)

Bennett, Richard, and Elton, John, *History of Corn Milling*, Vol. I and III (Simpkin, Marshall & Co, 1898 and 1900; Vol. II and IV, E.P. Publishing Ltd, 1973 and 1975)

Brook, Fred, *The Industrial Archaeology of the British Isles: The West Midlands* (Batsford, 1977)

Brunskill, R.W., *The Illustrated Handbook of Vernacular Architecture* (Faber & Faber, 1972)

Buchanan, C.A. and R.A., *The Industrial Archaeology of Central Southern England* (Batsford, 1980)

Buchanan, R.A., *Industrial Archaeology in Britain* (Allen Lane, 1980)

Burton, Anthony, *Industrial Archaeology Sites of Britain* (Weidenfeld, 1977)

Burton, Anthony, and May, John, *Landscape Detective* (Allen & Unwin, 1986)

Bush, S., *The Silk Industry* (Shire Publications, 1987)

Butt, John, and Donnachie, Ian, *Industrial Archaeology in the British Isles* (Paul Elek, 1979)

Cady, Michael (ed.), *Where To Go in the Countryside* (Automobile Association, 1985)

Chaucer, Geoffrey, *The Canterbury Tales* (trans. Nevill Coghill) (Penguin, 1951)

Clifton-Taylor, Alec, *The Pattern of English Building* (Faber & Faber, 1972)
Defoe, Daniel, *A Tour Through the Whole Island of Great Britain* (Penguin, 1971)
Eagle, Dorothy, and Carnell, Hilary, *The Oxford Literary Guide to the British Isles* (OUP, 1977)
Evans, George Ewart, *The Farm and the Village* (Faber & Faber, 1974)
Feiling, Sir Keith, *A History of England* (Macmillan, 1973)
Gardens of England & Wales 198- (The National Gardens Scheme, current ed.)
Gombrich, E.H., *The Story of Art* (Phaidon Press, 1972)
Grigson, Geoffrey, *Geoffrey Grigson's Countryside* (Ebury Press, 1982)
Hartley, D., *The Land of England* (Macdonald & Jane's, 1979)
Hartley, D., *Water in England* (Macdonald & Jane's, 1978)
Haselfoot, A.J., *The Industrial Archaeology of South-East England* (Batsford, 1978)
Hinde, T. (ed.), *The Domesday Book* (Century-Hutchinson, 1985)
Hoskins, W.G., *The Making of the English Landscape* (Book Club Associates, 1977)
Hudson, Kenneth, *Industrial Archaeology, a new introduction* (John Baker, 1976)
Hume, John R., *The Industrial Archaeology of Scotland, Vols I & II* (Batsford, 1977)
Joekes, R. (ed.), *The National Trust Guide* (Cape, 1984)
Major, J. Kenneth, (NT) *Watermills and Windmills* (Jarrold, 1986)
Marwick, Arthur (cons.), *Britain Discovered* (Mitchell Beazley, 1983)
Morgan, Kenneth (ed.), *The Oxford Illustrated History of Britain* (OUP, 1984)
Morris, Christopher, (ed.), *The Illustrated Journeys of Celia Fiennes* (Macdonald, 1984)
Mossman, Keith, *The Shell Book of Rural Britain* (David & Charles, 1978)
Ordnance Survey Leisure Guides, several publications, various eds. (Automobile Association/OS)
Pevsner, Sir Nicholas (ed.), *The Buildings of England, Wales etc by Counties* (Penguin, various dates)
Prentis, W.H., *The Snuff Mill Story* (published privately by the author)
Raistrick, Arthur, *Industrial Archaeology, An Historical Survey* (Eyre Methuen, 1972)
Reid, Kenneth C., *Water-mills and the Landscape* (Society for the Protection of Ancient Buildings, 1959)
Reynolds, J., *Windmills & Watermills* (Hugh Evelyn, 1970)
Rix, Martin and Alison (eds), *Gardens Open Today* (Viking Penguin, 1987)
Rollins, John G., *The Needle Mills* (Society for the Protection of Ancient Buildings, 1970)
Russell, Ronald, *Rivers* (David & Charles, 1978)
Seymour, J., *Forgotten Arts* (Guild Publishing, 1984)
Sixty Industrial Archaeological Sites in Scotland (Association for Industrial Archaeology, 1985)
Syson, L., *British Water-mills* (Batsford, 1965)

Syson, L., *The Watermills of Britain* (Batsford, 1980)
Trevelyan, Sir G.M., *English Social History* (Longman, 1978)
Vince, J., *Discovering Watermills* (Shire Publications, 1987)
Wailes, Rex, *Tide Mills*, Vols I & II (Society for the Protection of Ancient Buildings, 1956)
Watts, Martin, *Corn Milling* (Shire Publications, 1983)
Wenham, Valerie (ed.), *Properties of the National Trust* (National Trust, 1983)
Wenham, Valerie (ed.), *The National Trust Handbook 198-* (National Trust, current ed.)
Wilson, Paul, N., *Watermills, an Introduction* (Society for the Protection of Ancient Buildings, 1985)
Windmills & Watermills Open to View (Society for the Protection of Ancient Buildings, 1986)
Wright, Geoffrey, N., *Discovering Abbeys and Priories* (Shire Publications, 1985)

Index

General Index

Index of Mills

The following is a list of all the mills referred to in the text. Some no longer exist, some names are the alternatives by which certain mills are, or have been, known. The location of the mills is also given here – *not* in the general index.